THE
EVERYTHING®
TRAVEL GUIDE
TO ITALY

Dear Reader,

Oh, the cheese. Every spring when my plane is on its final descent into Rome or Genoa, I literally start to drool while thinking about mozzarella cheese. Yes, I know, I should be trying to decide whether to visit the historic Colosseum or the ruins of Pompeii or the canals in Venice, but there's just something about eating an *insalata Caprese* (salad in the style of Capri, with sliced tomatoes, buffalo mozzarella, fresh basil, and olive oil) in the land where it originated that makes it taste extraordinary. It's an incredibly good dish in a place where food is absolutely great.

And it keeps my belly full whether I'm exploring the cliffsides of the Cinque Terre or the stylish shops of Milan, the picturesque harbor in Portofino or the old walled city on Elba. I've cruised Italy's coastline, crossed its countryside by train, and walked its city streets until my feet went flat, and during every visit the nation has satisfied not just my belly, but also my mind and soul, offering a fantastic combination of history, nature, and beauty.

I hope this book helps you plan your own ideal vacation in Italy, even if you want to skip the *insalada Caprese* in favor of a Parma ham *panini* or a slice of Sicilian pizza. That's one of the many things I love about Italy as a vacation destination: It offers a bit of something for every traveler's personal taste.

Kim Kavin

Welcome to the EVERYTHING® Series!

These handy, accessible books give you all you need to tackle a difficult project, gain a new hobby, or even brush up on something you learned back in school but have since forgotten. You can choose to read from cover to cover or just pick out information from our four useful boxes.

Alerts

Urgent warnings

Facts

Important snippets of information

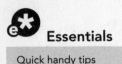

Essentials

Quick handy tips

Questions

Answers to common questions

When you're done reading, you can finally
say you know **EVERYTHING**®!

PUBLISHER Karen Cooper

DIRECTOR OF ACQUISITIONS AND INNOVATION Paula Munier

MANAGING EDITOR, EVERYTHING® SERIES Lisa Laing

COPY CHIEF Casey Ebert

ACQUISITIONS EDITOR Lisa Laing

DEVELOPMENT EDITOR Elizabeth Kassab

EDITORIAL ASSISTANT Hillary Thompson

EVERYTHING® SERIES COVER DESIGNER Erin Alexander

LAYOUT DESIGNERS Colleen Cunningham, Elisabeth Lariviere, Ashley Vierra, Denise Wallace

Visit the entire Everything® series at www.everything.com

THE
EVERYTHING
TRAVEL GUIDE
TO ITALY

A complete guide to Venice,
Florence, Rome, and Capri—and all
the breathtaking places in between

Kim Kavin

Avon, Massachusetts

For Miriam Toohey

An Everything® Series Book.
Everything® and everything.com® are registered trademarks of F+W Media, Inc.

Published by Adams Media, a division of F+W Media, Inc.
57 Littlefield Street, Avon, MA 02322 U.S.A.
www.adamsmedia.com

Contains material adapted from *The Everything® Learning Italian Book,
2nd Edition with CD,* by Ronald Glenn Wrigley, Copyright © 2009 by
F+W Media, Inc., ISBN 10: 1-60550-092-5, ISBN 13: 978-1-60550-092-8.

ISBN 10: 1-60550-166-2
ISBN 13: 978-1-60550-166-6

Printed in the United States of America.

10 9 8 7 6 5 4 3 2 1

Library of Congress Cataloging-in-Publication Data
is available from the publisher.

Maps created by Map Resources

*This book is available at quantity discounts for bulk purchases.
For information, please call 1-800-289-0963.*

Acknowledgments

This is my sixth *Everything® Guide* for Adams Media, and all six projects have come to me with help from literary agent Jacky Sach at Bookends, LLC. I am grateful for continuing support from her, as well as from Editor Lisa Laing and the entire team at Adams Media.

I have been fortunate to visit Italy at least once a year for the better part of a decade thanks to boating and travel magazine editors who send me off in search of interesting stories. Special thanks to Richard Thiel of *Power & Motoryacht* and Doug McWhirter of *Robb Report* for helping to fund my overseas adventures.

Thanks also go to my friend Elena Patriarca, who is always a pleasure to see when I'm in and around Genoa. Her help with local transportation and restaurants has been invaluable over the years. Special thanks to Glenn Wrigley, too. He wrote *The Everything® Learning Italian Book, 2nd Edition with CD*, from which parts of this book have been adapted by Adams Media.

My parents, Marc and Donna Kavin, and my sister, Michelle Kavin, are wonderful supporters of everything I do—and excellent distractions when I need a break from writing. I love and appreciate them dearly.

Last on this list but first in my heart is Sean Toohey, who always understands when I am still typing long past midnight. He is the partner of my dreams.

Top 10 Things to Do in Italy

1. Roar like a gladiator as you make your way through the arches and into Rome's Colosseum.

2. Prevent your mouth from falling agape as you look up at Michelangelo's Sistine Chapel ceiling.

3. Smooch beneath the city lights during a romantic sunset gondola ride along the Venice canals.

4. Shop for stylish new shoes in Milan before they become available anywhere else in the world.

5. Stop for a mid-morning espresso in a seaside village after hiking along the Cinque Terre.

6. Drive alongside locally built Maseratis and Lamborghinis (if you can keep up the pace, that is).

7. Cock your head for a straight-on view of the leaning tower in Pisa.

8. Stand on the old rock walls of Elba island and contemplate Napoleon's exile.

9. Explore what's left of Pompeii in the wake of the A.D. 79 Mount Vesuvius eruption.

10. Eat spaghetti with Bolognese sauce, mozzarella cheese, and a local Chianti. Throw some Parma ham on the side, and enjoy a cannoli for dessert. Save room for the next day's Sicilian pizza, penne with pesto sauce, and gelato. And the next day's Parma ham, provolone cheese, and biscotti.

Contents

Introduction

Civilization is believed to have existed within the current Italian borders for a mind-bending 200,000 years. Greek colonists were the first to call the land home before Ancient Rome emerged, blended in some ways with the Greek empire, and formed the basis for much of today's Western civilization. The layers upon layers of history and culture that were left behind—along with modern-day attractions and gorgeously preserved natural landscapes—today draw between 25 million and 30 million tourists each year. That's nearly half the population of the European Union itself, and it ranks Italy among the world's top half-dozen or so vacation destinations.

You could tour Italy for more than a month, visiting a different UNESCO World Heritage Site each day, and still not see them all in the span of a single trip. Many tourists say a week isn't even enough to shop for shoes in—let alone walk all around—a city such as Rome or Milan. Scholars have spent entire lifetimes researching single sites like the Colosseum and even single works of art by the Italian masters Leonardo da Vinci and Michelangelo. You could sample Chianti in and around the city of Florence for a year and never taste a drop from the same vintage, or enjoy life on the mainland for decades without crossing Italy's waterways to play on the islands of Sicily and Sardinia.

Given all that Italy has to offer, it's no wonder so many people visit—and then visit again and again. The trick to planning your own vacation in this land of plenty is outlining a doable itinerary that will get you to the areas that intrigue you most, without leaving you so exhausted that you feel too tired to truly explore and enjoy them. Trying to see all of Italy in a single vacation is plainly unimaginable, but learning about all of Italy and then picking and choosing what sounds best to you? Well, that's just smart planning.

For that reason, *The Everything® Travel Guide to Italy* is organized primarily by geographic region. If you're trying to envision your first visit to Italy and want to focus on a popular location such as Rome, you will find everything you need to create a memorable weeklong visit within the city limits. Or, if you're heading to Italy for the fourth or fifth time and want to explore some of the less-frequently visited regions, the following pages will help you determine where you might start and end to create a reasonable weeklong or monthlong schedule. Each chapter focuses on the prime tourist offerings in every region of the country, with special attention given to hotel and restaurant listings so that you can keep your budget in tune with your traveling wish list.

The Everything Travel Guide to Italy also includes full chapters on Italian food and wine, which are a huge part of the tourism experience and can be much more enjoyable if you understand what and how to order. Also in that vein, there is an entire chapter full of common Italian words and phrases. Yes, the people of Italy are accustomed to welcoming tourists, especially in the larger cities where English is often spoken, but the language of choice is still Italian, and you can get much friendlier (and faster) assistance if you take the time to learn a few key phrases.

Last, there are chapters about sample itineraries and options for visiting Italy by boat or cruise ship, or as part of international itineraries that include nearby nations. France, Germany, Switzerland, Austria, and Slovenia are exciting cultures unto themselves, each bringing into sharp relief what makes life in Italy so different and special.

Which is, of course, why you want to start your vacation in Italy—which is exactly what this book will help you do. Get ready to begin with a fast history lesson, one that will help you understand the centuries of civilization that gave birth to today's countless tourism options.

Italian Regions

CHAPTER 1

Buongiorno!

O r *buona sera*, if you're reading this at night. Good day, good evening, and welcome to Italy, a nation that has given birth to some of the world's greatest history, minds, foods, and wines. With at least a dozen primary regions and major islands to explore, including world-class cities that have stood for centuries, Italy offers almost every type of vacation you can imagine. Where else can you walk in the foot steps of an emperor, view some of the planet's finest masterpieces, shop for the latest fashions, and dine on classic regional recipes, all in a single day?

From Ancient Rome to the European Union

Archaeologists have found evidence supporting the notion that humans inhabited present-day Italy as early as 200,000 years ago, and it is believed that Greek colonies were established on the land as early as the eighth century B.C., just before the first communities of what would become Ancient Rome began to form. The massive Roman Empire started here and dominated most of Europe for some 1,200 years.

During the Middle Ages, the various regions of Italy were annexed and re-annexed to various neighboring empires while the first of Italy's city-states began to emerge, eventually becoming known as the four classic Maritime Republics. You will recognize their names even today: Venice, Pisa, Genoa, and Amalfi, each strategically located along the coastline where merchant ships traveled. By the 1400s, Italy had fueled the Renaissance that would last for 300 years, inspiring a renewed interest in learning and culture that soon spread across modern-day Europe.

❷ Question

What is a Renaissance man?
Generally speaking, the term refers to a person whose intelligence and knowledge are not restricted to a single subject area. Some of the best-known Italian Renaissance men included Leonardo da Vinci and Michelangelo, who painted, wrote, sculpted, designed architectural and engineering plans, and more.

Toward Modern Boundaries

Italy became a unified state in the late 1800s, though its borders continued to shift into the early 1900s. Fascist dictator Benito Mussolini rose to power in 1922 and remained in control until 1943. Italy was liberated from fascist rule in 1945 at the end of World War II.

After more territorial transitions in the wake of that war, the Marshall Plan helped rebuild Italy within the borders that we know today. During those same postwar years, Italy—along with Belgium, France, Luxembourg, Holland, and West Germany—became a founding member of the European Coal and Steel Community in the first step toward the economic unification of Europe.

Italy also has played a strong role on the world stage as part of the United Nations, into which it was admitted in 1955. The nation's soldiers have helped with peacekeeping missions from Somalia to Lebanon, as well as supporting the United States' Operation Enduring Freedom with 2,000 troops in Afghanistan in 2003.

The European Union

In 1993, a generation after the creation of the European Coal and Steel Community, Italy became one of the founding members of the European Union, which continues to grow and strengthen today. The Treaty of Maastricht established the multinational entity, stating that Italy and the other member states share an economic market that guarantees the free movement of people, goods, services, and capital. There are foreign policy components, as well, but in general each country still has its own systems of laws and government. When you visit Italy you are within the European Union, yet you are still subject to Italian customs and laws.

Fact

Italy is one of the countries in the European Union's euro zone, meaning places where the euro is the official form of currency. Italy adopted the euro in 1999, before which the lira had been the national currency. Lira had been used since 1861, and you needed to exchange nearly 2,000 lira to get a single euro when the new currency was adopted.

What's nice about the European Union for travelers is that once you enter, you don't need to get your passport stamped when crossing the borders between countries. Should you want to cross the northwestern Italian border with France to visit a beach on the Côte d'Azur, you can do so without international authorization.

Great Minds

Italy has produced some of the world's most celebrated thinkers, artists, and leaders. You will likely find countless references to the most renowned as you travel from region to region, so here's a quick primer on some of Italy's most prestigious citizens throughout history.

Julius Caesar

It's not every man who has a Shakespearean tragedy written in his name and a palace-style casino named after him in Las Vegas, but then again, it's not every man who starts a civil war that ends up making him the leader of the Roman Empire. Such is the story of Julius Caesar, who was proclaimed dictator for life, had a love affair with Cleopatra, and ruled until the Ides of March in 44 B.C., when his old friend Brutus (*et tu?*) assassinated him. You can view the whole sordid affair by watching the 1953 film *Julius Caesar*, which was nominated for Best Picture Oscar and for which Marlon Brando was nominated as Best Actor (he played Mark Antony).

 Fact

Julius Caesar learned about leadership and responsibility early in life, when his father died suddenly one morning while putting on his shoes. Caesar was just sixteen years old at the time, and he immediately became head of his entire family. The following year, he was named a high priest, but lost that designation before joining the army.

Galileo Galilei

The work of Galileo Galilei is widely renowned as part of the scientific revolution that took place in the 1500s and 1600s. He made vast improvements to the telescope that helped to confirm the phases of Venus, discover some of Jupiter's satellites, and analyze sunspots.

He caused a great deal of controversy when he claimed he could prove that the sun, and not the Earth, was the center of the known universe. His work greatly angered the Roman Catholic Church, which eventually forced him to recant his scientific testimony. He died under house arrest during the Inquisition, which sought to confine and destroy heretics.

Leonardo da Vinci

Leonardo da Vinci is best remembered as a painter, but he also was a mathematician, inventor, botanist, scientist, engineer, musician, architect, and writer. His two most famous works are the *Mona Lisa* and the *Last Supper*, and his lesser-known contributions include designs for a helicopter and a calculator, and the theory of plate tectonics.

Interestingly, da Vinci's drawings of the human body—including the iconic *Vitruvian Man*—were based on countless hours that he spent dissecting cadavers at hospitals in Florence, Milan, and Rome. He was one of the first people in history to draw a fetus still inside the womb.

Michelangelo

His full name was actually Michelangelo di Lodovico Buonarroti Simoni, and he is best remembered for his sculpture *David* and his Sistine Chapel frescoes. Michelangelo was ahead of his time, but he was also honored within it, becoming the first Western artist to have a biography printed before he died. Unlike his contemporary da Vinci, whose best-known works are spread throughout Europe, Michelangelo's *David* is on display at the Accademia di

Belle Arti Firenze, while his frescoes still grace the Sistine Chapel ceilings in Vatican City.

Dante Alighieri

This poet from Florence was typically called simply "Dante," and his *Divina Commedia*, or *Divine Comedy*, is renowned to this day as an exceptional detailing of a journey through Hell, Purgatory, and Paradise. How can a journey through Hell be called a comedy, you ask? Because in Dante's days (the late twelfth and early thirteenth centuries), any work not written in Latin was considered trivial. Dante wrote in what he called Italian, an altered regional dialect of Tuscany.

Niccolò Machiavelli

If you look up the word "Machiavellian" in the dictionary, the definition reads: "characterized by subtle or unscrupulous cunning, deception, expediency, or dishonesty." The word is often used in modern politics as part of the phrase "Machiavellian tactics," describing someone who places brute political force above morality.

 Fact

The modern use of the word "Machiavellian" really fails to honor the true viewpoints of the man himself. Machiavelli believed that sometimes, the ends justify the means when it comes to political power, but in general, he was far less of an extremist than the current definition implies.

Poor Niccolò brought this legacy on himself, not so much in his well-regarded work as a diplomat from Italy serving in France, but because he described such methods of retaining power in his work *The Prince*, which was not published until 1532, five years after his death, when he was no longer around to point out its more moderate themes.

Italy Today

Modern celebrities from Italy are a bit different from these historical figures, and most world citizens are far less likely to name a current-day philosopher or artist than they are to know the names Salvatore Ferragamo, Giorgio Armani, Gianni Versace, Enzo Ferrari, and Mario Andretti. These names are practically synonymous with what many tourists visit Italy to enjoy: high fashion and high speed.

Sensuous Style

Milan, a city in northern Italy, is widely renowned as one of the world capitals of fashion and design. Its Via Montenapoleone street in the Fashion District is home to the boutiques of some of the planet's most prominent clothing and jewelry designers, and other fashion districts in cities including Rome typically highlight styles that go on to sweep the world consciousness (and its citizens' pocketbooks).

Gucci, Ferragamo, Armani, Versace, Dolce and Gabbana, Valentino, Fendi—all of these top-end brands are Italian. Many of these brands have been established worldwide for decades (Ferragamo has been selling shoes in the United States since the 1920s), while others started out in Italy and took longer to capture the world fashion market (Fendi bags didn't make it into Bloomingdale's until the 1960s).

You will notice as a tourist in Italy—especially in the cities—that the locals dress up more than Americans typically do for simply walking around town or enjoying dinner at a restaurant. If you want to fit in, try to take your wardrobe up a notch. Baseball caps are frowned upon, for instance, and jeans are cut more like slacks than regular ol' Wranglers.

Go-Fast Thrills

Looking good in Italy doesn't stop with clothing, handbags, and shoes. You want to turn heads on the road, too, a philosophy embodied by Italian sports car manufacturers including Lamborghini, Maserati, Ferrari, and Alfa Romeo. The street-legal vehicles that these companies produce shatter speed limits in the United States and often look more like Batmobiles than cars.

 Alert

Just as on the streets of New York, Paris, or London, "Italian" fashion designs and purses being offered by Italy's cart vendors are typically fakes. You might assume that an Armani suit would cost less in the country where it is headquartered, but odds are if you're buying it on the street, the logo isn't real.

And Italy's infatuation with speed doesn't end there. If you're at all a fan of racing, then you know the name Mario Andretti. Born in Italy and later naturalized as an American citizen, Andretti is one of the most successful drivers in automobile racing history. He is the only driver ever to win the Indianapolis 500, Daytona 500, and Formula One World Championship, which are among his more than 100 career wins on major circuits.

In general, the love of fast driving permeates Italian culture. If you rent a car in Italy, expect to experience a very different style of driving than you're used to in the United States. Everything moves much faster on Italian roads, and you have to pay close attention lest you get run over between the time you spot an oncoming car and the time you get over into the slow lane. Even on narrow city streets, slowpokes receive honks and yells. You'll also get some odd looks if you fail to drive with your headlights on, even during the day, because many parts of Italy include highways replete with dark tunnels.

ⓔ✱ Essential

If you want to get a taste of life in the fast lane before visiting Italy itself, you can sign up for a day of driving with an instructor through the Mario Andretti Racing School. It operates in sixteen U.S. locations from Las Vegas to Miami and lets you get behind the wheel of real race cars. Learn more at *www.andrettiracing.com.*

Lay of the Land

Geographically speaking, Italy is divided into twenty regions. You might recognize some of those names, including Tuscany and Piedmont, and by the end of this book you will be familiar with far more. Though Italy is a small country compared with the United States, its regions are surprisingly diverse. Some are coastal, others are mountainous, and still others encompass large, metropolitan sprawls.

Within some of Italy's twenty regions lie the nation's biggest cities. Rome is the largest, with 2.7 million residents, and Milan is second, with 1.3 million residents. The next-largest cities, each with less than 1 million residents and listed in descending order, are:

- Naples
- Turin
- Palermo
- Genoa
- Bologna
- Florence

It might surprise you that Venice is not on this list. It has at least 100,000 fewer residents than Florence, with a count of about 270,000 during the last census. That's a good-size city, to be sure, but is more on par with Birmingham, Alabama, or Fort Wayne, Indiana, than with larger, better-known metropolitan areas in the United States.

Regions You're Likely to Visit First

The regions whose names you'll want to remember include some of the country's most famous cities. The Lazio region is home to Rome, the Campania region is home to Naples, the Liguria region is home to Genoa, the Tuscany region is home to Florence, and the Veneto region is home to Venice.

 Alert

In general, all the regions in Italy have the same laws, languages, and customs, but five of the twenty regions—including the popular tourist islands Sicily and Sardinia—are legally autonomous in certain matters of cultural, ethnic, and language peculiarities. You might find a Sicilian dialect, for instance, hard to understand even if you speak Italian.

Each major city is the centerpiece of tourism in these individual regions, but in most cases, you can go beyond the cities to find interesting local attractions, restaurants, and the like. Campania, for instance, has Naples as its prime tourist draw but also includes the ruins of Pompeii and the islands of Capri. The Lazia region, which includes Rome, is also home to the cities Gaeta and Formia, which are rich in ancient and Medieval history.

Judging Distances

Though Italy's regions are diverse, they're not always terribly far apart, at least in contrast with states like California and New York. Rome and Venice, for instance, are on entirely opposite coasts, but the driving distance between them is just 245 miles. From Milan to Rome is just shy of 300 miles, and from Naples to Rome is only 120 miles.

A half-day's drive (or less) will thus often get you from one major city or region to the next, and trains make travel even easier. For instance, you can easily take a train from Rome to Pisa and back in a single day if you want to see the leaning tower and nothing else within the Pisa city limits. High-speed trains that make no local stops between major cities are also sometimes an option.

Climate

Because Italy stretches more from north to south than from east to west, it has climates that vary depending on latitude. To the north, near the mountains, temperatures become far harsher during the winter months than they do in the southern coastal sections.

In general, the country is known as a summer destination (unless you're a snow skier). The months of June, July, and August tend to bring the least rainfall, though those months can also become oppressively hot. Tourists who try to push themselves from one attraction to the next are susceptible to heat exhaustion and heat stroke. July and August are also the busiest in terms of pedestrian congestion, as Italians themselves are on summer vacation. If you can visit in the spring, say between April and June, you'll find the country much easier to get around. Prices are typically lower at this time of year.

Temperatures in Rome

Rome is just south of the middle of Italy, on the western coast. Its daily temperatures rarely drop below 50°F, even during the winter months, when average nighttime lows are in the high 30s and low 40s.

During the popular summer vacation months, the average high temperatures in Rome are well into the 80s and 90s, with lows typically in the 60s and 70s.

Fact

Global climate change is affecting Italy much like the rest of the world, with summers seeming to get hotter every year. A 2007 European heat wave that included Italy pushed temperatures above 110°F, leading to wildfires and deaths. In the cities, overheated residents scrambled into the fountains to cool off.

Temperatures in Venice

Venice, on Italy's eastern coast, is farther to the north than Rome. Its daily high temperatures can drop into the upper 30s during the coldest winter months, with some lows below freezing from December through February. During the summer months, Venice daily highs tend to be between 75 and 85°F, with lows in the high 60s to low 70s.

Temperatures in Sicily

Sicily, the southernmost Italian island that hangs down below the tip of the mainland "boot," is temperate thanks to its coastal climate. Its average summer highs are in the 80s and 90s, with lows during July and August around 75°F. When winter comes to the island, daytime temperatures drop to about 60 degrees, with nighttime lows in the 40s.

Essential

If you want to know what the average daily temperature is likely to be in different sections of Italy during your travel dates, check out *www.knowital.com/weather/italy*. It lets you plug your arrival and departure dates into a search engine that analyzes the days against data from every city and region in the country.

Getting Here and Around

Most visitors to Italy arrive by airplane, and once in Italy travel by train, bus, or rental car. If you're taking part in a guided tour, you may travel by private tour bus, but for the most part Italy's public transportation system is well designed to help you get from pretty much anywhere you are to virtually anywhere else you want to be.

By Plane

There are more than 100 airports in Italy, with the biggest (and most likely to welcome international travelers) in Rome and Milan. You can find daily flights into Italy from dozens of connecting European hubs, as well as direct flights from major cities within the United States.

Leonardo da Vinci-Fiumicino Airport

This is the airport closest to Rome, located about twenty miles from the city's historic center and connected to the city's main transportation hub by a shuttle train, the Leonardo Express, that runs every hour during peak travel times. Nearly 33 million people went through this aiport's terminals in 2007, many of them flying on Alitalia airlines, which has its sole hub here.

Fiumicino, as it's often called, has been operating since 1961. Thanks to upgrades over the years, it now has five terminals serving dozens of airlines. The newest, Terminal 5, which opened in

2008, welcomes international flights from the United States on American Airlines, Continental Airlines, Delta Air Lines, United Airlines, and US Airways.

Terminal 5, which is where most U.S. visitors will fly into Rome's airport, is quite a distance from the older buildings within the complex. There is a free shuttle service, but expect to encounter significant transfer time if, say, you plan to connect to a regional flight after landing in Rome.

The airport's official website is *www.adr.it*, where you can find information about arrivals, departures, parking, and directions, all in English. If you want to search for airfares on other websites, the airport's international code is FCO.

Milan-Malpensa Airport

Italy's second-busiest international airport is Milan-Malpensa in the north. Nearly 24 million passengers embarked and disembarked here in 2007, with two terminals (divided into three sections) servicing dozens of airlines. Most visitors from the United States will enter via Terminal 1B, which is the end point of routes operated by American Airlines, Continental Airlines, Delta Air Lines, and US Airways.

 Alert

As of 2007, Alitalia had ceased its major hub operations at the Milan-Malpensa Airport. Only one long-haul route to the United States is expected to continue in the near future, from New York's John F. Kennedy International Airport (international code JFK).

The airport's official website is *www.sea-aeroportimilano.it*, where you can find departure and arrival information as well as maps and a virtual airport tour, all in English. If you want to search for flights on another website, the Milan-Malpensa airport code is MXP.

By Train and Bus

Italy's public transportation network is quite good, although trains are not always designed to accommodate the larger suitcases that international travelers tend to have. Within the airports in Rome and Italy, you will see signs (usually in English) directing you to train stations and bus stops that are within walking or free shuttle distance of the terminal. Maps are usually easily available, so you can plan your routes accordingly.

e! Alert

In most cases, you cannot book an online train ticket through the Trenitalia website less than a week before your travel date. If you get to Italy and decide to buy a train ticket at the last minute, you will have to go to a local train station, where the ticket sales agents may not speak English.

Within the cities, you will find local trains and buses. Between Italy's cities, you can often take high-speed trains that travel at close to 200 miles per hour. The high-speed trains are typically called TAV, which stands for Treno Alta Velocità, a special-purpose entity created specifically to build and operate the nation's high-speed train network.

The company Trenitalia lets you book both local and high-speed train tickets in advance of your trip at the website *www .trenitalia.it*. Some of the train routes cross international borders, so if you want to book a seat from, say, Genoa to Antibes, France, this is the place to log on. Note that you need to purchase a ticket *and* make a reservation for a specific seat on many of Italy's trains. For the most popular routes, including high-speed trains between major cities, the smart move to ensure a seat reservation is to have Trenitalia make the booking well in advance of your journey and mail the tickets to you in the United States. There is a fee for this service, but it beats finding your train of choice fully booked up once you get to Italy.

By Rental Car

Booking a rental car in Italy is just like booking a rental car in the United States. You make your reservation (often through a website like *www.expedia.com* or *www.orbitz.com*), go to the rental car agency section of the airport after your flight arrives, hand over a credit card and driver's license, and get behind the wheel.

Also as in the United States, your rental car rate and agreement will typically cover use of the car only. Insurance, gas, and any other charges will be billed as extras—and credit cards that have built-in insurance policies for U.S. car rentals may not apply in Italy. Be sure to check with your provider before you sign on the dotted line. In addition, be sure to specify that you need a car with an automatic transmission if you are not comfortable operating a vehicle with a manual transmission. Most rental cars in Europe have manual transmissions, and you may have to pay extra to get an automatic.

Essential

The cost of unleaded fuel in Italy (and the rest of Europe) has been substantially higher than the U.S. rate for many years. If a rental car seems inexpensive compared with a bus or train ticket, be sure to check the current price of gasoline and factor it into your total estimated travel expenses.

Most rental car agencies will provide you with free maps that list major highways. They are easy to follow, with routes marked as A-12, A-4, and the like. Road signs are of course in Italian, but with the letter-number system, the odds are you won't get lost pulling onto or off of a major highway. If you plan to do a lot of exploring on back roads, invest in a Michelin map for the region. You can purchase these before you leave at places such as *www.amazon.com*.

If you get onto a road that is part of Italy's Autostrade—paid highway system—then you will also have to factor toll charges into your driving expenses. This is similar to U.S. turnpike systems in which you take a ticket when you enter the roadway and pay when you pull off at an exit. Cash and major credit cards are accepted, but stay out of the Telepass lanes unless you have one of the automatic payment devices (which are like the U.S. equivalent of EZ-Pass cartridges).

Also be aware that some Autostrade fees can be quite high compared with U.S. tolls, especially if the euro is stronger than the dollar at the time of your journey. In some cases, you might have to pay as much as $20 U.S. for the privilege of using the roads. Be sure you have more than a few euro in your wallet when you drive up the Autostrade entrance ramp.

Rome Metropolitan Area

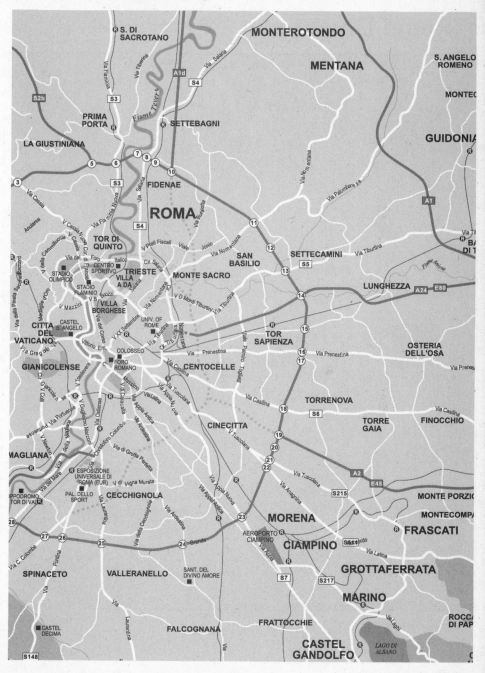

Rome Downtown

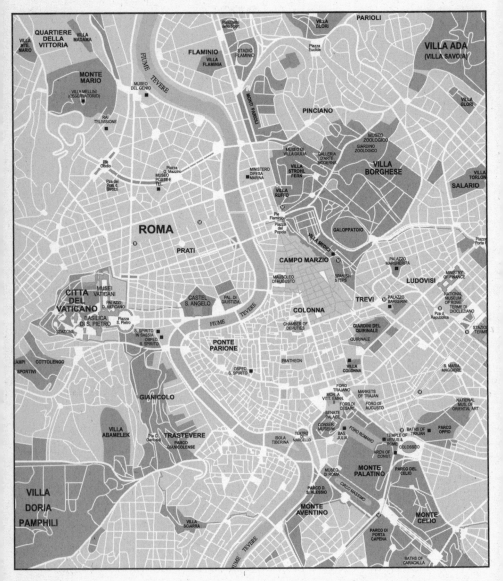

CHAPTER 2

Rome

When you think of a vacation to Italy, the Colosseum and Michelangelo's Sistine Chapel immediately come to mind. Both are located in the capital city of Rome, which was once the center of all Western civilization. Thousands of years' worth of history are here, including an old city center that is a UNESCO World Heritage Site. There is a pleasantly modern transportation infrastructure that makes the city easy to get around, as well as countless options for hotels and restaurants at all price points.

History of the City

Archaeologists and historians continue to debate the origins of Rome, but there is evidence to support its founding by settlers in the eighth century B.C.—the same time that mythology says the twins Romulus and Remus created the city. The original settlements grew into what would become the Roman Kingdom, Republic, and, finally, Empire, ruled by kings, senators, and emperors throughout centuries of conquest that spread its borders all across modern-day Europe.

At its height, the Roman Empire included what many historians estimate was at least 1 million citizens, but that number shrank to just 50,000—or even 20,000, by some estimates—at the time of the Middle Ages, after the empire's fall. The Italian Renaissance made its way to Rome in the second half of the fifteenth century, and, by 1861—even though Rome was at the time under control of the Roman Catholic Church's pope—the city became the capital of what we know today as Italy.

 Fact

The reason so much of Rome's history survives today is that it was one of the cities to escape the widespread destruction of World War II. There was some fighting, but no large-scale bombing of museums and archaeological sites. You can still see a good bit of the Renaissance (1400s to 1600s) and Baroque (1600s) periods in today's Roman streets.

After Benito Mussolini marched on Rome in 1922, the population again swelled to about 1 million people, and it continued to grow after Italy was liberated from dictatorship at the end of World War II. Today, there are more than 2.7 million Romans, nearly three times as many as there were at the height of the Roman Empire, though squeezed into a much smaller section of the Mediterranean coastline.

Birth of Tourism

The kind of mass tourism we associate with Rome today actually began in the 1700s, when the generations of Europeans who, along with their parents and grandparents, had been educated during the later Renaissance years began to understand and appreciate all the ancient sites within the modern city limits. Between that development and the continuing strong presence of the Roman Catholic Church, which draws followers to the city by the millions, Rome found itself a "hotspot" location. According to a report released by the city council of Rome in 2008, the city now receives 100,000 tourists a day, and tourists stay an average of three or four days.

❓ Question

How deep are the ancient city remains below the surface?
Not too deep at all, in some cases. City workers have found ancient roads just four inches underground, making it all but impossible in many locations—especially the old city center—to create new infrastructure without destroying remnants of the past.

Preserving the Past

Italy in general has strong preservation laws to protect the nation's archaeological heritage, and in no place are they more regularly enforced than Rome. For decades, city planners wanting to dig new transit tunnels or parking garages underground have waged virtual wars against archaeologists and preservationists seeking to protect the city's underground history. Workers digging out a new metro stop, for instance, might encounter a third-century complex of sculpture gardens. Should it be preserved? Documented and then moved? Knocked down without a word to make way for modern needs? The arguments rage on.

Despite the slow progress (or steady preservation, depending on which side you favor), modern Rome is a relatively easy city to get around. You can walk to and between many of the most popular tourist spots, especially if you're in decent shape and pack a comfortable pair of shoes. The underground Metro is also an inexpensive and easily accessible alternative, with stops at prime locations including the Colosseum, Vatican City, and the Spanish Steps. The Metro is not perfect—it doesn't stop near Trevi Fountain, for instance—but it can likely help you see most of the sites on your wish list.

Getting Around

If you arrive in Rome by airplane, you can take a taxicab or a train from the international airport into the city proper. Stazione Termini is the main train station, welcoming local as well as international trains, so the odds are you will enter the city here. The city's main bus station is directly across the street from this train depot, and a lot of the inexpensive hotels that cater to tourists are within walking distance. The network for buses and trams in Rome is extensive, with more than 8,000 stops.

 Alert

If you can walk, take a train, or ride a bus to get around Rome, do it—and skip the taxicabs altogether. The city is quite congested with traffic, not to mention designed with old roadways that aren't in an easy-to-manage grid system. A twenty-mile ride can take more than an hour, and the meter is always running.

Bus and Metro Tickets

There are vending machines where you can purchase bus and metro tickets at all the major stops, and you can also sometimes get tickets at local bars. Bus tickets can usually be purchased onboard. Tickets come in several varieties: one-way, daily pass, three-day tourist, and weekly pass. Prices range from €1 for a one-way ride to €16 for a weekly pass.

Whether you're riding the bus or the metro, you have to validate your ticket at the beginning of your journey so your fare can be accurately calculated when you arrive at your destination. Buses have onboard validation machines, while the metro stops have the machines in the terminal, before you get onboard.

Taxis

The officially licensed taxis in Rome are yellow or white and have meters to keep track of your time inside and the rate being charged. Rates change depending on the time of day, so you could pay more one day over the next for the exact same ride.

Rome has far fewer taxicabs per resident than most other modern cities, which can make hailing a cab on the street virtually impossible, especially at night. If you think you might need a taxi, talk with your hotel concierge about a recommended service, and keep the phone number handy so that you can call the driver as needed.

On Foot

Rome itself is huge, but the old city center where a lot of the favorite tourist attractions are located is actually quite easy to walk. It takes most people about 45 minutes, for instance, to walk from the Colosseum to Vatican City. From the Colosseum to the Spanish Steps is about a 30-minute walk.

If that level of physical exertion doesn't intimidate you, then go for it. The streets are typically clean and safe, and there's lots of beautiful architecture to enjoy along the way. You will quickly notice that a lot of other tourists are walking in the same places you are, with plenty of *trattorias* and other eateries lining the most popular routes so that you can make pit stops as needed.

The Colosseum

Most people who visit Rome make a beeline to its most famous archaeological site: the Colosseum. This elliptical amphitheater— a historic Giants Stadium, as it were—was the largest ever built by the Roman Empire, able to hold some 50,000 spectators at a time. It is 615 feet long by 510 feet wide. If you saw the movie *Gladiator*, then you know the kinds of bloody exhibitions that went on here in addition to plays, battle re-enactments, and other forms of entertainment.

Today, the Colosseum appears battered in many places, mostly because of earthquake damage and outright theft of stone. But you can take a tour inside, one led by an archaeologist if you like, and learn not just the history of what happened inside the building's walls, but also the fascinating way in which they were constructed.

 Alert

Lines for entry into the Colosseum can be long, and scam artists often prey on the most recent tourists to arrive, saying that the wait is longer than it really is and that once you get inside you will not be able to sign up for a guided tour. Ignore them and be prepared for them to insult you if you fail to purchase their "services."

Construction and Usage

There were no backhoes or cement mixers when construction of the Colosseum began in 70 A.D. It was completed a decade later, making extensive use of arches to support the heavy slabs of limestone, brick, and marble that were lifted by rope, pulley, and brute strength—and then bound together with iron clamps in many places—to create the structure's multiple levels.

The Colosseum's location was the former site of a private lake fancied by the emperor Nero, whose ruling style was characterized by tyranny and extravagance (he's the man they say "fiddled while Rome burned"). The emperor Vespasian began the Colosseum's construction and his son, Titus, finished it, arguably returning the center of the city to the use of the people from the times when Nero had kept the land for himself.

Gladiators fought inside the Colosseum until about 435, and animal hunts were popular forms of entertainment there until about 523. People entered the arena much as they would a modern one, looking for their seat section and row. However, they had shards of pottery rather than paper tickets. There were eighty entrances at ground level, each numbered. If there had been a parking lot outside, you can bet it would have been designed as an early example of color coding. ("Where is the chariot, dear? Blue 23?")

✅ Fact

To celebrate the opening of the Colosseum, some 5,000 to 9,000 wild animals were brought in to battle against gladiators during a 100-day extravaganza. Senators and ambassadors had the best view of the slaughter, as the first tier of Colosseum seating was reserved for them. The wealthy class sat in the second tier, and the general public up in the nosebleeds.

During Medieval times, the Colosseum was used for housing and workshops until a great earthquake in 1349 that destroyed the southside wall. Much of that original stone was used to rebuild hospitals and other buildings in Rome, and a religious order eventually moved in to the remains of the Colosseum, where they lived until the early 1800s. It was not until the rule of Benito Mussolini, in the 1930s, that the arena substructure was fully excavated and exposed.

Touring Today

Some 40 billion Italian lira were spent during the 1990s to help restore what's left of the Colosseum for tourism purposes. Romans understand that it is an iconic symbol of their city, one that draws millions of visitors and tourist dollars each year, and thus are highly motivated to prevent further deterioration inside the arena.

The insides are too dilapidated to use for events anymore, but big-name performers such as Paul McCartney and Elton John have "played the Colosseum" in recent years, using the exterior as a backdrop.

The official guided tours are sold through a ticket stand inside the building. They are quite good, typically led by archaeologists, and often include a broad discussion of Roman history as well as an introduction to the Colosseum itself. You need no appointment; just walk in as you would to a museum and wait for the next tour to begin. English-language tours are regularly scheduled, especially during the prime summer months.

Many online travel agencies sell advance-purchase tickets for Colosseum entry, but they often come with built-in fees that can be as much as the on-site tickets themselves. Usually, the wait to enter is no more than an hour, and you get a view of the Colosseum's exterior the entire time, so weigh that option against the fees when you decide whether to buy in advance.

Old City Center

The old city center is right near the Colosseum, so you can plan to see both in a single day. The Palatine—the birthplace of Rome, according to mythology—looks down over the remains of the Roman Forum.

Question

Was there really a cave at Palatine?
Apparently, yes. Archaeologists reported in early 2007 that they had found the legendary place while trying to restore the home of Augustus, the first Roman emperor. There has been no documentation yet on whether anyone named Romulus or Remus actually existed there.

The Palatine

Legend says that Palatine Hill is where city founders Romulus and Remus were found, inside a cave. From as early as 510 B.C., many wealthy Romans made their homes here, which is why you can tour the remains of palaces and temples today. The views from this area are spectacular, and you can access many spots where there are winding paths and gardens. There's also an on-site museum full of artifacts and artworks from the Palatine itself.

 **Essential**

Since the Pantheon continues to serve as a working Catholic church, be sure to dress appropriately even if you only want to wander through as a tourist. Sleeveless and backless shirts are a no-no, and if you are wearing shorts, they should come down to cover your knees. Pants or long skirts are a better option.

Roman Forum

The Forum was the area around which civilization in Rome evolved. This is where government leaders met, criers detailed the day's news to the people, and temples were built for worship. Think of a modern-day business and civic district—one where the people wore flowing robes to the taverns after a long day's work. Much of the Forum has been destroyed, but with a map in hand, you can visualize what used to be there as you make your way around.

The Pantheon

To the northwest of the Roman Forum is the Pantheon, often cited as the best-preserved building from the times of Ancient Rome. It was built as a temple to all the gods of that time and has been continuously used ever since, most recently as a Catholic church since the seventh century.

Mass is still celebrated here, if you want to become a part of the building's history instead of just touring around it. The interior is spectacular, and its construction is often cited as the Romans' most important architectural achievement. The concrete dome weighs about 5,000 tons and is so large that it may have been designed to symbolize the heavens.

The Spanish Steps

One of the most popular gathering places for tourists in Rome is the 138 treads known as the Spanish Steps, which rise from one side of Piazza di Spagna. The steps are north of the Colosseum and Forum areas, just south of a metro line stop and Villa Borghese, the city's largest public park featuring fountains, statues, and museums.

 Fact

The Spanish Steps were actually built with money donated by a French diplomat. The nearby piazza is named after the Spanish embassy, which used to be situated there, but the staircase itself leads to Trinità dei Monti, which is a French church.

The Spanish Steps were built in the early 1700s and are widely recognized as one of the tallest, widest outdoor staircases in western Europe. The piazza is a bit older, dating from the early 1600s. On one corner is the home where English poet John Keats lived and died in the early 1800s. (It's now a museum that you can tour; go to *www.keats-shelley-house.org* for more information.)

Fontana di Trevi

Trevi Fountain—at eight stories high, the largest Baroque fountain in Rome—is not to be missed. It draws flocks of tourists the way food scraps draw pigeons, but don't let the masses deter you. The sculptures that line the fountain are among the most beautiful in Italy, and the photo opportunities are worth elbowing your way down to the front of the crowd.

Be sure to have a few coins with you when you get to the water's edge. Legend states that if you toss a coin into Trevi Fountain, you will return to Rome someday. A lot of people believe this to be true: About €3,000 make their way into the water every day.

Religious Highlights

Religion and history go hand in hand, and thus, Rome is awash in religious monuments and touring opportunities. The biggest, of course, is the enclave of Vatican City—including St. Peter's Basilica and the Sistine Chapel—which will be explained in detail in Chapter 3.

Question

Did Michelangelo carve Christ the Redeemer in one try?
Nope. The great sculptor had to abandon his first attempt while it was still in rough form because he found a black vein running through the slab of white marble. It marred the area that would have become Christ's cheek.

Basilicas offer interesting opportunities to explore historic artwork in addition to the city's religious tradition. Some good options include the Basilica of St. Peter in Chains and Santa Maria sopra Minerva, both of which are home to works by Michelangelo.

Basilica of St. Peter in Chains

This basilica, built in the middle of the fifth century, is best known as the home of Michelangelo's statue *Moses*. The basilica takes its name from the fact that it was built to house the relic of chains that bound St. Peter in Jerusalem. They're not open and in public view, but the statue of *Moses* is, and is well worth a look, since Michelangelo considered it to be his most lifelike creation.

Santa Maria sopra Minerva

This is the only Gothic church in Rome, and it's close to the Pantheon. The building houses Michelangelo's *Christ the Redeemer* sculpture, which stands to the left of the main altar. Renaissance painter Fra Angelico is buried here, as is Pope Paul IV.

Top Museums

If you prefer to view your artwork in museums rather than in churches, Rome will not disappoint. You could visit a museum or gallery each day for an entire week's worth of vacation, if you so choose, each housing important historical works.

National Museum of Rome

The National Museum of Rome is home to one of the world's foremost archaeology collections. You will find great works of art and sculpture here, as well as a unique numismatic collection that shows the evolution of currency in Italy, including some extremely rare coins.

Some of the works you can view here include historic church frescoes, the sculptures *Suicide of Gaul* and *Tivoli General*, and mosaics taken from the villa of Livia, wife of Rome's first emperor, Augustus. The museum's website is *www.roma2000.it*.

Museum of Roman Civilization

This museum is dedicated to highlighting ancient Roman civilization. It attempts to document ancient Roman life as completely as possible, using a combination of reconstructed works, casts, and models. You read that correctly: What you're seeing in this museum is not original.

Essential

If you visit the Museum of Roman Civilization, be sure to check out its model of Imperial Rome, which is built at a scale of 1:250. The vast reconstruction by architect Italo Gismondi is mesmerizing, with an intact Colosseum and sprawling city streets all around.

Collections are divided into fifty-nine sections. The museum's first fourteen rooms tell the complete story of the history of Rome. Next is a section on Christianity, followed by sections about everyday Roman life. The English version of the museum's website is at *http://en.museociviltaromana.it.*

Villa Giulia National Etruscan Museum

This museum is, as its name implies, actually a villa. Pope Julius III built it in the mid-1500s, though little of that original design survives today. The on-site museum was founded in 1889 to collect pre-Roman antiquities, most of which come from the Etruscan and Faliscan civilizations. Among the works you can view here are the almost life-size funerary monument called *Bride and Groom*, the Pyrgi Tablets (writings that provide evidence of Phoenician influence in the Western Mediterranean), and the *Apollo of Veii* statue.

Capitoline Museums

This group of art and archaeological museums is situated in Piazza del Campidoglio, atop Capitoline Hill. The creation of the buildings dates back to 1471, when Pope Sixtus IV donated a group of bronze statues to the people of Rome.

The three main buildings that stand today are Palazzo Senatorio, built in the 1100s, Palazzo dei Conservatori, built in the mid-1500s, and Palazzo Nuovo, built in the 1600s. Within these buildings you can view the *Statue of Hercules* in gilded bronze, the *Bust of Medusa*, and the *Statue of Eros Stringing His Bow*. More details are available in English at *http://en.museicapitolini.org*.

Borghese Gallery

The Borghese Gallery is named for Cardinal Scipione Borghese, the nephew of Pope Paul V, whose collection of paintings, sculpture, and antiquities forms the basis of this museum's offerings. It's an easy museum to get around quickly, with just twenty rooms on two floors.

 Fact

Michelangelo Merisi da Caravaggio, whose works are displayed at Borghese Gallery, lived to be just thirty-nine years old. He was pugnacious and belligerent, often carrying a sword around town to pick fights. He killed a man during a 1606 brawl in Rome, and had to flee with a bounty placed on his head. Caravaggio died the following year.

Borghese was a collector of Bernini sculptures and Caravaggio works, both of which fall within the Baroque period. He also was a collector of Raphael paintings. What's interesting about the sculptures at this site is that many are still displayed in the areas where they were originally purchased to stand. Learn more at *www.galleriaborghese.it.*

Museum of Castel Sant'Angelo

This building also goes by the name Mausoleum of Hadrian, as the Roman Emperor Hadrian originally commissioned it between 135 and 139 A.D. as a tomb for himself and his family. It served as a fortress, a papal state prison, and a castle at various times. It became a museum in the twentieth century.

Tourists are allowed to visit all the rooms, including the jail and the popes' apartments, and examine the collections of weapons and documents. Frescoes and sculptures are also on view.

National Gallery of Modern Art

This is the one art museum where you can get your imagination out of ancient Rome and into more modern times. The works here are representative of the Neoclassic and Romantic eras, and the displays include the largest collection of works by 1800s and 1900s artists such as Balla, Fattori, and Burri. In keeping with the timeline that is the museum's focus, you can also find works by foreign artists including Cézanne, Duchamp, Degas, Van Gogh, Pollock, and Monet. The National Gallery of Modern Art is close to the Villa Giulia National Etruscan Museum, so they make a nice one-two punch if you want to plan a morning of museum hopping.

Where to Stay

You can do a day, a week, or even a month in Rome on almost any budget. There are hostels for a few euro if you're trying to travel on a shoestring, or you can go first-class elegance with prime-location hotels full of modern amenities.

The price code for the hotel listings below is $=€100 or less; $$=€100 to €150; $$$=€150 to €200; $$$$=€200 or more per night, per room.

The Beehive
$

Located northeast of Stazione Termini, this is a small hotel owned and operated by American ex-pats from Los Angeles, California. There are just eight rooms, and one of those is a dormitory-style setup that sleeps eight people. All of the rooms share bathrooms, though if you want your own apartment, the couple offers three that can be rented by the room or in their entirety, about fifteen minutes' walking distance from the hotel.
www.the-beehive.com.

Hotel Palladium Palace
$$–$$$$

This large hotel is within walking distance of Stazione Termini and includes an on-site gymnasium, conference room, and panoramic terrace. There is a WiFi hotspot in the lobby as well as a wireless keyboard in each room. Laundry service is available, as is a shuttle service to and from the airport. Occasionally, special offers and last-minute deals are posted on the website.
www.hotelpalladiumpalace.it.

Hotel Julia
$–$$$$

Hotel Julia has been operating since 1949 inside a small 1800s palace. There are thirty-three rooms with direct phone lines, satellite television, and air conditioning. Free WiFi is available in the rooms as well as the public areas, and a buffet breakfast is served daily. Room rates vary widely depending on the season, with "economic singles" costing anywhere from €40 to €90 for the same exact accommodations.

www.hoteljulia.it.

Hotel Locarno
$$–$$$

Built in 1925, the Hotel Locarno's main building houses forty-eight rooms, with most of the deluxe rooms and suites in an extension building that brings the property's total number of rooms to sixty-six. Each has a private bathroom, air conditioning, WiFi access, satellite television, a safe, a mini-bar, and a hair dryer.

www.hotellocarno.com.

Hotel Portoghesi
$$$–$$$$

The same family has owned and operated this hotel for a century and a half, upgrading it over the years so that rooms now include private telephones, air conditioning, satellite television, and WiFi access. There is a roof garden if you want to relax with a cold drink on a sunny day, away from the crowds.

www.hotelportoghesiroma.com.

Where to Eat

Rome is filled with restaurants, and the ones nearest popular attractions typically offer menus in English as well as Italian. Those restaurants are more touristy (and likely more expensive) than the ones you'll find down side streets, but they do generally offer a good taste of the local cuisines.

The price code for the restaurant entrees below is $=€25 or less; $$=€26 to €50; $$$=€51 to €75; $$$$=€100 or more.

Dune Restaurant
$

The Dune is within easy walking distance of Trevi fountain and offers local dishes as well as international cuisine. You can get small or large dishes here, including soups, salads, and omelets. The homemade pasta menu will make you feel deliciously carb guilty just for looking at it.

www.dunerestaurant.it.

Antico Arco
$$–$$$$

There's a wine bar plus four dining rooms at this out-of-the-way, upscale restaurant that consistently wins rave reviews from clients who appreciate how the menu changes with each season. Traditional Roman dishes are the essence of what's offered, but foodies looking for interesting twists on the local cuisine will not be disappointed.

www.anticoarco.it.

La Terraza dell'Eden
$$$$

If you want to spend some serious euro for one night's farewell dinner in Rome, La Terrazza dell'Eden is a good choice. It's the elegant rooftop restaurant of Hotel Eden, serving high-end Mediterranean cuisine with spectacular city views and soft piano music. There's a lovely bar here, too, if you want to enjoy a nice chianti before dinner.

www.starwoodhotels.com.

Agata e Romeo
$-$$$

Back in the late 1800s, the Agata family used to serve roasted pig. Today, the restaurant boasts fine chefs of both Italian and French culinary schools, as well as a thriving catering business in the private homes of Roman nobles. The wine list is extensive and worldly, and has been featured in *Wine Spectator* magazine. This restaurant also has received noteworthy ink from *Travel + Leisure*, the *Los Angeles Times*, and *Marie Claire*, to name a few.

www.agataeromao.it.

Ad Hoc
$-$$

One of the great things about this restaurant, in the heart of Rome, is that it offers a private room for no more than five people—a wonderful way to experience authentic Italian cuisine if you are on your honeymoon or traveling with close friends or family. The owners claim that everything is made fresh, with no frozen ingredients, and the pasta is cooked with olive oil instead of butter or cream, so you can feel free to indulge without the guilt.

www.ristoranteadhoc.com.

Vatican

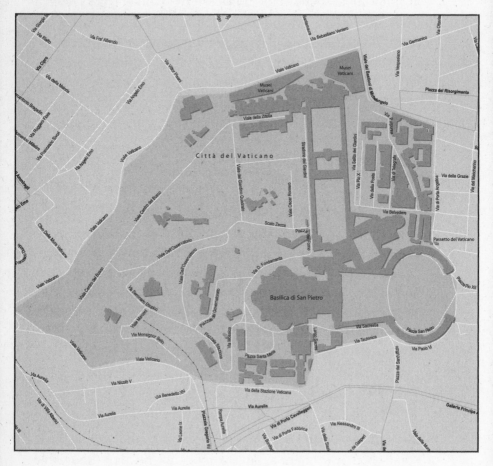

CHAPTER 3

Vatican City

If you looked at Vatican City on a map, you would likely think it was part of the city of Rome. Geographically, it seems to be, but legally speaking the 110-acre, walled-in site is a sovereign city-state. In fact, it is the smallest independent state in the world. This is the place the pope calls home, the location of St. Peter's Basilica, and the site of the Sistine Chapel. Even if you are not Catholic (or not religious at all), the sheer grandeur of Vatican City and the treasured artworks inside its buildings can make for a fascinating day of touring.

History of Vatican City

The history of Christianity runs deep and rich within the boundaries of what we know today as Italy. At one time, an entire swath in the central part of the current country's borders was known as the Papal States, stretching from modern-day Rome to Venice and organized with the pope as both spiritual and civil ruler. Those states existed until 1870, when, after about a decade of territorial handovers, the last of the church-run land was absorbed into what would become today's nation of Italy.

Vatican City itself was not recognized until 1929, creating what from the early 1860s until that year was known as "the Roman Question." When Rome became capital of the newly formed Italy in 1861, nobody within the former Papal Sates or within the new

Italian government quite knew what to do with the religious leaders or the walled-in area where they lived. The pope would not recognize the Italian king's right to govern them inside of Rome, even though their land was inside the very city that had just become Italy's capital. Thus, the pope and his fellow religious leaders refused to leave their compound until the question was resolved, which took a solid generation of negotiations.

 Fact

One of the conditions of the Lateran Treaty, which created Vatican City, was that the pope had to pledge perpetual neutrality in foreign affairs and abstain from mediating any such controversies unless invited by all parties to do so. Hence the pope's continuing presence as a moral guide, not necessarily a negotiator, on the world stage.

The Lateran Treaty, signed by Benito Mussolini on behalf of Italy, officially created Vatican City in 1929, recognizing the full sovereignty of the Holy See—the central government of the Catholic Church since the early days of Christianity—within the boundaries of the newly formed city-state. Thus, Vatican City and the Holy See are two distinct entities, but they are intertwined for practical purposes. For instance, ambassadors who come from Vatican City are said to represent the Holy See, not Vatican City as a state. The pope has total legislative, judicial, and executive power in Vatican City, where he lives inside the papal apartments just off St. Peter's Square.

Modern Life

If you walk up to Vatican City while touring the streets of Rome, you certainly don't feel like you're leaving one country and entering another. There are no passport windows or other obvious borders, just a sudden swarm of tourists inside a walled compound that has been an intimidating presence since its earliest years. You'll know you're getting close when the price of a gelato goes from €2 to €10, and when pizza shoots up from €10 to €20. If you're traveling on a budget, be sure to dine before making your way to the city's immediate outskirts.

Essential

If you want to join the 800 or so people with current citizenship in Vatican City, then you will likely have to get a job working inside the Vatican. Typically, once a person's employment by the Vatican has ended, his or her citizenship is revoked. Some Vatican citizens hold dual passports, with the other one usually being from Italy.

Day-to-Day Business

Vatican City does have its own police force, separate from that of Rome, and it issues its own stamps and coins (a Vatican version of the euro). The millions of tourists who purchase stamps at and mail letters from the Vatican City post office each year contribute greatly to the nation-state's income.

There is an ATM in Vatican City, but it gives instructions for making deposits and withdrawals in Latin, making it perhaps the only one of its kind on the planet. So you can get an ATM receipt as a souvenir of your visit, but unless you are an expert in ancient Roman languages, you may accidentally take out more money than you had intended in the process. As with any government entity, Vatican City has a website. You can check it out at *www.vaticanstate.va*.

Tourism

An estimated 4.2 million people visit Vatican City each year, making it among the top forty destinations in the world. (About the same number of people visit the Statue of Liberty in New

York and the Grand Canyon in Arizona annually.) There are no official statistics about how many of these visitors are Catholic; many people visit Vatican City not for religious reasons, but to appreciate the architecture and masterworks housed within the city walls.

❗ Alert

You can't just walk into a Mass at St. Peter's Basilica and ask to have your baby baptized. You have to make reservations in advance, and the only way to do so is by fax. When dialing from within the United States, that number is (011) 39 06 698 85793.

By sheer numbers, 4.2 million visitors to a space of just 110 acres is overwhelming, and you can expect to find crowds at Vatican City pretty much year-round. Mass is celebrated several times a day, seven days a week, with the biggest crowds attending services during Easter and Christmas. During national holidays in Italy, there have been as many as 10,000 people standing in serpentine lines that wind through the nearby streets and alleyways, waiting to get inside St. Peter's Basilica and the Vatican Museums.

As of this writing, Mass was being celebrated at St. Peter's Basilica from Monday through Saturday at 9 A.M., 10 A.M., 11 A.M., noon, and 5 P.M., and on Sundays and holidays at 9 A.M., 10:30 A.M., 11:30 A.M., 12:15 P.M., 3 P.M., 6 P.M., and 7:30 P.M.

Respectful Tourism

You will need to respect the dress code at Vatican City in order to enter locations including St. Peter's Basilica—even if you're only taking a self-guided tour and not attending a celebration of Mass. There are monitors who look at the people lined up to enter the church, and anyone who fails to meet the dress code can (and will) be refused entry. The rules are as follows:

- No skirts above the knee
- No shorts
- No bare shoulders
- No bare feet

A nice scarf or shawl wrapped around your shoulders over a T-shirt and jeans will do the trick, and nearby vendors on the street can provide you with a cheap pair of long slacks if your plans include leaving Vatican City and continuing to tour Rome in shorts on a hot summer day.

Also, be prepared to put backpacks, purses, and other items through metal detectors before entering tourist destinations within Vatican City. Personal searches are sometimes requested if the guards on duty note anything suspicious.

St. Peter's Basilica

St. Peter's Basilica takes its name from St. Peter, one of the twelve apostles of Jesus who was the first bishop of Rome and, thus, the first in the line of papal succession that continues today. The basilica is one of four major basilicas in Rome, and is the most dominant structure in all of Vatican City.

 Fact

St. Peter's is a basilica, not a cathedral, because it is not the seat of a bishop. Basilicas, by definition, are large or important churches upon which the pope has conferred special ceremonial rites. St. Peter's certainly fits that bill in size alone, covering nearly six acres of land and being able to hold some 60,000 people.

Visiting St. Peter's Basilica is a must for anyone interested in architecture or art. The building itself bears the fingerprints of Michelangelo, and countless treasured masterworks are housed inside. The sheer expanses of marble in the place are astounding.

Construction

The building that you can tour today is not St. Peter's Basilica in its original form. The first structure was a 350-foot-long, fourth-century church built over a small shrine that was believed to mark St. Peter's burial place. This original basilica was neglected over the years, and was badly in need of repair by the late 1400s. It was Pope Julius II, in 1505, who finally decided to raze the original structure and build a new one. He held a contest to find the best design, and the work that began under his reign continued well into the 1600s, with a large number of religious leaders and artisans contributing to the building that stands in Vatican City today.

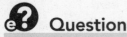 **Question**

Is the dome at St. Peter's Basilica the tallest in the world?
Yes, it is. At its highest point, it rises 448 feet above the floor. It's a massive structure, too, not just in height alone. The dome's internal diameter is 136 feet, the length of a twelve- or thirteen-story building if it were laid on its side.

Most famous in this group is Michelangelo, who, in 1547, took over the building program at St. Peters while it was in a state of mid-construction. Michelangelo thus did not conceive the massive dome that impresses so many visitors today, but he did help to execute its construction and in doing so lent his own artistic sensibilities to its design.

The grand façade on the outside of St. Peter's Basilica came later, under the watch of Baroque architect Carlo Maderna. It is made of travertine stone with massive Corinthian columns, all of which create a dominant presence as you approach the basilica from St. Peter's Square outside.

📢 Alert

As of this writing, cameras are allowed inside St. Peter's Basilica, but you usually won't be allowed to use a flash. Many visitors try to lie down on the ground and take a photograph looking up at the massive dome, but this is forbidden. Security guards will insist that you get back up immediately, whether you've clicked the shutter or not.

Tombs, Artworks, and Relics

You could spend an entire lifetime studying the tombs, artworks, and relics located within St. Peter's Basilica. Ninety-one popes are buried here, including Pope John Paul II, who died in 2005. There are a pair of holy water basins that date to the early 1700s, Michelangelo's statue *Pietà* (which depicts a grieving but graceful Mary holding the limp body of Jesus after the crucifixion), and dozens of statues that each tell a part religious history and tradition.

Unless you are a religious scholar, you probably won't be able to understand or appreciate everything you're seeing without a guide. It doesn't cost anything to walk into the basilica for a self-guided tour, or you can pay €10 for a guided look at the excavations around St. Peter's tomb. Reservations must be made at least a week in advance. Contact the Ufficio Scavi at 06 698 85 318 or *scavi@fsp.va*. The gift shop on site has entire books describing the sculptures and basilica itself if you would prefer to buy that and work your way around at your own pace. If you want to read such a book during your plane ride over to Italy, shop online at the Vatican's website, *www.vaticanstate.va*, which includes a bookstore.

The Sistine Chapel

The Sistine Chapel is located within the Apostolic Palace, which is where the pope lives. It makes regular appearances on television as the home of the papal conclaves, which are the deliberations that go on before a new pope is elected.

When you enter Vatican City with St. Peter's Basilica directly before you (as almost everyone does), the Sistine Chapel will be to your right, inside the Vatican Museums. The chapel itself is toward the end of the guided tour of the museums that is well worth its purchase price. As with St. Peter's Basilica, you will be required to meet a dress code. No bare backs or shoulders, no bare feet, and no exposed knees.

Alert

Hours of operation for tours of the Sistine Chapel are typically listed as ending between 12:20 P.M. and 3:20 P.M. daily, but final ticket sales and admissions are a half-hour to an hour before that, to ensure that the last people in line get enough time to walk around before the chapel closes. If you want to be sure to get in, arrive closer to the daily 8:45 A.M. opening.

If you plan to visit the Vatican Museums and Sistine Chapel during a time when lots of tourists are expected, then the official Vatican website you should visit first is *http://biglietteriamusei.vatican .va/musei/tickets/*. Pay the online booking fee and print out your tickets at home before you even get on the plane to Europe. Your tickets will include a time when you are allowed to enter the museums through a special line, which often has about twenty people in it as opposed to several thousand people in the regular line. You can make reservations for English-speaking guided tours through the website, too. The advance-purchase surcharges can save you hours of waiting once you arrive.

Construction

The chapel as it stands today was completed in 1481 after about eight years of construction. It is not the original; that was demolished to make way after it fell into a state of disrepair. The current chapel appears to be similar in proportion to the original, which records indicate existed as early as the 1360s.

Outside, the Sistine Chapel doesn't look nearly as impressive as buildings such as St. Peter's Basilica. The chapel has a brick façade with no decorations or exterior entrances (you enter through the Papal Palace). Inside, though, grandeur reigns; the chapel's walls have served as canvases for some of the most impressive artistic works in modern human history.

Artworks

There are frescoes and tapestries throughout the Sistine Chapel, all done by various and combinations of revered Renaissance artists including Michelangelo, Raphael, and Botticelli. The most famous works inside the chapel are Michelangelo's frescoes on the ceiling and his end-wall composition *The Last Judgment*.

Michelangelo's Frescoes

Pope Julius II actually wanted Michelangelo to paint the twelve apostles on the ceiling of the Sistine Chapel, but the artist lobbied for a more substantial challenge that included representations of creation, man's downfall, and the promise of salvation. The resulting work took nearly four years to complete—Michelangelo worked on it between 1508 and 1512—and incorporated more than 300 figures. Some of the scenes within the entire ceiling fresco are famous unto themselves, including *Creation of Adam*, which shows a bearded, elderly God touching his right index finger to Adam's left hand.

The Last Judgment

Pope Clement VII commissioned Michelangelo to paint *The Last Judgment* on the Sistine Chapel's altar wall, but it was Pope

Paul III who oversaw the work after Clement died. The work took the artist from 1534 until 1541 to complete, depicting the second coming of Christ and the apocalypse.

 Fact

Nowadays, cartoons are what children watch on Saturday mornings, but during the Renaissance the word referred to preparatory sketches or drawings. Thus, the artworks that Raphael created for the weavers to follow in creating the Sistine Chapel tapestries are called cartoons. The Raphael cartoons now hang in a London museum.

Interestingly, the scene as it appears today is not exactly how Michelangelo painted it. He was true to anatomical form in his renderings, but they were later deemed obscene and ordered blurred, work undertaken by one of his apprentices. Because he painted loincloths over some of Michelangelo's depictions of genitals, the apprentice earned the nickname "the breeches maker."

Raphael's Tapestries

Renaissance painter and architect Raphael Sanzio (known today almost exclusively by his first name) was commissioned in 1515 to create a series of tapestries for the Sistine Chapel. Pope Leo X wanted the ten tapestries, called *Acts of the Apostles*, to fill the lower portion of the chapel's walls, and it took weavers four years to complete the large works that Raphael designed.

Interestingly, Michelangelo and Raphael were competitors in the art scene of their time, and thus Raphael went to great lengths to try to ensure that his tapestries would "outdo" Michelangelo's ceiling frescoes. As the tapestries only hang in the Sistine Chapel for limited time periods nowadays, you will have to get lucky with the timing of your vacation in order to judge for yourself which artist's work is the most enduring.

Stanze di Raffaello

Raphael's rooms are a group of reception rooms inside the Apostolic Palace in Vatican City that contain frescoes painted by the Renaissance artist and, after his death, assistants from his workshop. Pope Julius II commissioned the work in the early 1500s as a redecoration, apparently unhappy with the frescoes that his predecessor had enjoyed.

Today, the works are among the most extraordinary pieces in Vatican City, and are available for viewing by the public. You can walk through the four rooms to see the frescoes on your way to tour the Sistine Chapel and Vatican Museums.

Question

Which of the frescoes did Raphael finish first?
Disputation of the Holy Sacrament, which is in the Room of the Segnatura. If walls could talk, this fresco would have countless stories to share, as it was the original centerpiece of the room where the supreme papal tribunal held its meetings.

Hall of Constantine

This is the largest of the four rooms, with the frescoes representing Christianity's victory over paganism. While impressive, the artwork was not begun until Raphael had died, so if your goal is to see an authentic piece by the Renaissance artist during your tour, admire this room quickly and then keep on walking.

Room of Heliodorus

The theme of this room is the heavenly protection that Christ granted to the church. There are four paintings in this room, and in each of them, Raphael originally included the likeness of Julius II.

It's believed this was because Raphael was thankful for the chance to showcase his artistic talents on such a large scale, much as one of today's new rap singers might mention a bigger star who gives him a shot at a few lyrics on a hot new album.

Room of the Segnatura

This was the first of the frescoes that Raphael completed, taking inspiration from the fact that the room would be used to house the pope's library collection. There is a theme of wisdom, along with artistic references to theology, philosophy, and law.

Stanza dell'incendio del Borgo

Named for the *Fire in the Borgo* fresco inside the room, this space is primarily the work of Raphael's assistants. The artist did the original designs, especially for that namesake fresco, but it was his apprentices who completed that artwork, as well as all the others in this section of Raphael's rooms.

Vatican Library

If you had to put a date on when the collection of the Vatican Library began to come together, it would be sometime in the late thirteenth century. The popes of that century's latter decades undertook the mammoth task of trying to reconstruct a new collection of historical texts after the original archive of the Roman Catholic Church—which, by some accounts, dated to the fourth century—was dispersed for unknown reasons in the early 1200s. Formally speaking, the Vatican Library as it exists today was established in 1475, but that inauguration came thanks to the combining of longstanding collections of Greek, Latin, and Hebrew works. The building that houses those original works and all those that have been added until the present is the building that still stands in Vatican City today, commissioned in the late 1500s.

The current collection at Vatican City includes some 75,000 manuscripts and about 1.1 million printed books. That's certainly not the largest collection in the world (by comparison, the Library of Congress boasts more than 61 million manuscripts and some 32 million books), but some of the holdings are extraordinary, including the *Codex Vaticanus*, which, while incomplete, is believed to be the oldest known manuscript of the Bible.

e! Alert

Vatican Library was temporarily closed to the public in the summer of 2007, while a rebuilding and restoration process got under way. The scheduled date of completion and reopening is September 2010. If that's close to your travel dates, check to ensure work is on schedule by calling (011) 39 06 6987 9402 from the United States.

Gaining Admission

Unlike St. Peter's Basilica and the Sistine Chapel, you can't just walk up to the Vatican Library, get in line, and wait your turn for a chance to go inside. Texts that are centuries old are delicate, rare, and fragile, and for those reasons the Vatican imposes strict guidelines about who can gain entry.

In general, the library's own rules state that admission is intended for "qualified researchers and scholars from around the world, particularly professors and researchers from universities and other institutions of higher education, and other learned persons known for their writings and scholarly publications." Still, undergraduate students are rarely given access, and even graduate students can have a tough time making the cut.

Even those who do gain permission to use to the library for research will not necessarily have the right to simply browse. The library's own rules, for instance, prohibit people who show a need to review printed books from even entering the Manuscripts Reading Room. If you think you have what it takes to fill out a successful application to enter the Vatican Library, then you can call for more information from the United States by dialing (011) 39 06 6987 9402.

Vatican Secret Archives

All of that sounds shrouded enough, but there is yet another layer of preserved information inside Vatican City: the Vatican Secret Archives. Pope Paul V ordered about 35,000 volumes removed from the Vatican Library in the 1600s, and these became known as the Secret Archives. Nobody knows for sure how many volumes are in the Secret Archives, since publication of so much as an index listing them is forbidden.

Today, you can access the Secret Archives for research if you meet the tough criteria set by the Vatican (similar to the criteria for doing research in Vatican Library), and—perhaps more crucially—if you already know about the existence of a specific document that you wish to research. Unless you're a biblical scholar, good luck with that one.

Vatican Museums

More than 4 million people a year visit the Vatican Museums, whose visitor route includes the Sistine Chapel and Raphael's Rooms and ends with entry into St. Peter's Basilica. According to the Vatican, the museums originated with a group of sculptures collected by Pope Julius II in the early 1500s. As you already know from earlier sections in this chapter, Julius II was a fan of then-contemporary artists Michelangelo and Raphael. Thus, it's no surprise that the museums include decorative works by both. You can also find works here by Leonardo da Vinci and Fra Angelico.

There are a baker's dozen sections in the Vatican Museums:

- Gregorian Egyptian Museum
- Gregorian Etruscan Museum
- Classical Greek and Roman Antiquities
- Pio Christian Museum
- Picture gallery
- Tapestries
- Ceramics
- Miniature mosaics
- Modern Religious Art
- Missionary-Ethnological Museum
- Museo Sacro (previously part of the Vatican Library)
- Gregorian Profane Museum
- Vatican Historical Museum

There are both guided and audio tours available; audio tours are offered in eight languages, including English. As with most museums, you'll also find a gift shop and bookstore, along with a cafeteria and pizzeria to help recharge your engine should you decide to try to at least take a cursory look at all the collections in a single day.

Note that if you intend to see the Sistine Chapel, it will be included in your ticket price when you purchase entry into the Vatican Museums. If you want to get a better idea what kinds of works you will be able to see throughout the museums, then check out the (albeit limited) virtual tours at the Vatican's website, *www.mv.vatican.va*.

If you're visiting the Vatican Museums with a group, opt for the "radio services" option of the audio tour. It is a multichannel broadcast system that lets everyone in your party wear headphones and hear the guide at the same time, thus eliminating any confusion about which audio recording refers to which artwork.

Northeastern Italy

CHAPTER 4

Northeastern Italy

There have been many names for Venice, the city that is, by far, the most popular tourist destination in northeastern Italy. No matter what name you know Venice by—"Queen of the Adriatic," "City of Bridges," or "City of Light"—it is one of the most magnificent metropolitan areas in the country and, by many people's account, in the entire world. There's no doubt your trip to northeastern Italy will include this historic center, and hopefully, you will also have time to explore beyond its borders to nearby Padua, Verona, and Vicenza.

Lay of the Land

For the purposes of this book, northeastern Italy comprises two regions: Friuli-Venezia Giulia and Veneto. The former is as far northeast as you can get in Italy's "corner" before you cross the Italian border and enter Austria and Slovenia, while Veneto, to Friuli-Venezia Giulia's west, is the region that includes Venice. It receives 20 million tourists a year who are drawn there because of the city's history, charm, and beauty.

Venice Marco Polo Airport serves the region, including some international flights from the eastern United States on Delta Air Lines and US Airways. Local airlines also make connecting flights here from Rome and Milan, and you can get to in-country and international trains via a bus service that runs between the airport and the nearby Venice-Santa Lucia and Mestre-Venice railway stations. Full schedules, as well as links to train operators, are at the airport's website, *www.veniceairport.com*.

If you plan to fly to Venice and stay for a few days, skip the rental car. There are ferries that can get you and your vehicle to some places, but even the locals use small boats and a good pair of comfortable shoes to make their way amid the dozens of canals.

✴ Essential

If you want to experience Venice as a city of water from the moment you arrive, then consider taking a water taxi instead of a traditional one with wheels from Venice Marco Polo Airport to your hotel. The fee is €98 for four passengers: not cheap, but certainly scenic. You can make reservations via the airport's website, *www.veniceairport.com*.

If you are visiting Venice as a day trip from another part of Italy and already have a rental car, you can leave it at one of two parking lots/garages that serve the city: Tronchetto and Piazzale Roma. The cost is about €25 per day for parking, and the lots are open twenty-four hours a day, every day of the year. Ferries and public transport boats will get you from the lots to the city itself, and from there you can explore as the locals do: on foot. For directions and reservations, the Trochetto website is *www.veniceparking.it*. If you can stick with that parking area, do so; it's typically a lot less harried with fewer crowds than the Piazzale Roma site.

Venice

There is no city in the world like Venice, if only for the simple reason of geography. The city is built not on a broad stretch of land, but on 118 small islands atop a lagoon. About 150 canals run amid and around those islands, including the Grand Canal, which snakes through the city from north to south like a backward "S." More than 400 bridges connect one island to the next, with *vaporetti* (public transportation boats) and gondolas cruising all around. The city has been known for its relationship to the water since its earliest days, when it was a major shipping hub on the Mediterranean and its leaders controlled large swaths of inland territory as well.

✅ Fact

Marco Polo is perhaps the most famous Venetian trader, known as one of the first westerners to traverse the Silk Road to China. He left Venice in 1271 with his father and uncle, who also were traders, and didn't make it back home until some twenty years later. His book about his travels apparently inspired Christopher Columbus to seek a western route.

Historic Power

While there are records indicating the existence of people in modern-day Venice before the fifth and sixth centuries, it was then that barbarian invasions farther inland caused settlers to flee into the lagoon area that comprises the city today. By the 1100s, Venice was a city-state just like Genoa to the west, a prime trading center on the seafaring route between western Europe and Asia. At the peak of its power in the 1300s, Venice had some 36,000 sailors running as many as 300 ships that could be converted from commercial to wartime uses as needed to defend territory and shipping routes. The city's decline in power began in the 1400s, when explorers discovered new ocean and land routes to Asia as well as the New World.

The French soldier Napoleon Bonaparte conquered Venice and ended its history as a republic in 1797. Austria took control of the land the following year, after Napoleon signed the Treaty of Campo Formio. Control changed hands a few more times until 1866, when

Venice, along with the rest of the Veneto region, became part of the new state of Italy.

Tourism as we know it today began in the late 1800s, when the beaches in Venice's Lido section (where the Venice Film Festival takes place) became popular. The city was generally spared from major bombings during World War II, though floods and general neglect have contributed to the continuing demise of many of the city's historic monuments, buildings, and artworks. You may have heard reports that Venice is sinking, a reality that residents began to notice in the mid-1900s as they were forced to move out of first floors and into the upper levels of some homes. The cause of the sinking was underground water pumping that is now prohibited, and by some estimates, the sinking is now under control.

 Question

How did underground water pumping cause Venice to sink?
As industrial companies sucked water out of the aquifer beneath the lagoon on which Venice sits, the soil left behind began to compact, sort of like a sponge that has been squeezed dry. The buildings atop that soil sank down a little at a time until the water pumping stopped.

Modern Perils

Global concerns about climate change and rising sea levels are particularly important to Venice and the tourists who enjoy visiting there, especially as flooding becomes more commonplace. According to the British-based relief organization Venice In Peril (*www.veniceinperil.org*), locations that flooded ten times a year in 1900 now flood as many as sixty times a year. The regular water level in the city is about ten inches higher than it was in 1897, with the constant wear eating away at the bricks at the base of some buildings. Donations are being accepted to help preserve historic sites, and the Italian government contributes regularly to restoration programs.

The Venice Water Authority has a plan for a series of inflatable "gates" that would prevent water from coming into the Venice lagoon from the sea when high water is in the forecast. If you want to watch a video of how this would work, go to *www.pbs.org* and search for "Venice gate" in the website's *Nova* section.

Touring Tips

Venice is divided into six sections: Cannaregio, Castello, San Marco, Dorsoduro, San Polo, and Santa Croce. Trying to find anything by street number in any of these districts is virtually impossible because the system that Venice uses is unlike any other in the world. Ask a local water taxi driver to take you to the location of your choice, and you'll find it just as easily (if not more easily) than you would by trying to decipher street names and maps.

Alert

Gondolas are a romantic option for touring the Grand Canal in Venice, but they're used mostly by tourists nowadays—and thus have price tags designed to get the most out of you during your visit. Look for larger water taxis and ferries with guides if you don't mind sharing the view with others, and you'll save a good bit of money.

The Grand Canal

One of the absolutely must-do activities in Venice is a ride along the more than two-mile-long Grand Canal. Nowhere else on the planet can you see buildings rising right out of the water. A guided tour is a must; the dozens of buildings, palaces, and other structures that you will see could take a lifetime for you to learn. Even cursory students of architecture will find a feast for the eyes in this part of the city.

Bring your binoculars if your trip to Venice will fall during the first Sunday in September. That's when the annual Historical Regatta is held on the Grand Canal, with gondoliers sailing in costume and other Venetian boats competing in various events while thousands of spectators watch from onshore and from floating stands.

St. Mark's Square, St. Mark's Basilica, and Doge's Palace

This trifecta of sightseeing delights is in the San Marco district, all within a stone's throw of one another. You will start in the square, also known as Piazza San Marco, which is the principal square in all of Venice. Think tourists, cameras, and pigeons. Grab a cool drink and maybe a panini from a local vendor, and sit back and watch the show of people go by. It's surprising how loudly the human voices echo without the noise of nearby car traffic from cars as there would be in other cities.

 Alert

St. Mark's Square is the lowest point in Venice. As such, it is typically the first to flood when high water comes into the Venice lagoon from the Adriatic Sea. The Venetian phrase for such high-water occurrences is *acqua alta*, so if you see predictions for that—or even for heavy rain—consider skipping the square until the water level subsides.

St. Mark's Basilica (which enforces a strict dress code) is filled with gilded mosaics and marble expanses. Also inside is the Pala d'Oro, an altarpiece set with nearly 2,000 emeralds, rubies, pearls, and other precious gems and stones. The building itself is a marvel of Byzantine architecture and was, for some time, known as the "church of gold" because of its artworks and symbolism of wealth and power.

Connected to St. Mark's Basilica is the Doges' Palace, known locally as Palazzo Ducale. At one time, this was a governmental building that included offices and prisons. Today, it is a museum that you can tour room by room, viewing everything from classic oil paintings to former inmate cells. If you want to leave the crowds and view the lesser-known parts of the palace, ask for the *itinerari segreti* (secret itinerary), which will get you to places such as a former torture chamber.

Peggy Guggenheim Collection

American art collector Peggy Guggenheim lived in Venice for about three decades, until her death in 1979. She had previously lived in Paris and owned a gallery in London, and she was married to German dadaist/surrealist Max Ernst, so it's not surprising that she amassed a collection of works by such renowned artists as Pablo Picasso, Salvador Dali, René Magritte, and Jackson Pollock.

That collection is now on display in Venice's Dorsoduro section, inside Guggenheim's former home—an unfinished eighteenth-century Grand Canal palace. Special exhibitions regularly take place, so check the museum's website, *www.guggenheim-venice.it*, to see what will be on display during the dates of your trip.

 **Essential**

If you have a membership card from New York City's Solomon R. Guggenheim Museum, bring it with you to Venice. All Guggenheim Museum members get free admission to view the Peggy Guggenheim collection (regular admission for other patrons is €10).

Basilica di Santa Maria Gloriosa dei Frari

This is one of the greatest churches in Venice, easy to access from the San Polo and Santa Croce sections of the city. The church that originally stood here was completed in the early 1300s, but the modern structure was built during the course of nearly the entire century that followed. The exterior is Italian Gothic, and the masterworks inside include pieces by Renaissance artists Giovanni Bellini, Donatello, and Titian. As with all the other churches in Italy, be sure you are dressed appropriately before entering. No bare shoulders or bare legs above the knees.

Padua

If you've read William Shakespeare's *Taming of the Shrew*, then you've heard of Padua, which is where most of the action in that play takes place. Padua is about twenty-three miles west of Venice and is home to more than 200,000 people who are regularly counted as residents of the Venetian suburbs. You can reach Padua by rental car, bus, taxicab, or train, though a portion of the city's center is closed to all traffic except pedestrians and bicycle riders. The train ride from Venice (there's one arriving every fifteen minutes or so) is just twenty minutes long and brings you into Padua's main station, Padova Centrale.

 Fact

Allied bombing during World War II destroyed several sites in Padua, including the Chiesa Degli Eremitani church, which dated to the thirteenth century and housed frescoes by Renaissance artist Andrea Mantegna. Some art historians say this was the largest cultural loss Italy suffered in the entire war.

History

In a region full of antiquities, Padua claims to be the oldest city in northern Italy. Nobody knows for sure whether that's true, but certainly the city is longstanding. Artifacts dating back to before the common era have been found here. Attila invaded with the Huns in the fifth century, a constitution was established in the eleventh century, and a university was founded in 1222. The Venetians took over as rulers of Padua in the early fifteenth century and remained in control until the Venetian republic fell just before the turn of the nineteenth century. As with Venice, Padua was under Austrian control for a time, eventually becoming part of Italy in 1866.

Professors and alumni of the university in Padua include Copernicus and Galileo. It houses what is believed to be the world's oldest botanical garden, established in 1545 and still in its original site. According to the university, there are some 6,000 plants there today. You can tour the garden for €4 year-round, except on holidays, when it is closed. Details are online at *www.ortobotanico .unipd.it*.

Touring Tips

The main sights worth seeing in Padua are religious. Perhaps the best known is Scrovegni Chapel, which was originally built as a private chapel for a wealthy banker named Enrico degli Scrovegni. He commissioned Renaissance painter Giotto di Bondone to paint a fresco called *Last Judgment* that covers an entire wall and other works of art. Guided tours are available in Italian, or you can make special arrangements for English-speaking tours if you are visiting with a group. The official website is *www .cappelladegliscrovegni.it*.

Another site worth seeing is the Basilica del Santo, which was completed in the early 1300s and to this day is Padua's largest church. It is where the corpse of St. Anthony of Padua lies, and thus is an important location of pilgrimage for many visitors.

Beyond touring the interior of the church, which houses many artworks, you can make arrangements for a guided tour of the courtyards, which are absolutely gorgeous. Book directly online through *www.basilicadelsanto.org*.

 **Alert**

You must make reservations to tour Scrovegni Chapel at least twenty-four hours in advance, and you can do so online at *www.cappelladegliscrovegni.it*. If you plan to visit the chapel on a Monday, you must make the reservation the previous Friday. On the day of your tour, you must collect your ticket at least one hour before your scheduled tour.

Verona

To the west of Padua is the city of Verona, which Shakespeare made famous in his tragedy *Romeo and Juliet*. Verona is home to some 250,000 people, roughly the same population as Padua. It dates to at least 550 B.C. and, like its neighboring areas, fell to Napoleonic and then Austrian rule before becoming part of Italy in the late 1800s. The entire city was named a UNESCO World Heritage site in 2000 because of the sheer number of monuments from antiquity, Medieval times, and the Renaissance. It also is noted as an exceptional example of a military stronghold.

Verona Arena

The amphitheater in Verona was completed around 30 A.D. and is the third largest in Italy (behind the Colosseum in Rome and the amphitheater at Capua). It reportedly once held 20,000 to 25,000 spectators at a time, and the interior is largely intact even though the exterior was badly damaged by an earthquake in 1117. Today, the arena seats about 15,000 spectators both on stone steps around the perimeter and in modern, padded chairs on the main level.

Depending on when you visit, you might catch an event here—anything from operas to fairs and ballets. Such events tend to take place between June and August. You can check the schedule for your travel dates at *www.arena.it*.

Casa di Giulietta

Don't let the spelling of Giulietta throw you off; that's how Shakespeare's fictional character Juliet Capulet was known in some early editions of his *Romeo and Juliet* tragedy. Casa di Giulietta, or "Juliet's House," is the site of what is said to be the inspiration for the balcony scene (you remember the words: "What light through yonder window breaks?"). That's unprovable, of course, but it doesn't stop tourists from paying a few euros apiece to take a look.

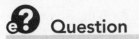 Question

Is opera the only kind of music performed at Verona Arena?
No—rockers sometimes take the stage, too. Patrons of the past have been able to sit on the stone steps (wearing Roman-style togas, if they so chose) and listen to everyone from The Who to Kiss and Pearl Jam.

The house is right near the city's main shopping street, Via G Mazzini, so can make for a nice diversion from buying souvenirs even if you don't believe the hype.

Basilica di San Zeno

Though the original church on this site dates to 380 A.D., the large, well-known church as it stands today was completed in the late fourteenth century after being rebuilt following the great earthquake of 1117. The church is known for its Romanesque architecture, its bronze entrance doors (which can only be viewed well from inside), and its Andrea Mantegna triptych (an artwork divided into three pieces) known as the San Zeno Altarpiece. If you plan to visit this church, be prepared to walk a bit. It's outside the city center.

Vicenza

The city of Vicenza is between Venice and Verona but is much smaller and only has about 120,000 residents. It shares a similar history with its nearby sister cities, and was ruled by (and thus shares the same stories as) Venice beginning in 1404. Today, the United States Army keeps a post here known as Caserma Ederle ("Camp Ederle"), which is the headquarters of the Southern European Task Force and the 173rd Airborne Brigade.

Most tourists who visit Vicenza arrive with at least a cursory knowledge of architecture and a desire to see the buildings Padua native Andrea Palladio designed in the 1500s. The movement known as Palladian Architecture was named for him, which consists of designs based on the symmetry and perspective of formal classical temples by the Ancient Greeks and Romans. The style is known well beyond Italy, and designers in England and the United States have embraced it over the centuries.

Essential

If you want to have good luck in love and in life, then join the thousands of people who walk up to the bronze statue of Juliet at Casa di Giulietta and rub her right breast. Doing so is said to be lucky.

Villa Capra

Palladio designed this Renaissance villa—also known as "La Rotonda"—for a priest who retired from the Vatican and decided to build a home in the Venetian countryside in 1565. Palladio died in 1580 before the villa was complete, but the design is associated with him today nonetheless. The interior is as magnificent, if not more so, than the exterior, with a domed room that is reminiscent of fresco-dominated cathedrals.

Villa Capra is still a private home, owned by a former professor of architecture at the University of Virginia. It's open to the public for interior tours only on Wednesdays, and the exterior gardens are open daily.

ⓔ✔ Fact

President Thomas Jefferson's self-designed Monticello, near Charlottesville, Virginia, is based on Palladian architecture that Jefferson saw while traveling in Europe during the late 1700s. Jefferson's architectural designs for the University of Virginia were also based on Palladio's work.

Basilica Palladiana

This building is located in Vicenza's central Piazza dei Signori and features one of the earliest examples of what came to be known as a Palladian window. Though Palladio didn't invent the arched design, he did use it extensively in his structures. There's a large hall inside the basilica that is used today for exhibitions and events.

Teatro Olimpico

Palladio's last work was this theater, which is widely considered the first covered theater of modern times. It is the oldest surviving example of a Renaissance theater, and the architect himself never got to see it completed; he died just six months after construction began. It is still used for productions today, though only in the spring and fall because there is no heat or air conditioning inside. If you want to see whether a production is planned during your travel dates, visit the theater's official website, *www.olimpico.vicenza.it*.

Palazzo Chiericati

This palace is currently the home of Vicenza's museum and art gallery. Most of the artworks inside are by local artists, as opposed to the masters whose works you can see in the region's basilicas.

Other Must-See Spots

Outside this region's main cities of Venice, Verona, and Vicenza, you can find interesting locations for day trips or half-day trips that you might want to combine with a visit to the cities themselves. Two of the most interesting options are the Wine Road in the Euganean Hills and the town of Treviso, home of clothing designer Luciano Benetton.

 Fact

In 1991, Benetton teamed with the toy manufacturer Mattel to create Benetton Barbie. The two companies worked together again in 2006 to launch Benetton Fashion Fever Barbie. (And if you're interested, there are Benetton clothes for Ken, too.)

Euganean Hills Wine Road

The Strada del Vino Colli Eugenei, as it's known in Italian, is a route you can follow by rental car with a map from the tourist office in Padua. Unfortunately, the route's website (*www.stradadelvinocollieuganei.it*) is only in Italian, so unless you speak the language, you'll have a tough time researching the wineries and their vintages in advance of your trip. The website operated by Italy and Wine suggests semi-private and private tours of the area with English-speaking guides; learn more at *www.italyandwine.net*.

There also are cute little villages and scenic walking routes in this area, making it an interesting option for local bed-and-breakfast-style overnight trips. This is well outside the normal tourism zones, though, so if you don't have a good grasp of the Italian language, you might have a tough time getting the things you want and need.

Treviso

This city of less than 100,000 people is ideal for a day trip. Accommodations are limited inside the city limits, and a train ride from Venice is the easiest way to get here.

While there are plenty of historic sites to see, the city is the proud home of the Benetton Group, a global clothing brand founded in 1965 and made popular in the United States during the 1980s. There is a large store in the center of town where you can find designs that haven't yet gone global.

Where to Stay

You could easily book a hotel room in Venice and make day trips to Verona, Vicenza, and the surrounding areas, but there are good options in the outlying cities if you want to get away from the bulk of the crowds along Venice's Grand Canal.

The price code for the hotel listings below is $=€100 or less; $$=€100 to €150; $$$=€150 to €200; $$$$=€200 or more per night, per room.

Locanda Antico Fiore
$$$–$$$$

This hotel, housed in a 1700s building, is in Venice's San Marco district near St. Mark's Square and its popular tourist sites as well as the Grand Canal. You can arrive by water taxi for a true Venetian experience. Rooms come in twin, double, and family varieties, each with private bathroom, air conditioning, telephone, and television.
www.anticofiore.com.

Hotel Giorgione
$$$$

A bit farther from the hustle and bustle of the San Marco district is this hotel, which is in the Cannaregio section of Venice. You can walk from here to St. Mark's Square in about ten minutes, but then leave the main tourist district behind each night. The building dates to the early 1800s, and each room has its own bathroom, air conditioning, television, and telephone. A nice touch is the complimentary umbrella for you to use during your stay.
www.hotelgiorgione.com.

Hotel La Residenza
$-$$$

This hotel is in Venice's Castello district, inside a fifteenth-century mansion with rooms that were renovated in 2001. Each room has a bathroom, television, air conditioning, and telephone. The hotel's location is east of St. Mark's Square, which you can get to on foot as long as you don't mind a bit of a walk.
www.venicelaresidenza.com.

Hotel Maxim
$-$$$$

Hotel Maxim is in Verona and has 185 guest rooms configured with either one double or two single beds. Each room has a private bathroom, free modem connections for laptop computers, air conditioning, and television. There is WiFi on site, too, and breakfast is included in the room rate. Children five and younger can stay in your room for free.
www.maximverona.it.

Hotel Giardini
$–$$

Located in Vicenza, this hotel has just eighteen rooms, each with a private bathroom, air conditioning, television, and telephone. The building is in the middle of the old town center, allowing you to walk to many of the Palladian architectural sites. Though the hotel is small, it does take online reservations.

www.hotelgiardini.com.

Where to Eat

Venice will offer your most metropolitan dining experiences in this part of Italy, but there are good meals to be had in the outlying cities and towns as well.

The price code for the restaurant entrees below is $=€25 or less; $$=€26 to €50; $$$=€51 to €75; $$$$=€100 or more.

Avogaria
$$–$$$$

Avogaria is one of Venice's trendy, modern restaurants, serving Venetian, Italian, and international cuisine. If you're a vegetarian, you'll appreciate the relatively large number of dishes available alongside meat and pasta entrees. The wine list is quite good as well, featuring selections from Italy's various grape-growing regions.

www.avogaria.com.

Centrale
$$$-$$$$

Celebrity sightings are commonplace at this Venice restaurant and lounge, where a private gondola entrance and security services are on the menu alongside traditional Venetian cuisine. If you don't want to blow your budget on the entrees, order some appetizers at the wine bar, which features about 200 bottles on its own menu. *www.centrale-lounge.com.*

Piola
$-$$

You might recognize the name Piola from its restaurants in New York City, Miami Beach, and Atlanta, but the thin-crust pizza recipes all come from Treviso, where the company opened its first restaurant in 1986. There are dozens of topping combinations available, plus salads and pasta dishes. *www.piola.it.*

CHAPTER 5

North-Central Italy

The Lombardy region, which includes the fashionable city of Milan, dominates north-central Italy. You will find countless national monuments here along with a handful of UNESCO World Heritage Sites, impressive cathedrals, Leonardo da Vinci's *The Last Supper*, and—oh, yes—some of the best shopping and most stunning scenery that Italy has to offer. Even the celebrities flock to this part of Italy, with no less than megastar George Clooney owning a fifteen-bedroom villa on Lake Como. Sounds like a region worth seeing at least once in your life, no?

Lay of the Land

The Lombardy region has been home to civilization since at least the second millennium B.C., and, seemingly since its creation, has been a much-fought-over part of what we know today as Western Europe. Its people fell under control of the Roman Empire as a province in 194 B.C., when the Romans brought the first major systems of transportation, agriculture, and trade to the region. They considered Lombardy so important geographically that for a time Milan was used as the capital of the Roman Empire. The name Lombardy, though, would actually come after the empire's fall, when a Germanic tribe known as Lombards invaded in the 570s. Charlemagne annexed the land in the late 700s for his Frankish Empire, and the Lombards didn't regain their independence until the 1100s, when they formed the Lombard Leagues in a revolt against the Roman Empire's Frederick I. France and Austria waged war over Lombardy in the early 1500s, and some of the territory was at times controlled by the Republic of Venice. Napoleon took control in the late 1700s, the Austrians got Lombardy back in the early 1800s, and then finally, in 1859, Lombardy as we know it today became part of the Kingdom of Italy.

Today, Lombardy is a major center of commerce, with its local economy making up as much as 20 percent of Italy's entire gross domestic product. Companies with headquarters and operations in Lombardy operate in the fields of machinery, textiles, wood, rubber, petrochemicals, weaponry, silk, lace, agriculture, and fashion. About 1.3 million people live in Milan alone, making it by far the region's largest urban area.

 Fact

Philosopher and author Pliny the Elder, who died in the 79 A.D. eruption of Mount Vesuvius, was from Lombardy. He wrote "Naturalis Historia," a thirty-seven-book series that would become the model for modern encyclopedias. It included entries about everything from cane sugar to gold mining to artwork.

Malpensa International Airport in Milan is where you want to land if you are flying directly to Lombardy instead of coming from Rome, Venice, or another major Italian city. The airport, which is second only to Rome's in terms of international traffic, handles nearly 24 million passengers a year. Airlines with direct service to the Milan airport from the United States include Alitalia, American Airlines, Continental Airlines, Delta Air Lines, and US Airways. The English version of the airport's official website is *www .sea-aeroportmilano.it/en*.

From Malpensa airport, you can catch trains, buses, and taxis, or grab a rental car to explore the Lombardy region. It's about a forty-minute train ride from the airport to the Milan Cadorna railway station, where you can pick up the Milan subway system. The bus ride to Milan Central Station, where you can catch long-haul Trenitalia trains, is about an hour without traffic. If you plan to tour Milan only, you can get by with public transportation and taxis instead of a rental car.

⊛ Essential

No matter what method of transportation gets you to the Lombardy region, make one of your first stops a snack vendor selling gorgonzola cheese. It is said to have originated in the town of Gorgonzola, near Milan. In this part of the world, you can sometimes even find slices of pizza with gorgonzola cheese as a topping.

Milan

The word "milliner"—whose definitions include selling hats and dresses to women—derives from the city name Milan. That, in and of itself, should give you a clue as to just how seriously this city takes fashion. The street called Via Montenapoleon is home to many flagship stores from the world's best designers, and Milan's Piazza Duomo is arguably the planet's oldest shopping mall. Milan's annual Fashion Week is on par with those held in Paris and New York. Sightseeing in Milan includes people-watching as much as anything else, and if you want to do it right, you'll be looking through a pair of stylish sunglasses yourself—both during the daylight hours and in the nightclubs after dark.

There is history and great art here, too, including the impressive Duomo di Milano cathedral, the La Scala opera house, countless museums, and Leonardo da Vinci's masterwork *The Last Supper.* You could easily make a week out of a vacation in Milan alone; at the least, the city offers an interesting few days' worth of touring and shopping.

Duomo di Milano

Duomo di Milano, also known as Milan Cathedral, is the second-largest church in Italy (after St. Peter's Basilica in Vatican City) and the second-largest Gothic cathedral in the world (after the Cathedral of Seville in Spain). It was commissioned in 1386 and completed in the early 1800s when Napoleon Bonaparte ordered it finished after centuries of slow progress. It was not until 1965 that the last gate was inaugurated.

 Fact

American writer Mark Twain visited Milan in the 1860s and described Milan Cathedral in his book *Innocents Abroad*. He could barely contain his enthusiasm in describing the cathedral, about which he wrote: "What a wonder it is! So grand, so solemn, so vast! And yet so delicate, so airy, so graceful!"

You can tour the cathedral in a couple of ways. The main cathedral floor is open every day from 8:30 A.M. until 6:45 P.M., and its stained glass windows are worth seeing on their own. Audio guides are available for an extra charge to help you make sense of what you're seeing inside. The more interesting tour—if you're okay with heights—is atop the cathedral roof, which you can access by stairs for €5 or by elevator for €7. (It's between 150 and 165 steps, according to various counts.) You'll see not just pinnacles and spires here, but also sculptures that aren't visible from other vantage points.

As with other churches in Italy, remember to dress appropriately for these tours. Cover your shoulders and legs above the knees. More details are available in the English section of *www.duomomilano.it*.

La Scala

This famous opera house was inaugurated in 1778 and rebuilt substantially after World War II bombing. The Romantic composer Giuseppe Verdi often saw his Italian operas performed here, with some—including his last work, *Falstaff*—making their premieres inside La Scala. It continues to host productions today, in addition to being the home of a museum that will thrill any lover of theater. If you're lucky enough to get a ticket to a performance during your visit, you will appreciate the major renovations the opera house underwent between 2002 and 2004. They included rebuilding its stage, enhancing its acoustics, and adding monitors to the seats that let the audience follow the production in English as well as Italian.

Alert

The La Scala museum lists its hours of operation as 9 A.M. till 12:30 P.M, and 1:30 P.M. till 5:30 P.M., daily except for holidays. However, the last entrances are actually allowed at noon and 5 P.M., giving patrons enough time to look around before the building closes for lunch and, later, for the day.

The museum is adjacent to the opera house in the Piazza della Scala, which is famous for the countless pigeons that absolutely adore the tourists who buy seed to feed them. Inside the museum, you can see costumes, set designs, instruments, and all kinds of other items associated with La Scala in particular and theater in general.

Guided tours of the opera house are available, as are booklets that will help you understand the items in the museum. Details are available in English at *www.teatroallascala.org/en*.

The Last Supper

Leonardo da Vinci's painting *The Last Supper* is housed inside Santa Maria delle Grazie church, which is listed as a UNESCO World Heritage Site. The painting is quite massive, measuring fifteen feet tall by twenty-nine feet wide. It covers an entire back wall of the church.

Da Vinci painted *The Last Supper* between 1495 and 1498, and efforts to restore it to its original grandeur first began in the late 1700s. Some of the restoration attempts actually caused additional damage, and by 1970, work had begun to correct the work anew. After more than two decades of additional restoration efforts, *The Last Supper* once again became available for public view in 1999—though you have to book several days in advance by telephone (011 02 894 21 146) if you want a ticket to see it.

e? Question

Why has *The Last Supper* been so ravaged by time?
Part of the reason is the way da Vinci painted it. True frescoes were painted on wet plaster, which hardened and held up over the years. Da Vinci painted *The Last Supper* on a dry wall that he covered with sealant and then painted atop. It started to deteriorate just a few years after he completed it.

Museums

There are too many museums to visit in Milan in a week (some would argue in a lifetime), but a handful are worth a look even if you have limited time in the city. Two in particular—Museo Nazionale della Scienza e della Tecnologia Leonardo da Vinci and Museo Poldi Pezzoli—are good options if you're traveling with children.

Museo Nazionale della Scienza e della Tecnologia Leonardo da Vinci

This is the largest science and technology museum in Italy, founded in 1953 and named after Leonardo da Vinci, who, though primarily known today as a painter, was also a master of building things. The museum houses a collection of machine models based on his designs, as well as interactive exhibits, theater performances, a walk-inside submarine, and workshops designed for adults and children alike.

Fact

The Museo Poldi Pezzoli has an interesting offering if you're traveling with children: an audio tour called "The Museum for Curious Kids." It's designed for children ages eleven to fourteen to help them discover interesting items throughout the permanent collection. Programs for younger children are also available.

The museum is open every day except Mondays starting at 9:30 A.M. The last entrances are allowed at 4:30 P.M. on weekdays and 6 P.M. on weekends. More information is available in English at *www.museoscienza.org/english*.

Museo Poldi Pezzoli

This museum is named for Gian Giacomo Poldi Pezzoli, part of a family that inherited a palace in Milan's center because of work done collecting taxes on behalf of the Austrian government. That palace is now the Museo Poldi Pezzoli, housing a collection that dates back to the family's personal acquisitions from the 1800s. The palace first opened to the public in 1881.

You can view early arms and armor, decorative works, paintings, jewelry, tapestries, and glasswork. Among the better-known paintings are Botticelli's *Madonna and Child*. Hours are Tuesday through Sunday, 10 A.M. till 6 P.M. Learn more at *www .museopoldipezzoli.it*.

Shopping

The Milanese call the area defined by the four streets Via della Spiga, Via Sant'Andrea, Via Montenapoleone, and Via Allessandro Manzoni "the Golden Quad," a tip of the tongue to all the high-priced, high-fashion designers and jewelers who have boutiques and shops here. Just some of the brand names you will find include:

- Gucci
- Prada
- Versaci
- Roberto Cavalli
- Dolce & Gabbana
- Chanel
- Tiffany
- Cartier

The shops are generally open from 10 A.M. till 7 P.M. daily, except on Sundays, when they're closed. Sales take place in January and July, when the narrow streets are packed with pedestrians battling it out for the best bargains—if you can call them that, what with prices for high fashion starting in the hundreds if not thousands of euro nowadays.

Brescia

The city of Brescia, home to about 190,000 people and thus Lombardy's second-largest city, is pretty much due east of Milan, an easy ride by car or train. As with Milan, history in this area is rich with conquerors and plundering, and thus you will find cathedrals, ruins, and a castle for your touring pleasure. Not everything dates back to earlier days, however. In 1769, lightning struck one of the city's churches, which happened to be used in part as a storage location for a reported 200,000 pounds of gunpowder. The resulting explosion destroyed as much as one-sixth of the city and killed several thousand people.

Even still, a good number of historic sites remain. Those that should be atop your to-see list include Colle Cidneo, Duomo Vecchio and Duomo Nuovo (the old and new cathedrals), and the Roman ruins at Monastero di Santa Giulia and Basilica di San Salvatore.

Colle Cidneo

Colle Cidneo means "Hill of Cidneo," the site that was, for many centuries, the heart of Brescia's defense forces. You can imagine the thousands of soldiers standing on high, looking down over the plains, prepared to defend their families and neighbors against any and all intruders. Today, this historic center is still home to Brescia's Castle, which now houses a pair of museums that you can tour to learn more about the region's history and see examples of the many weapons that were used by local soldiers throughout time.

Not far from the castle is the Church of San Pietro in Oliveto, whose marble façade dates to the 1500s. The artwork inside is by local painters and is worth a look even though it isn't on par with other Renaissance works at larger churches in the region.

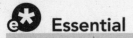 **Essential**

> Colle Cidneo is northeast of the modern town center in Brescia, close enough to walk if you're fit. Another option, though, is riding a bicycle—and they're available for free, along with free audio guides (in English) to the city, at the Brescia Tourism Office. Details are available online at *www.comune.brescia.it.*

Duomo Vecchio and Duomo Nuovo

These two churches are right next to each other, just off Piazza Paolo VI, and can easily be toured one after the other.

Duomo Vecchio—"the old cathedral"—was built on the ruins of a basilica that was demolished in the 1100s. The cathedral is an example of Romanesque architecture (which evolved into the Gothic style) and is noteworthy because of its circular shape.

Duomo Nuovo—"the new cathedral"—was also built on the site of an earlier cathedral. Work was completed in 1825, some 200 years after building commenced. Because the cathedral took so long to build, its architectural style is far from uniform and, thus, typically of less interest to art students than the Duomo Vecchio.

Monastero di Santa Giulia and Basilica di San Salvatore

Brescia's City Museum is housed inside the complex known as Monastero di Santa Giulia and Basilica di San Salvatore, which is east of the main city piazzas and south of Colle Cidneo (and well within walking distance of both). Here you can see Roman mosaics and a jewel-encrusted cross from the era of Lombard rule. Some scholars believe the complex is one of the best remaining examples of High Middle Ages architecture in all of northern Italy.

Pavia

Pavia is a city of about 70,000 people located due south of Milan, and easily reachable from there by car or train. The city is best known as the home of the University of Pavia, which dates to the 1300s and counts explorer Christopher Columbus among its alumni. Pavia's other calling card is its status as a production center for a great deal of Italy's rice. If you're a fan of risotto, this is a darn good place to get it about as fresh from the earth as possible, at almost any restaurant that catches your fancy along the city streets. The two main tourist sites here are Certosa, which is a Carthusian monastery from the 1300s and 1400s, and Castello Visconteo, a late-1300s castle that today is home to Museo Civico, the city's museum.

Fact

Albert Einstein wrote his first scientific work, "The Investigation of the State of Aether in Magnetic Fields," while living in Pavia with his family in the late 1800s. He was supposed to be at a boarding school in Munich, but used a doctor's note to persuade school officials that he was allowed to leave to be with his family in Italy.

Certosa

This monastery complex is noted for its Gothic and Renaissance architecture. It was under construction from the 1390s until the early 1500s. There is a noteworthy collection of stained glass windows here along with sculptures, frescoes, and other works you would expect of the Renaissance era.

Monks still live on the complex, so while you can look around, admission is by donation instead of purchased ticket, and you'll find no guided or audio tours. Remember to dress appropriately, with covered shoulders and long pants or a skirt that dips below your knees.

Castello Visconteo

Galaezzo II Visconti, part of the Visconti dynasty that ruled the city of Milan from 1277 until 1447, built this castle as a primary residence for his family in 1360 after taking over the city of Pavia. Though the structure itself is beautiful, Visconti himself was known as downright sadistic, being infamous for instituting a form of torture that predated the "breaking wheel," upon which people were strung and then stretched and beaten to death over several days' or even several weeks' time.

Today, thankfully, no such horrors take place at Castello Visconteo, which now houses Pavia's Museo Civico, or city museum. Here, you can see collections of art and archaeological relics that detail the city's past, including a good bit about the Visconti family's era of command.

Bergamo

Bergamo is northeast of Milan, easily accessible by car or by train. Though Bergamo is quite close to its fellow Lombardy city of Milan, it actually was under the control of Venetians for much of its history.

Alert

The Orio al Serio International Airport serves Bergamo. It welcomes Italian and international flights, but none from the United States. If you are traveling from another Italian city or from another European city, it's possible for you to fly here instead of into Milan. The airport's website, with English available, is *www.sacbo.it.*

Today, a walled hilltop known as the "upper town" remains in Bergamo, in addition to the "lower town," which is a modern city that is home to about 115,000 people. The two towns are connected by cable cars, roads, and walking paths. Parking is extremely limited in the upper town, so most tourists opt to walk or take the cable cars.

Upper Town

Città Alta, as the upper town is known, is on a hilltop and surrounded by walls from the 1600s. Piazza Vecchia is the old town square, which is where you will first end up no matter where you enter the walled city itself. From there, you can get to the two museums inside the city walls as well as to the Palazzo della Ragione (which houses an eighteenth-century sundial), the Romanesque Basilica di Santa Maria Maggiore, and the Rocca (a castle that dates to the 1300s).

⊛ Essential

Comfortable walking shoes are a must in Bergamo's upper town, especially if you want to hike up to the best lookout spots for a view of the lower town. There are signs marking the best walking routes, which can include steep stone steps. Bring water, a lightweight camera, and a small pair of binoculars if you want to make the most of the schlep.

The Museo di Scienze Naturali Enrico Caffi (the Caffi Natural Science Museum) has interesting sites, but not much for you to see or understand in English. The Museo Civico Archeologico (the Archaeological Civic Museum) is also mostly in Italian, although it offers an interesting glimpse into the walled city's history and remains. Both museums are inside the former citadel, which has an impressive courtyard if you'd prefer to stroll outside.

Città Bassa, as the lower town is known, is a modern city that expanded greatly during the twentieth century. You won't find many historical sites in this section of Bergamo, but, as with most modern cities, you can enjoy a couple of art museums.

The Accademia Carrara is an art gallery and academy with about 1,800 paintings that date to the fifteenth century. You can also see collections of bronzes, sculptures, porcelain, and furniture here. The gallery has been open to the public since the late eighteenth century and housed the art academy until the early twentieth century, when it moved to another nearby building.

Nearby is the Galleria d'Arte Moderna e Contemporanea (GAMEC), which opened in 1991 as a facility for showcasing more modern and contemporary works. This museum has a website with an English translation where you can sample a bit of the permanent collection and view the schedule for upcoming exhibitions: *www.gamec.it.*

Other Must-See Spots

You could get lost in Lombardy for years and still not enjoy everything its ancient and modern cities have to offer—not to mention its northern tourist section of lakes that sit at the base of the Alps at Italy's border with Switzerland. If you must choose just a couple other places to check out during your vacation, consider the star-studded Lake Como and the small city of Cremona, where you can learn about the history of the Stradivari violin.

 Fact

Lake Como has been featured in several recent hit movies. The lake doubles for the planet Naboo in *Star Wars II: Attack of the Clones;* "the Night Fox" is said to live on Lake Como in *Ocean's Twelve;* and secret agent James Bond recuperates at a Lake Como hospital after being tortured in *Casino Royale.*

Lake Como

You can take an hour-long bus ride to Lake Como from Malpensa airport in Milan, or arrive by train from Milan's Stazione Nord. Once you arrive, there are ferries and hydrofoils to get you around the large lake (it's the third biggest in all of Italy). You will find opportunities to rent sailboats, windsurfers, and other watercraft, or you can simply enjoy the view while riding the ferries and hydrofoils as they pass by extravagant villa after villa long the shore.

Keep your eyes peeled for celebrities, too. George Clooney has a villa here, and many Hollywood stars visit for work and pleasure alike.

Museo Stradivariano

You might know the name Stradivarius when it comes to violins, but that's the Latinized version of the surname Stradivari, as in Antonio Stradivari, who hails from the small Lombardy city of Cremona and is world-renowned for the violins he created there in the late seventeenth and early eighteenth centuries. Today's orchestra professionals still consider his violins among the best ever created, and they have become expensive works of art for collectors. One garnered more than $3.5 million at auction in 2006.

The Museo Stradivariano houses examples from Stradivari's workshop, where he made violins, cellos, guitars, and violas. It's open every day except Mondays and is near Cremona's civic museum, which also has a small collection of violins that include a Stradivari.

Where to Stay

Milan is the obvious central location for booking a hotel if you want to tour the Lombardy region, but it's expensive to stay there, especially anywhere near the main tourist attractions—and there are good, budget-friendly options in the outlying cities.

The price code for the hotel listings below is $=€100 or less; $$=€100 to €150; $$$=€150 to €200; $$$$=€200 or more per night, per room.

Hotel Spadari
$$$$

Located right near the Milan Cathedral and the opera house, this hotel offers rooms with single or double beds, private bathrooms, desks, and sofas. The hotel has a decidedly contemporary feel, which can be a nice break after a day of touring historical sites. Special attention has been paid to the décor; the walls are lined with fine artwork and sculpture.

www.spadarihotel.com.

Hotel de la Ville
$$$$

This hotel, in the heart of Milan's tourist district, is a favorite among the designers and celebrities who visit the city for its annual Fashion Week. If you want top-dollar luxury, this is the place, with an in-house bar that's tailor made for people-watching. *www .delavillemilano.com.*

Hotel Excelsior
$

Located near the Pavia train station and within walking distance of its city center, this hotel's rooms have air conditioning, Internet access, and a large room where you can have breakfast before heading out for the day.

www.hotelrizpavia.com.

Hotel Arli
$–$$$

Founded in 1973 in Bergamo, this fifty-six-room hotel is in a good location for touring both the upper town and the lower town without a car. Rooms have air conditioning, and some non-smoking rooms are available. There is a gym on site as well as laundry service and buffet-style breakfast. Rollaway beds are available for €25 in addition to the regular room rate.

www.arli.net.

Hotel Posta
$

This is a good budget option on Lake Como, located right between the historic center and the lake itself. There's an on-site restaurant, and the rooms are promoted as "tidy and comfortable" (which in this case means small but clean). You'll have a private bathroom and television.

www.hotelposta.net.

Where to Eat

Milan is the fashion capital of Italy (and of the world, the Milanese would argue), so be prepared to spend a pretty euro if you want to dine in the heart of that city. In the suburbs, of course, you'll find more financially feasible options.

The price code for the restaurant entrees below is $=€25 or less; $$=€26 to €50; $$$=€51 to €75; $$$$=€100 or more.

The Chedi
$$$–$$$$

This chic Milan restaurant has an Asian décor and a seasonal menu that fuses interesting combinations of Italian and Asian cuisines. Think goose liver wrapped in lemon leaves and coffee beans, or ravioli filled with foie gras and spinach. The kitchen is exhibition style, so you get a bit of a show along with your meal.
www.thechedimilan.com.

Ristorante Noce
$–$$

Located in Brescia, Ristorante Noce specializes in fish, meat, and homemade pasta, including shrimp and lobster from Sicily. The tasting menus (there are three: local, meat, and fish) give you a chance to sample multiple dishes from the region and Italy in general. The restaurant has only thirty seats, so reservations are recommended.
www.ristorantehotelnoce.com.

Ciccio Passami l'Olio
$

This Bergamo restaurant is in the middle of a colorful bed and breakfast. The cuisine is Mediterranean with meat and fish specialties, but you can also order fresh pasta and choose from among the half-dozen or so salads. Fixed menus are an option if you don't want to order a la carte. Be sure to save room for the homemade tiramisu.

www.cicciopassamilolio.com.

CHAPTER 6

Northwestern Italy

Three regions—Aosta Valley, Piedmont, and Liguria—comprise northwestern Italy, which is, for touring purposes, most accessible from Milan and Lombardy to the east or from Florence, Livorno, and Tuscany to the south. Northwestern Italy is bordered on its north and west sides by Switzerland, France, and Monaco, making this section of Italy a rich blend of history, culture, and natural beauty. There's the bustling city of Genoa, the charming seaside harbor at Portofino, and the preserved trails along the Cinque Terre, just to name a few must-see attractions.

Lay of the Land

Geographically speaking, this section of Italy is quite diverse. To the far northwest is the Aosta Valley, which is, as its name implies, a valley that sits in the shadows of the towering Alps. (You might recognize the names Mont Blanc and Matterhorn, two of the best-known peaks in the mountain range that crosses the Italian border into Switzerland.) Northwestern Italy also includes a good bit of Mediterranean coastline, including the onetime powerhouse shipping mecca of Genoa as well as the colorful and far more subdued coastal towns from Portofino to the Cinque Terre. In between the Alps and these seaside civilizations are great stretches of agricultural land in the Piedmont region, which is known as a top Italian wine producer and is home to the industrial city Turin.

Historically speaking, this part of Italy was briefly ruled by France in the early 1800s, when the French annexed the entire Piedmont region as well as Liguria, which had previously been under the control of the Republic of Genoa. Both regions reverted to Italian control in 1815 thanks to the Congress of Vienna, which redrew European borders after Napoleon was defeated. There has long been a strong merchant history in the area, with goods being brought from Piedmont down to Genoa's waterfront docks, where merchant families set sail to distribute them and earn their fortunes.

Today, Genoa is the top tourist city in the area and is a good place to stay if your goal is to tour along the coast with a city as your base. Turin is about 100 miles northwest of Genoa and makes a better metropolitan hotel choice if your ideal vacation in this part of Italy includes the Alps. You can fly, drive, or take a train between the two cities with ease; second-class train tickets typically cost less than €20 each way. If you want to escape the crowds, there also are countless smaller hotels and villages beyond and between these two main cities.

 Fact

Turin hosted the XX Olympic Winter Games in February 2006. The official logo displayed the name Torino, which is how Italian people know the city, but all English-speaking countries referred to it then, and now, as Turin.

Genoa

Genoa, which today has nearly 1 million people living within and near its city limits, started out in ancient times as a fishing village. Its political and economic power had expanded greatly by the 1500s, when the city served as a crucial Mediterranean trading seaport.

Genoa's most famous native seaman was Christopher Columbus, whose writings indicate that he went to sea as early as age ten.

The city declined in importance as a trading center after Columbus set sail and "discovered" the Americas. Around the same time, the Portuguese explorer Vasco de Gama reached India, and the business of international trade slowly shifted away from the Mediterranean waters that had previously enjoyed shipping commerce almost exclusively. With the loss of business, Genoa's strategic importance faded. Today, the city's ports are still used for some trade, but you're just as likely to see (or disembark from) a cruise ship here as you are to spot a container ship along the arc-shaped waterfront.

e✔ Fact

The city of Genoa celebrates its native son with a Christopher Columbus monument in Piazza Acquaverde, and Italian-Americans take great pride in celebrating Columbus Day each October. It is ironic, then, that this Italian hero was actually sailing for Queen Isabella of Spain in 1492, when he made landfall in the modern-day Bahamas.

Porto Antico and Aquarium

You can walk along the marinas in Genoa's old harbor—called Porto Antico—for free, marveling at everything from cruise ships to local fishing boats. Each May, the Marina Molo Vecchio hosts one of the world's top boat shows, bringing some of the newest, largest, and most expensive motoryachts afloat well within picture-taking distance. On any given day throughout the summer season, the waterfront is abuzz with fishermen tending to their nets alongside street vendors offering the latest knockoffs. Restaurants are located along the quays, as are Internet points where you can pay a few euro to get onto the World Wide Web. During summer weekends, there are often festivals here, celebrating everything from music to fast food and games. School field trips are also a common sight, with swarms of children holding hands and walking in line one after another.

The most popular attraction in this part of the city is the Acquario di Genova (Aquarium of Genoa). It's the largest in Italy and the second-largest in all of Europe, and it offers all the sea creatures you would expect along with a large, round biodome that is home to a tropical forest. Though the aquarium's website (*www .acquariodigenova.it*) and most of its on-site signage are in Italian, the facility is easily understandable and a good deal of fun for English-speaking tourists with even a basic knowledge of marine life.

🅴❗ Alert

Don't be startled if you ask to get online at an Internet store in Genoa and are asked to present your passport in addition to paying the hourly computer usage fee. Just as with local hotels, these shops use your passport number as your form of identification, as part of your "rental agreement" with them.

The harbor area is across a main highway (with pedestrian crossways) from the city itself, which is marked by a confusing maze of narrow, hilly streets and alleys that can be a bit dark and creepy if you're not used to walking up and down them. To be honest, the city has a reputation for being dirty and replete with pickpockets who target tourists, but in recent years, there has been clear improvement on both fronts. If you remain aware of your surroundings and use common sense, you should be just fine.

Downtown Genoa

There are plenty of sights worth seeing in Genoa, but if you have time for only two, then consider heading straight for Le Strada Nuove and the Museo d'Art Orientale.

Le Strada Nuove, in the city's historic center, became a UNESCO World Heritage site in 2006. It made the list based in part on its combination of Renaissance- and Baroque-era palaces, which were built at the height of the city's worldwide power. By law, these palaces were constructed as venues for hosting foreign dignitaries, who returned to their homelands with stories about the wonderful buildings. In time, through the constant influx of influential visitors and their word-of-mouth campaigns back home, the Genoa architectural style became a model throughout Europe. Think open staircases and grand courtyards, all with spectacular views. Three of the palaces—Palazzo Rosso, Palazzo Bianco, and Palazzo Tursi—can be toured. The Palazzo Rosso, for instance, displays two centuries' worth of paintings and frescoes. Admission is €8. Its website (which has an English translation) is *www.museopalazzorosso.it.*

 **Essential**

When you're done with a day of touring in Genoa, stop at any local restaurant and ask for their homemade pesto sauce atop linguine or ravioli. Genoa is the birthplace of the basil-based, green-hued sauce, which is often the only kind of pasta sauce you can order. Yes, this is Italy, but tomato sauce comes from other regions.

Another interesting touring opportunity is the Museo d'Arte Orientale, which, with about 20,000 pieces, boasts one of the largest collections of Asian art in all of Europe. They range from armor to paintings and musical instruments. Most of the museum's signage is in Italian, like its website (*www.museochiossonegenova.it*).

Cinque Terre

Cinque Terre is Italian for "five lands," and thus describes the region south of Genoa, along the coast, where five villages are linked by a walking trail. The area is so beautifully preserved that the villages, coastline, and surrounding hills were named a UNESCO World Heritage Site in 1997. The committee rightly stated that the area represents "the harmonious interaction between people and nature to produce a landscape of exceptional scenic quality that illustrates a traditional way of life."

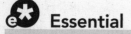 **Essential**

If you plan to walk the trail through all five villages of the Cinque Terre, be sure you are in good physical condition before you start out. Some of the trails are rated as challenging or difficult, and some include dozens or even hundreds of steps. Do not count on handicapped accessibility, either.

Getting There and Getting Around

It's this traditional way of life that you will see if you visit this area by train or ferry from Genoa. The train stops in each of the five Cinque Terre villages: Monterosso, Vernazza, Cornislia, Manarolo, and Riomaggiore. You can pick up the trail system in the middle or walk it from end to end.

The most popular sections of the trail are fee-based (you can pay a few euro for a twenty-four-hour pass on all trails), and other portions are free—though they tend to be the less-traveled, harder sections. No matter where you start or end, there are lots of inns and bed-and-breakfasts waiting to accommodate you and all the other hikers, plenty of whom jam the trail during the peak summer months of July and August.

For more information, the main Cinque Terre park office is near the Riomaggiore train station, but you can also visit the smaller park offices in any of the other villages to get a trail map. There is a park office website, *www.parconazionale5terre.it*, but it offers information only in Italian.

Wines of the Cinque Terre

Almost everywhere you look in the five villages, you'll find a wine bar offering Cinque Terre (a dry white) or Sciacchetrà (a dessert wine). They're made from the grapes that you will see growing on the terraced hillsides as you hike. After you spot even one vintner tending to his vines atop six-foot-high retaining walls, you will certainly appreciate the effort that goes into making these wines, and perhaps you will be able to enjoy them all the more with a serving of traditional fish stew.

Portofino

If you prefer upscale flair and superstar sightings to trail-filled seaside villages, then skip the Cinque Terre and head to Portofino, whose harbor is perhaps the best known in all of Italy for multimillion-dollar megayachts squeezed side-by-side. As you might imagine based on that level of clientele, Portofino's tourist-laden restaurants and hotels are not for the faint of pocketbook. Still, there's a reason those in the know choose to come here: The colorful harbor is absolutely mesmerizing in its beauty.

ⓔ✔ Fact

Universal Studios tried to capture the charm of Portofino's harbor—including cobblestone streets and outdoor cafes—when it built the Loews Portofino Bay Hotel in Orlando. If you want to sample the Italian ambience before you fly to Europe, you can book a room near the theme park in Florida for about $300 per night.

There are a few churches that you can tour in Portofino, but the main activity is caféing—yes, that's café being used as a verb—in which you spend hours sipping your espresso or cappuccino and watching the crowds of perfectly primped jetsetters meander along the harborside. Sure, there are a good number of T-shirt-wearing tourists around, but the overall scene is well-to-do. Wear a wide-brimmed hat or a pair of fancy leather sandals and you'll fit right in. There are shops along the harbor where you can rent small boats for day trips, often with skippers, and snorkeling trips are also an option.

Cuneo

Cuneo, a city of about 55,000 people, is west of Genoa, almost at Italy's border with France. It's widely renowned for its rum-filled chocolates. On the local menus, the sweets appear as "Cuneesi al rhum," and they're well worth the indulgence of calories.

You can find a lot to do in and around Cuneo, including museum tours, wineries, castle tours, and parks full of hiking trails. Ideally, you would take a train here from Genoa and then continue north, using the train line to Turin for longer itineraries. Fall is an excellent time to visit, with the annual chestnut fair in early October marking the start of the festival season.

Regional Wines

Barolo, Barbaresco, Dolcetto, and Barbera are the reds you might know from this part of Italy, and if you are at all a wine connoisseur, then you know the best of these bottlings come at a high price if you order them in the United States. Visiting the source has its perks, and that includes tastings and offerings at far more reasonable rates.

⚠ Alert

> Many of the wineries in this region close for at least a few days each week in January. Some of the wineries close for the entire month. If you're planning to visit during that time of year, it's imperative that you call ahead to your winery of choice, lest you arrive to find the proprietors off on their winter vacation in the Caribbean.

Some of the wine cellars are worth visiting even if you don't care to taste their vintages. The Barolo Regional Wine Center, for instance, is inside a castle that contains a cultural museum. A good resource for planning tours to wineries such as this is the website *www.cuneohotel.info*.

Castles and Museums

There are a dozen or so castles and museums to tour within easy travel distance of Cuneo. Some of the structures date to the 1400s and 1500s, while others hold important cultural significance.

One castle you might want to visit is Castello di Serralunga, northeast of Cuneo. It was built in the 1300s and has a moat you need to cross via a drawbridge. Another interesting option is Castello Reale, located in Racconigi about halfway between Cuneo and Turin. You can see the royal residence's paintings and sculptures, and you can also tour the substantial gardens. Still another good touring choice is Forte di Vinadio, located west of Cuneo. It's a massive military fort that U.S. and British forces bombed extensively during World War II (you can still see the scars today). As with winery tours in this region, a good source for English-speaking castle tours is *www.cuneohotel.info*.

Other Must-See Spots

As you no doubt have figured out by now, the northwestern section of Italy is so diverse that you could travel here for months and still find new, interesting sights every day. A few more places you might want to put on your list are Turin, Valle D'aosta, and Gran Paradiso National Park.

Turin

The city of Turin is home to about 900,000 people. It hosted the 2006 Winter Olympics, but the city is best known for its strong manufacturing base. Fiat is based here, and the Lingotto building—which is now a multipurpose tourist facility with a concert hall, shops, and more—was previously the largest car factory in the world.

Most visitors make a stop at the Cathedral of St. John the Baptist, where the Shroud of Turin—believed to be Jesus' burial cloth—is kept. A tour takes you beneath the church, where you can see artifacts related to the shroud and view a video about it.

 Fact

One of the pieces you can see at Museo Egizo is a mummy that the museum's team discovered in an Egyptian tomb. The mummy was found along with items believed to be needed in the afterlife, including loaves of bread, clay pots, bandages, head rests, and sandals.

Another popular tourist destination in Turin is Museo Egizo, which houses one of the largest collections of Egyptian antiquities outside of Egypt. About 500,000 people visit each year, looking at everything from paintings to papyrus collections. The museum is the only one of its kind outside of Cairo, specializing solely in Egyptian art and culture. There are exhibitions, guided tours, and educational programs on-site. You can learn about them by viewing the English version of the museum's website, *www.museogizio.it*.

Also worth a look is the Museo Nazionale del Cinema, which showcases not just Italian films throughout history, but also the cameras and sets used to create various movies. There's an on-site theater that hosts screenings and special events such as discussions with filmmakers. You can also take a ride up the glass elevator to the rooftop terrace. Details are available in English at *www.museonazionaledelcinema.it*.

Question

What is *patois*?
Patois is regional language spoken by more than half the people who live in the Aosta Valley region. Although Italian is of course spoken here, French is, too, thanks to the proximity of the border. *Patois* is a Franco-Provençal dialect typically spoken as a second language among the area's residents.

Valle d'Aosta

The Aosta Valley is at the base of the Alps, and as such attracts travelers interested in winter sports. The best-known resorts are in Courmayeur and Breuil-Cervina, but there are plenty of smaller, lesser-known options as well. There are castles galore, too, since this area was a place that dignitaries were keen to stop and enjoy as they made their way across the Alps throughout the centuries.

All levels of skiers, from beginners to experts, can find challenging slopes in the valley, and you can get an Aosta Valley Lift Pass that will let you ski or snowboard at multiple resorts, sometimes crossing international borders into Switzerland and France.

A good website with ski maps and more information about the valley is *www.skiitaly.com*, produced by the Activelifestyle Travel Network.

If you visit here, be sure to pack the warmest layered clothing you can find. The climate is considered severe. The higher you go, of course, the colder it gets, and some of the peak areas are designated as tundra—yes, tundra, like what you find in the Arctic. You can rest assured that if you're staying in a main resort area, there will be plenty of shops ready to sell you a well-insulated new parka with mittens to match.

Gran Paradiso National Park

This national park is Italy's oldest, named for the Gran Paradiso mountain that is within the park borders. The land was originally set aside as a hunting preserve for the Alpine ibex, which looks sort of like a ram and was thought to have therapeutic properties, such as a heart bone that could protect people against violent death. There are still about 4,000 ibex living in the park, which was established in 1922 and today encompasses nearly 175,000 acres, including fifty-nine glaciers.

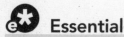 **Essential**

If you plan to hike along the trails at Gran Paradiso National Park, then bring a good map and leave your favorite Fido at home. The park requests that all hikers stick to the marked lanes instead of tramping all over the local vegetation, and dogs are forbidden, even on a leash, because some pets have mauled the native animals in the past.

You can camp here, or go hiking for the day and then stay at one of the many hotels just beyond the park's borders. Entrance to the park itself is free. The northern section of the park is most popular with tourists thanks to picnicking areas, easily accessible lodging, and spectacular views. There's a botanical garden on site, and interpretive guided walks are available during the most popular tourism months of April through October. Another interesting option for touring is the Ecomuseum Copper Forge, which dates to 1675 and gives you an idea of how the locals worked with copper using blast furnaces in the pre-industrial age. Learn more at the park's website (which is offered in English), *www.pngp.it.*

Where to Stay

Genoa is this region's largest city and is the easiest to reach from the United States. There are plenty of hotel options that make it a good base for exploring the broader area. Turin and Cuneo also are safe bets, as are the resorts in the Alps and the bed and breakfasts along the Cinque Terre coastline.

The price code for the hotel listings below is $=€100 or less; $$=€100 to €150; $$$=€150 to €200; $$$$=€200 or more per night, per room.

Hotel Alexander
$–$$$

For a clean room in a safe part of Genoa at a reasonable price, it's hard to beat the Hotel Alexander. It's within walking distance of both the main train station and the harbor area, including the aquarium. Each room has a private bathroom as well as a television, refrigerator, and telephone. The hotel is on a main street, so ask for a room on one of the upper levels if you're sensitive to city noise.

www.hotelalexander-genova.it.

Hotel Bristol Palace
$$$–$$$$

A more upscale choice in Genoa is the Hotel Bristol Palace, a renovated palace that's close to the museums, shops, and aquarium. You will feel like nobility of the early 1900s as you descend the grand staircase each day. A restaurant is on-site, as are a twenty-four-hour porter, WiFi access, laundry service, satellite television, in-room safes, and pretty much every other luxury you might desire.

www.hotelbristolpalace.it.

Le Petit Hotel
$–$$

In Turin's old town, Le Petit Hotel is within walking distance of theaters and museums. Some staff members speak English, and there is a restaurant on-site. All rooms have private bathrooms, hairdryers, telephones, Internet access, mini-bars, and satellite television. Air conditioning and safes are also available, but not in every room, so be sure to request them if they're important to you.

www.lepetithotel.it.

Hotel Palazzo Lovera
$–$$$

This is a rebuilt palace in Cuneo where Pope Pio VII was once held as Napoleon's prisoner. There are forty-seven hotel rooms plus a small gymnasium and a restaurant. Package deals are available if you want to include massages, cooking classes, cheese tastings, and the like along with your hotel stay.

www.palazzolovera.com.

Hotel Carla
$–$$

Located in the village of Levanto within Cinque Terre national park, this hotel has thirty-six rooms plus a restaurant where you can enjoy homemade pastas and vegetable pies. All the rooms have private bathrooms as well as telephones, safes, and televisions. You'll be within walking distance of the Mediterranean coastline and a short taxi ride away from the Cinque Terre trails.
www.carlahotel.com.

Hotel Mont-Blanc
$$–$$$

This nineteenth-century hotel is in the Aosta Valley village of Chamonix, where you can walk or take a hotel shuttle to the ski slopes daily. There are thirty-two rooms and eight suites on site, plus a restaurant that serves buffet breakfasts and five-course dinners. Local wines are a highlight, with more than 15,000 bottles in the hotel's collection. Special rates are sometimes available if you book directly online through the Best Mont Blanc Group.
www.bestmontblanc.com.

Where to Eat

Genoa's proximity to the Mediterranean Sea—as with the Cinque Terre and Portofino—means that virtually every local restaurant you find will have freshly caught fish and shellfish on the menu. The farther you go inland in this part of Italy, the more you'll find meat dishes as the more standard fare.

The price code for the restaurant entrees below is $=€25 or less; $$=€26 to €50; $$$=€51 to €75; $$$$=€100 or more.

Ristorante Pizzeria Punta Vagno
$–$$

Despite its name, this Genoa restaurant actually specializes in fresh fish dishes. You can also find pasta and beef offerings on the menu, along with a handful of pizza options including a sausage pie with gorgonzola cheese. If you want a truly authentic local experience, order the seafood soup.

www.puntavagno.it.

Osteria di Vico Palla
$

For a menu of local cuisine that changes depending on what's available at the local markets, try the Osteria di Vico Palla in Genoa. The menu is presented on a chalkboard, with fish and meat dishes being the primary options. As this is Genoa, you'll usually find a nice pasta dish with pesto sauce, as well.

www.vicopalla.it.

La Terrazza
$$$$

If you're going to splurge on a big-euro dinner in Portofino, then do so at La Terrazza, where the views of the harbor are outstanding. The seafood and pasta dishes are impressive, as is the wine list, and you can enjoy a lingering meal over candlelight just like Frank Sinatra and Elizabeth Taylor used to do back in the day. The restaurant has no website, but you can learn more at:

www.portofino.ws.

CHAPTER 7

Bologna

The city of Bologna is the capital of Italy's Emilia-Romagna region, which sweeps across the top of the boot from east to west, just south of Milan and Venice. Like the rest of Italy's major cities, Bologna dates back centuries and offers countless historic churches and sights for touring. Medieval, Baroque, and Renaissance architecture abounds, along with moving modern marvels including Maseratis and Lamborghinis, both of which are built nearby. Students at the University of Bologna help keep the city young. If you're curious, this is also the birthplace of delicious Bolognese sauce.

Lay of the Land

Bologna has been an accessible city since 187 B.C., when the trade route Via Amelia was built to connect the region with the present-day Venice area along Italy's northeastern shore. Over the centuries, Bologna has rivaled Venice, Florence, and Milan in terms of population. The Germans even used Bologna as a transportation hub during World War II, until U.S. forces overtook the city in 1945. Bologna's strategic importance, geographically speaking, has in many ways been its greatest asset in terms of development. It's a place where people want to go, or at least go through, and as such bears the imprints of many generations.

Today's transportation infrastructure thus includes highways, railways, bus stations, and airports, all of which make it easy for you to get to Bologna. You can easily find enough to do in and around the city for a few days, or you can make Bologna a one-day stop during a broader vacation itinerary.

Arriving by Air

Guglielmo Marconi Airport, which is colloquially known as Bologna Airport, is just four miles northwest of the Bologna city center. About 20 million passengers fly annually through here, making it the third-busiest airport in all of Italy.

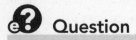 **Question**

Who was Guglielmo Marconi?
Marconi was an Italian inventor who lived from 1874 until 1937 and who is best known as the father of modern-day radio. He shared the 1909 Nobel Prize in physics, something that no doubt surprised the friends who had him examined in a psychiatric hospital after he first told them he had discovered a way to send messages through the air.

No American-based airlines have routes that fly directly here, but you can pick up flights after stopovers elsewhere in Europe through Air France, Alitalia, British Airways, and Lufthansa. The privately owned Milan-based carrier EuroFly (*www.eurofly.com*) sometimes has seats available on direct flights from New York to Bologna, but they are catch as catch can. They are often made available on search sites such as *www.expedia.com*.

The airport's official website, with an English translation, is *www.bologna-airport.it*. It includes a complete listing of airline carriers with routes here, as well as arrival and departure information.

Arriving by Train

Bologna Centrale is the main train station in the city, serving about 58 million people each year. It's a principal railway junction in Italy, with tracks running both north-south and east-west. About 500 trains pass through each day. (By comparison, New York City's Grand Central Terminal runs about 660 commuter trains each day.)

Even if you don't arrive or depart Bologna by train, the station is worth a visit. It was built in 1876, and the interior features towering ceilings and arched doorways. There's a decent restaurant on the mezzanine floor if you want to take a look around and have lunch before moving on to other nearby sights. You also might take a moment to visit the section of the station rebuilt after the 1980 terrorist bombing that killed 85 people and wounded more than 200 when an improvised explosive device detonated inside a waiting room full of late-morning commuters. Most of the wreckage has been renovated, though a piece of scarred flooring and a large crack in the wall remain, as a memorial to those who were killed. The station's main clock, too, has been left permanently at 10:25 A.M., the time of the explosion. Details about arrivals, departures, and other services are available in English at *www.grandistazioni.it*.

Arriving by Bus

Bologna has an extensive bus system that includes a shuttle service to and from the airport. There are also intercity buses that you can take from Milan or Ancona. The main bus depot in Bologna is right near the train station. An interactive map of the in-city bus routes is available in English at *www.atc.bo.it*, where you can also find ticket information, airport shuttle schedules, and a printable map.

Getting Around

Once you arrive in Bologna, you can easily explore the city on foot. Ask a local to point you toward Piazza del Nettuno or Piazza Maggiore, which are in the main part of the city just south of the scenic Parco della Montagnola (a large park) along the main road Via dell'Independenza.

If you are in good physical condition and have a comfortable pair of shoes, you'll be just fine for an entire day of touring. Otherwise, refer to the previous section about bus routes and plan your sightseeing to correspond with the available public transportation. Taxis are an option here, but can quickly get expensive. Remember: Many of the city streets are centuries old. Modern-day congestion is therefore amplified, especially at peak times in highly trafficked tourist spots.

Towers of Bologna

You've probably heard of Italy's leaning tower of Pisa, but tower building became something of an obsession in Bologna from the 1100s through the 1300s. Historians continue to argue about exactly how many towers existed at the height of the construction boom, but estimates range from about 80 to nearly 200. The towers were built as symbols of wealth for those who lived in them, as well as to serve as defensive watch posts against invaders. Feudal serfs did much of the back-breaking labor to erect the monuments year after agonizing year. Some of the towers took as long as a decade to complete.

 Fact

After World War II Allied bombings on Bologna, local volunteers would stand at the top of Asinelli Tower to see where the worst damage had occurred, directing rescue efforts from their bird's-eye post. This is ironic, given that when the towers were built, the lofty vantage points were used to coordinate attacks against enemies on the ground.

Today, fewer than twenty of the original towers remain. All the others were intentionally demolished, absorbed into other structures, or collapsed under their own weight. The two most famous remaining towers are Asinelli, at 318 feet tall, and Garisenda, at 157 feet tall, known together as "the Two Towers" that serve as the city's symbol. They stand (well, lean, actually) in Piazza di Porta Ravegnana, east of Piazza Maggiore, and are just twenty feet apart at their bases.

Unfortunately, because the Garisenda tower leans so much, it is considered unstable and therefore inaccessible for public tours. Asinelli, though, has 498 steps that you can climb for an admission fee of a few euro. The view from the top is worth the cardio workout, especially if you're planning to indulge in a plate of homemade pasta with the local Bolognese sauce later.

If the steps aren't for you, stand below the towers at street level and try to take a photograph while looking up. Bring the widest-angle camera lens you own. Taking this photograph is akin to capturing the entirety of a skyscraper from ground level.

Historic Churches

There are nearly a dozen historic churches in Bologna, but a few of them are more popular with tourists than others. The most notable, San Petronio Basilica, is the fifth-largest church in the world and is worth seeing for its sheer size.

San Petronio Basilica

Nearly 30,000 people can fit inside San Petronio Basilica, which is named in honor of Bologna's patron saint, Petronius, and is located in Piazza Maggiore. Construction and decoration of the mammoth building stretched from the late 1300s until well into the 1600s, in part because of an effort to build a cross higher than the one of St. Peter's Basilica in Rome. The Roman Catholic Church leaders didn't like this regional challenge to their central authority, of course, so work on San Petronio was halted, originally leaving the façade incomplete. It was not until 1954 that the basilica was finally consecrated.

There are two organs inside San Petronio Basilica, which was known throughout the centuries as a place where great music was performed. The organs date to 1476 and 1596, and they remain in excellent condition for their age.

Also noteworthy is a fifteenth-century fresco depicting the scene in Dante's *Inferno* that describes Muhammed being devoured by demons in Hell. In 2006, the Italian police caught Muslim terrorists plotting to destroy the church because they considered the fresco an insult to Islam. No backpacks or large bags are allowed inside the church today. Note that there is no place for you to leave them securely outside the church, either; your best bet is to leave them at your hotel.

ⓔ✸ Essential

During your tour of San Petronico Basilica, note the way the sun falls on the meridian line along the left aisle. The line is actually a sundial designed in the 1600s by astronomer Giovanni Domenico Cassini. He was the first person to observe four of Saturn's moons, and he shares credit for the discovery of the Great Red Spot on Jupiter.

San Petronio Basilica is a working church, so tourism opportunities are limited when services are taking place. In general, you can get inside between about 7:30 A.M. and 12:30 P.M., and then again from about 3 P.M. until 6 P.M., with slight variations to those hours depending on the season. Also, be sure to adhere to an appropriate dress code. Cover your shoulders and knees to show respect.

Basilica of San Domenico

Wolfgang Amadeus Mozart is the most famous cultural name associated with this church, which was built in the thirteenth century and became a prototype of construction for Dominican churches in other parts of the world. The remains of Saint Dominic, founder of Catholic religious order of Dominicans and the patron saint of the Dominican Republic, are buried here inside a shrine.

Mozart played the organ in the church's Rosary Chapel while studying with Bologna native Giovanni Battista Martini, who also taught Johann Christian Bach (the youngest son of world-renowned composer Johann Sebastian Bach). Mozart wasn't a regular; he only stopped in to play a few times during the month he studied at Bologna's music academy. Apparently, that was more than enough for the authors of history books to take notice.

Arcades

No, not the quarter-slurping type of arcade. The arcades in Bologna are covered walkways built to shade pedestrians from rain, snow, and the sweltering summer sun. There are nearly twenty-four miles of these arcades in Bologna's historic center (and even more just beyond its borders), making the city as famous for its protected walkways as it is for the towers that cast leaning shadows atop them.

❶ Alert

If you're physically challenged, the steps along the Portico of San Luca are a tourist opportunity you would be better off skipping. You can still get up to the top of the hill, where the sanctuary is located, by way of a road, and then view the portico itself from a distance as you look over the entire city of Bologna.

The definition of an arcade is a walkway covered by arches or vaults, and the longest one in Bologna—and perhaps the world— is the arcade that leads up a hillside to the Madonna of San Luca Sanctuary. There are 666 arches along this walkway, known as the Portico of San Luca, which was built from the mid-1600s to the late 1700s. Even if the sanctuary itself doesn't interest you, the walk is quite lovely—and there's a great view of Bologna from the top of the hill, perfect for taking keepsake photos.

Modern Marvels

Vast churches, serpentine arcades, skyscraping towers—all of these sights within Bologna's borders are symbols of wealth and power from generations past. Today, the world's movers and shakers often own mammoth buildings and donate mightily to cultural institutions and municipal projects, but they also put their fortunes into extreme playthings, such as sports cars. Some of the most prominent builders of these toys are located just beyond the Bologna borders—so many so, in fact, that the region is known as the "Land of Motors."

Lamborghini

Automobili Lamborghini S.p.A. is in the village of Sant'Agata Bolognese, which has just 6,500 or so residents but is known the world over by car aficionados who worship the models that have been built here since the early 1960s. The company was founded by Ferruccio Lamborghini, a tractor manufacturer who had a love of fast cars. His preferred brand was Ferrari, but he kept having trouble with the clutches on the models he brought home. He took his complaints to none other than company founder Enzo Ferrari, who told him that a man of his occupation was in no position to criticize a world-class carmaker. Lamborghini went back home and fixed the clutches himself—using his tractor parts, no less—and then went on to build what he deemed better and faster cars than Ferrari, just to prove that he could.

Today, the Lamborghini brand name is synonymous with extreme speed. The first Lamborghini model, the 350 GT, went 170 miles per hour. The company's newest speedster, the Reventón, hits a top speed of 214 miles per hour. (The price? A cool $1.4 million.) And yes, that's a Lamborghini that Bruce Wayne, Batman's alter ego, is driving through the streets of Gotham in the 2008 world-wide blockbuster *The Black Knight*.

The company inaugurated a museum in 2001, and it is open for public tours. You can see the original 350 GT here, along with other collectors' favorites and small-scale models and designs from throughout Lamborghini history. Entry is €10 for adults, €7 for students, and free for children age ten and younger who are accompanied by an adult. (Small children, typically those younger than six, are not allowed on the factory floor for tours.) The museum is open Monday through Friday, with various holiday closings throughout the year. A complete schedule with hours is online at *www.lamborghini.com*.

✅ Fact

Ferruccio Lamborghini's zodiac sign is Taurus, which is known for its determination, stubbornness, creativity, and resourcefulness. Taurus is the inspiration for the bull on the modern Lamborghini crest, and some of the maker's models, such as the Muira and Islero, are named for fighting bulls and breeders.

Ferrari

Ferrari S.p.A. continues to go strong in Maranello, to the west of Bologna. The sports car builder was founded in 1929 by Enzo Ferrari, who actually wanted to focus on race cars instead of personal roadsters. Allied forces bombed his factory during World War II, and the location was rebuilt in 1946. Ferrari's first road car, the 125 S, was produced in 1947 as a way to replenish lost income. Ferrari himself remained loyal to racing above all and often resented the wealthy people whom he felt were buying his vehicles for prestige, with no real understanding of or appreciation for how they worked.

Now owned by the Fiat group, Ferrari welcomes paying customers from all over the world, whether they're gear-heads or not. A Ferrari museum called Galleria Ferrari opened in 2005. There, you can see not just production models but also some of the race cars that have kept the brand name famous for decades. Expect to see a lot of red, which is Ferrari's signature color. Also be prepared to drop a pretty penny in the gift shop on the way out, unless you want to continue going through life without the benefit of a Ferrari Barbie or logo-embroidered bathrobe.

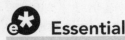

Essential

For true sports car lovers, TheBigDay company offers a three-day package that includes a factory tour in the region plus a Ferrari, Lamborghini, or Maserati for you to drive along the local streets. It's not cheap, at about €2,500 per person—but that's still six or seven figures less than actually buying one of these cars. Learn more at *www.thebigday.com*.

The Ferrari museum is open seven days a week excluding some holidays, with an entrance fee of €12 for adults and €8 for children. Learn more at *www.galleria.ferrari.com*.

Maserati

Maserati was founded in Bologna in 1914 and is now headquartered in Modena, just north of the city. Racing cars were the factory's primary output until 1957, when road cars such as coupes and roadsters began rolling off the production line in greater numbers. Today, the company is owned by Fiat, sharing the corporation's luxury car division with Alfa Romeo.

Maserati doesn't have a museum itself, but you can tour the Panini Collection, a private institution that houses about forty cars from a collection started by the original Maserati brothers. Interestingly, the Panini family is best known for producing Parmigiano Reggiano cheese, and thus they keep the world's most extensive collection of Maseratis in a building next to their cow barn. There's no website, but you can get more information (about cheese and sports cars alike) in English by calling (011) 39 359 51073.

Ducati

If you prefer two wheels to four, then Ducati Motor Holding S.p.A. inside the Bologna city limits is the place to visit. The company was founded in 1926 by three brothers who originally made radio components; the original motorcycles came off the line in 1950. The first Ducati motorcycle went just forty miles per hour. Today's models go more than 180 miles per hour. They're known for their flashy good looks, even making a cameo appearance as the toy of choice for the fictional Hollywood star Vincent Chase in the blockbuster HBO series *Entourage*.

You can see current Ducati models, as well as their predecessors, at the Ducati Museum at the factory headquarters. Opened in 1998, the museum displays the motorcycles around an illuminated racetrack for a truly memorable presentation. Side rooms detail Ducati history and people who have played an integral role in design and racing efforts. Guided tours are available twice a day in English from Monday through Saturday, and they include the factory as well as the museum. There is no entry fee. Details are online at *www.ducati.com*.

Other Must-See Spots

No trip to Bologna would be complete without at least a quick look at one of the oldest universities in the world. The National Art Gallery, which contains works by masters such as Raphael, is another must-see attraction.

University of Bologna

The University of Bologna is believed to have been founded around 1088, which would make it one of the oldest universities in all of Western history—if not the oldest. Some notable students drawn by the university's international reputation throughout the centuries include the poet Dante, the astronomer Copernicus, and United States founding father Benjamin Franklin. Today, the university has about 100,000 students studying everything from engineering to agriculture to medicine. It is modern in its teachings and historic in its presence.

A good number of museums and libraries on campus are open to the public. Most of them fall under the umbrella of the Museums of Palazzo Poggi. Exhibitions rotate and cover many topics, with some recent offerings including "Art and Anatomy from Leonardo to the Enlightenment" and "Fossils, Alphabets, and Ruins." The museums are closed on Mondays, and hours vary on other days of the week. Entry is free. Details are online in English at *www .museo.palazzopoggi.unibo.it.*

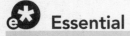 **Essential**

If you have any questions about the items you see on display at the Museums of Palazzo Poggi, you can e-mail them directly to scientists currently working on campus, who will do the appropriate research and get back to you—for free. The e-mail address for this "Ask the Experts" program is *poggidoc@alma.unibo.it.*

National Art Gallery

Locally known as Pinacoteca Nazionale, the National Art Gallery, which is north of the University of Bologna, has a large number of pieces by Bolognese artists, many of whom became famous during the Italian Renaissance.

One of the most important pieces in the museum's collection is "Ecstasy of St. Cecilia," painted by Raphael in the early 1500s. The artist originally completed the work for Bologna's Church of San Giovanni in Monte, where it was an altarpiece before being moved to the museum. Admission is €4, and the museum is open every day except Sunday and Monday. Unfortunately, the official website (*www.pinacotecabologna.it*) is available only in Italian, but an English translation is in the works.

Where to Stay

Bologna has many hotels inside its city limits, but if you're visiting primarily to get a look at the sports cars being built outside of town, you might choose a more remote locale—one that, say, overlooks the Ferrari test track.

The price code for the hotel listings below is $=€100 or less; $$=€100 to €150; $$$=€150 to €200; $$$$=€200 or more per night, per room.

Best Western Hotel San Donato
$$

This hotel overlooks the Two Towers and is within easy walking distance of Piazza Maggiore. Though the building dates to ancient times, the fifty-nine rooms located on three floors are renovated for modern needs, with each featuring air conditioning, hair dryers, and satellite television. Laundry service is available, as are non-smoking rooms.

www.hotelsandonato.it.

Hotel Porta San Mamolo
$$-$$$

There are forty-three rooms in this hotel, and the ones on the top floor have private terraces that overlook the city of Bologna. There are handicapped accessible rooms, and all rooms have air conditioning, Internet access, satellite television, private telephones, and, in some cases, plasma televisions. There's an attached restaurant, and in-room breakfast is available.

www.hotel-portasanmamolo.it.

Planet Hotel
$-$$$$

Located in Maranello, Planet Hotel overlooks the Ferrari factory and test track, with a foyer decorated in Ferrari memorabilia to make sports car fans feel immediately at home. There are just twenty-five rooms, each with private bathrooms, Internet access, air conditioning, and private telephone lines. Non-smoking rooms are an option, as are rooms with Jacuzzi tubs.

www.planethotel.org.

Where to Eat

Pretty much any *trattoria* on the local streets can make a good Bolognese sauce here, but Bologna also offers a good deal of international cuisine that's on par with what you'll find in other major Italian cities.

The price code for the restaurant entrees below is $=€25 or less; $$=€26 to €50; $$$=€51 to €75; $$$$=€100 euro or more.

Ristorante Pappagallo
$$-$$$

Located just across the piazza from the Two Towers, Ristorante Pappagalo has been dishing out traditional Bolognese cuisine since 1919. They make the meals the same way their ancestors did, using handed-down recipes for everything from cheese and porcini mushroom flan to guinea fowl with white grapes.

www.alpappagallo.it.

Cantina Bentivoglio
$

This Bologna wine bar and restaurant features live jazz performances every night. The cuisine is traditional, and the wine list always features at least 400 labels from Italian and international vintners. There are about a dozen different local-themed desserts, such as almond biscuits and mascarpone cream, making this a great spot to have dessert and a few drinks.

www.cantinabetivoglio.it.

Osteria Francescana
$$$–$$$$

If you're in Modena looking at high-priced cars, you might as well also sample some top-dollar cuisine. Chef Massimo Batturo opened this restaurant in 1995 and continues to create the kinds of traditional yet creative dishes that earned him two Michelin stars in 2005.

www.osteriafrancescana.it.

Tuscany

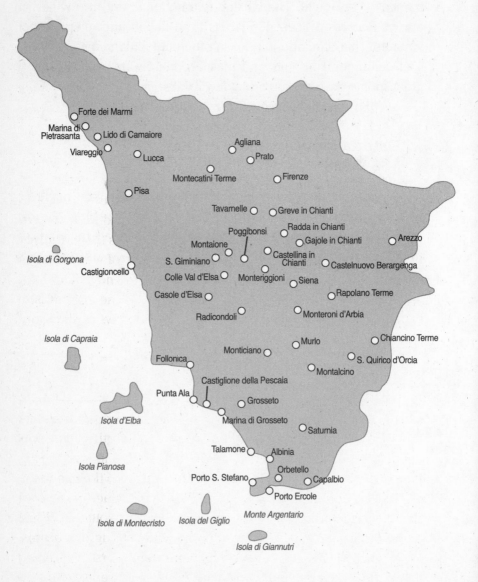

CHAPTER 8

Tuscany

Continuing your path south from Bologna and the Emilia-Romagna region, you come to Tuscany, whose western border is the Mediterranean coastline. The cities of art that gave birth to the Renaissance are here, including Florence and Pisa, and the region is well-aware and supportive of its history as the birthplace of opera composer Puccini, as well as the home of world-famous Carrara marble and long-enjoyed thermal spas and hot springs. You can tour countless churches, indulge in one fine artistic experience after another, or simply take in the views of cities and sprawling countryside alike.

Lay of the Land

Like all of Italy, the Tuscany region experienced various takeovers and wars throughout its history and for a great length of time was under control of the Roman Empire. It came into its own beginning in the 1400s when the arts and culture began to flourish in the city of Florence, in particular. Tuscany is the birthplace of the poet Dante and the artists Michelangelo, da Vinci, and Botticelli. While these names are today sprinkled prominently throughout art history books, Renaissance artists in general were at first considered low-grade craftsmen. It was not until the end of the Renaissance that their works began to command higher prices, as the value of art and culture rose both within Tuscany and beyond. It's that same appreciation for all things beautiful that draw millions of tourists to Tuscany each year. Between April and October, visitors outnumber the 360,000 or so residents of Florence.

 Fact

Tuscany is so renowned for its cultural beauty that it shows up in American pop culture with some regularity. The 2003 film *Under the Tuscan Sun* starring Diane Lane was a $43 million domestic blockbuster, and during the seventh season of *Seinfeld*, the character Maestro bragged that Jerry could never find a villa in Tuscany.

Getting Here

There are two main airports in the Tuscany region: Galileo Galilei International Airport in Pisa, and Peretola Airport outside Florence.

Galileo Galilei, which sees nearly 4 million passengers each year, offers service from the United States through Delta Air Lines as well as connecting international flights on Air France, British Airways, and Lufthansa. There are also connecting buses and trains to Pisa's main station, as well as to the Santa Maria Novella station in Florence. You can find flight schedules, train schedules, airport maps and more in English at *www.pisa-airport.com*.

Peretola Airport is much smaller—it has only a single runway—and offers no international service from the United States, but you can pick up regional flights from Rome. There is no connecting train service, but buses run into the city of Florence every half hour most of the day. The airport's website is *www.aeroporto.firenze.it*, and it offers an English translation.

Getting Around

Once in Tuscany, you can take buses or trains from one city to the next. It's about an hour's train ride, for instance, from Florence inland to Pisa on the coast. Train and bus service becomes spottier when you head into the countryside, but if your plan is to stick to Tuscany's cities, you will not need a rental car. You can book single-ride tickets or multiple-day train passes through *www.raileurope.com* or *www.italiarail.com*. If the countryside is your final destination, consider a rental car that's sturdy instead of one that's the least expensive. Many of the roads around the vineyards, for instance, are gravel instead of paved. Also keep in mind that manual transmissions are the norm, so you must specify if you want an automatic—and you may have to pay a little extra.

Question

Why isn't Peretola Airport named after someone famous, as other Italian airports are?
It actually is. Though the facility's official name is Peretola Airport, it's sometimes referred to as Amerigo Vespucci Airport, in honor of the Italian explorer who proved that Christopher Columbus had not sailed to Asia, but instead to a previously unknown continent.

Once you are in the city of your choice, you will be able to get around to the main cathedrals, monuments, and other tourist attractions on foot. That's one of the greatest things about visiting such storied locations: They were mostly laid out before "urban sprawl" became so much as a thought in any residential planner's mind.

Florence

The historic center of Florence was added to the list of UNESCO World Heritage Sites in 1982, when the city was deemed "the symbol of the Renaissance" based on its 600 years of cathedral building and master artwork creations. In truth, though, the story of Florence begins much earlier than the Renaissance—way back in 59 B.C., when Julius Caesar founded a settlement called Florentia as a home for his veteran soldiers. The army camp's location, between Rome and the agricultural lands to the north, soon helped the settlement grow into a center of commerce. By the time Michelangelo, da Vinci, and Botticelli burst onto the scene in the 1400s, the city was home to 60,000 to 80,000 people.

After various struggles that for a time had Tuscany falling under the authority of Austria, Florence emerged as Italy's capital in 1865 and kept the title for six years, after which Rome succeeded it. Tourism began to grow in the early 1900s, until German forces occupied Florence for a year during World War II. Allied troops fought for the city's liberation, and since the end of the 1940s, Florence has flourished as a travel destination.

❊ Essential

In Florence, take a moment to consider the placards placed on the walls of some buildings, noting the high water mark from a 1966 flood of the Arno River, which crested at about twenty-two feet in some parts of the city. The damage doesn't appear bad today, but countless lives were lost, at least 3 million books were damaged, and some 14,000 pieces of art were ruined.

You could spend a lifetime in Florence uncovering its history and admiring its architecture, but if you have only a few days to explore, the five must-see sights are Uffizi Gallery, the Galleria dell'Accademia, Florence Cathedral, Campanile, and Ponte Vecchio.

Uffizi Gallery

Housing works by Botticelli, da Vinci, Michelangelo, and Raphael, the Uffizi Gallery is one of the most important art museums not just in Italy, but in the world. It was built as a palace of offices in the mid-1500s (*uffizi* means offices in Italian), and the ruling Medici used the space for displaying its artistic treasures until the family fell out of power. The collection remained in their wake, and the site was opened as a public museum in 1765, after which its curators continued to collect important pieces. The museum is currently working to complete a massive expansion to finally bring the majority of works out of storage and into the light of day.

Masterworks on Display

The Botticelli works typically on display include *The Birth of Venus*, an instantly recognizable canvas to even the most peripheral of art students. It depicts the flowing-haired blonde goddess emerging nude from the ocean atop a shell, an iconic portrayal that has been recreated in film and television alike.

🅴❗ Alert

Ticket reservations for touring the Uffizi are essential, especially during the jam-packed tourist month of July. People without reserved tickets have had to wait as long as five hours in the hot summer sun before entering the popular exhibitions. Check the website (*www.polomuseale.firenze.it*) for the most up-to-date information.

Da Vinci's works include the early oil-on-wood *The Adoration of the Magi*, which historians cite as one of the artist's earliest efforts at chiaroscuro, or the contrast between light and dark. There was some controversy about the work in 2002, when a restoration technician claimed that da Vinci had only drawn the lines beneath the paint and not done the brushwork himself, but that claim has not been corroborated.

Michelangelo's *Doni Tondo* is also part of the Uffizi collection. It is the artist's only known preserved panel painting in its original frame, which is round. Michelangelo completed the work before taking on the Sistine Chapel in Vatican City.

The Raphael work that most patrons visit at Uffizi is *Portrait of Leo X*, considered by many to be the artist's greatest masterpiece. It is one of the last works he composed without assistance before his death. When he first displayed the portrait in the early 1500s, it created a sensation because it portrayed the pope in a group setting with two cardinals, instead of on his own in a more regal pose.

Museum Admissions

The Uffizi is open Tuesday through Sunday from 8:15 A.M. until 6:30 P.M. It is closed on Mondays, as well as on New Year's Day, May 1, and Christmas Day. During the popular summer tourism months, the museum sometimes extends its evening hours until 10 P.M. on weeknights. If that's the case, the hours are posted on the website, *www.polomuseale.firenze.it*. Exhibition prices typically range from €6 to €10.

Galleria dell'Accademia

This museum, which is within walking distance of the Uffizi, is home to Michelangelo's magnificent marble sculpture *David*— which has been housed here since the late 1800s. It stands just inside the museum's entrance and is one of the first stops on the tour, housed within a spectacular domed enclave built specifically for it. At seventeen feet tall, *David* towers above all the tourists, leaving a lasting impression.

You can't get close enough to touch the statue, but you can walk all the way around it and spend some time sitting on nearby benches, pondering every knuckle and muscle that Michelangelo carved. If you purchase the museum's audio tour, you can also hear the story of how the statue was moved through the streets to its current location to protect it from the wind and rain that used to batter it when it stood outside.

Countless online travel agencies sell advance-purchase tickets for the Galleria dell'Accademia. Surcharges apply, and the lines at this museum tend to be shorter than at the Uffizi. Weigh your financial options against the thought of a half-hour's wait when deciding whether to buy in advance.

Florence Cathedral

The Florence Cathedral's proper name is Basilica di Santa Maria del Fiore, originally designed in the late 1200s. The dome was completed in the 1430s, and the current façade was finished in the 1880s. It is neo-gothic with white, pink, and green marble panels, plus three massive bronze doors that date to the turn of the twentieth century.

❓ Question

How did Raphael die?
Legend has it that he enjoyed an evening of unbridled sexual relations with his longtime girlfriend that left him exhausted to the point of fever, then lied to his doctors about the root of his illness and was given a type of medicine he didn't need, which actually killed him. He was thirty-seven years old.

Inside, the sense of space and volume is extraordinary. Arches in the cathedral are 75 feet tall, and the cathedral itself is just a hair more than 500 feet long (if stood on one end, it would rival modern skyscrapers). There is less artwork in this church than many of the others you can tour in Italy, but Florence Cathedral is noted for its forty-four stained glass windows.

At the website *www.operaduomo.firenze.it*, you will find hours and fees (in English) for visiting the various parts of the cathedral. There's the main cathedral, the dome, the bell tower (also known as the campanile), and the archaeology site, each with different hours and costs of entry. The cathedral itself is free to visit and has an entrance for people who use wheelchairs. Note that if you want to tour the dome, there are 463 stairs and no elevator. The view is worth the effort if you have the stamina.

 Fact

Stained glass dates to ancient times, but it didn't come into its own as an art form until the Middle Ages. During those years, the population was largely illiterate, so stained-glass "pictures" were used to describe the stories of the Bible. These story-telling pictures soon took on the form of windows in churches, including prominent use in Florence Cathedral.

Campanile

The word "campanile," derived from the Italian *campana* (bell), means a free-standing bell tower. The world's tallest free-standing campanile is at the University of Birmingham in the United Kingdom, but Italy is well known for its campaniles, too, including the Leaning Tower of Pisa.

Giotto's Bell Tower is the campanile in Florence, located next to the Florence Cathedral. It's just shy of 280 feet tall and is named for Giotto di Bondone, a local painter who is widely recognized as one of the first Renaissance artists. He died in 1337, some twenty-two years before the tower was completed. The artist who was in charge of finishing the tower failed to include a spire Giotto had designed, so the artist went to his grave believing his namesake creation would actually be 400 feet tall.

Again, consult the website *www.operaduomo.firenze.it* for hours and fees, including dates when the tower is closed.

Ponte Vecchio

This Medieval bridge, one of Europe's oldest (the name translates as "old bridge"), crosses the Arno River and offers a view of the river from its midpoint. The structure is unusual in that it has shops built along it that once housed butchers and fishmongers who threw their waste over the side and into the river. Later, the shops became the workplace of goldsmiths and silversmiths, and today, jewelry sellers dominate the landscape. Interestingly, this is the only bridge in Florence that Hitler's troops left standing during their 1944 retreat from the city. Rumor has it that the dictator himself gave the order to let the historic bridge stand, though he did authorize destruction of all the buildings at its ends, thus blocking any access to it for the Allies.

Alert

Like the dome in Florence Cathedral, Giotto's bell tower offers outstanding views of Florence from its top—but without the benefit of an elevator. It's 414 treads to the top of the bell tower, from which you can look down on the dome. Also note that a wire cage that is in place atop the bell tower for safety reasons might interfere with your photographs.

Today, you will find not just shops but also street performers and portrait artists along the bridge—especially during the warm summer months, when tourism peaks. It's free to walk across the bridge and look around, but expect to pay a pretty euro if you stop at any of the nearby shops or restaurants, all of which are considered to be part of the tourist district.

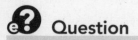 **Question**

How old is Ponte Vecchio?
The answer depends on how you determine age. The structure you can walk across today dates to the 1300s, but other bridges have been built across this section of the Arno River since the 900s. Records show that floods destroyed bridges here in 1117 and 1333, making the existing structure likely the longest standing.

Lucca

The Tuscan city of Lucca is best known for its Renaissance-era defensive walls, which remain intact even though the modern city has expanded well beyond them. Lucca is not as well known today as its sister cities Florence and Pisa, but in fact was the second-largest city state (after Venice) to remain independent until Napoleon arrived in the early 1800s. The city has a rich cultural heritage, too, and is the birthplace of composer Giacomo Puccini, who wrote *La Bohème* and *Madame Butterfly*.

Views from Above

There are two good locations for enjoying a bird's-eye view of the city. One is the Torre delle Ore, a thirteenth-century clock tower that will require you to hoof it up 207 steps. The other is the Palazzo Guinigi, which is slightly more formidable with 230 steps. At either place, you'll pay about €4 for the privilege of exhausting your thigh and calf muscles, but you'll get great photos. Both locations are in the city center, within walking distance of each other.

Views from Around

The city walls, built for military purposes, today are a tourist attraction unto themselves. (They've even been used for car races.) The rim is less than two miles around, which makes it a good leg-stretching distance for walking, jogging, or even bicycling. As with the Ponte Vecchio in Florence, the walls in Lucca are a free attraction well worth the visit.

Puccini Opera Festival

About eleven miles from Puccini's birthplace of Lucca is the hamlet of Torre del Lago, which hosts an opera festival in his honor every July and August. Some 40,000 visitors visit the hamlet's open-air Teatro dei Quattromila to enjoy performances near the home where Puccini lived and worked (and which is a tourable museum).

✹ Essential

If you're a Puccini fan, then check out the section of the festival's website (*www.puccinifestival.it*) that offers suggested itineraries for viewing not just the places where the composer lived and worked, but also the statues that have been erected in his honor. One is in Lucca, and there are others in surrounding Tuscan towns.

The festival has been held since 1930, but it was not on an annual basis until 1966. Since then, many of the world's greatest opera performers have taken to the stage, including Placido Domingo, who conducted *Madame Butterfly* in 2004.

Seats for the opera performances range from about €30 to about €160. You can buy them online through the festival's website, *www.puccinifestival.it*. It offers all information in English, including performance dates and opera synopses.

Pisa

Most travelers know of Pisa thanks to its famous landmark, the Leaning Tower. Even so, there is more to see here than the bell tower, especially if you are interested in historic churches. The Piazza dei Miracoli ("Square of Miracles), where the tower is located, also is home to the city's cathedral.

The Leaning Tower

No, it wasn't supposed to lean like that. Pisa's bell tower was meant to stand straight as a proud man's spine, but alas, its poorly laid foundation and the lousy dirt underneath left it listing after just three tiers were completed in the 1170s. Today, after centuries of being eased into new positions by gravity and manmade forces, the tower stands some three feet higher on one side than the other. It leans at an angle of about four degrees, having endured more than a few schemes to keep it stabilized.

The most recent effort was in 1990, when the tower was closed to the public and its angle was altered by removing some of the dirt underneath one side. That and other stabilization efforts made the tower stable enough to be reopened to the public in 2001. According to engineers at the time, it will be safe for at least another 300 years. In 2008, after more dirt was removed from beneath one side, engineers revised the previous estimate, saying it will be stable for another 200 years. Only time will tell which set of workers is correct—but both agreed to leave the tower with a tilt.

Only a limited number of people are allowed up into the tower at a time, for obvious reasons of weight and stability. If you want to make sure you're among them, you can reserve tickets for a predetermined time slot from any online vendor who deals with tours of Italy, or buy them in the mornings at the museums in the piazza. Go early to avoid the rush. Combination tickets will get you into the tower, the cathedral, and other piazza sites.

Piazza dei Miracoli

Beyond the Leaning Tower, Piazza dei Miracoli offers the Duomo, Baptistery, and Camposanto, an interesting combination of churches and cemetery with beautiful architecture and artwork.

Duomo

The Duomo is a Medieval cathedral whose construction began in 1063. A massive fire in the 1500s destroyed many of the Medieval artworks that used to be housed inside, but the artistic portions of the cathedral itself were either restored, rebuilt, or replaced. Like the Leaning Tower, which was built on similarly lousy soil, the cathedral lists—but not nearly as much as the world-famous landmark.

 Fact

The Leaning Tower of Pisa almost met its demise during World War II, when the Allied forces discovered that invading Nazi troops were using it as an observation post. As the story goes, a U.S. Army sergeant had the authority to call an artillery strike, but he withheld, thus preserving the tower as the monument it is today.

Baptistery

Opposite the Duomo is the Baptistery, a round, Romanesque building dedicated to St. John the Baptist. It's the largest baptistery in all of Italy, and if you count the statue of St. John the Baptist at the top, the baptistery is a hair taller than the Leaning Tower. There's not much artwork to see inside, but the sheer volume of the baptistery's interior makes it worth a look.

Camposanto

This walled cemetery dates to the thirteenth century and was originally filled with impressive frescoes. Unfortunately, the wooden roof was destroyed and many of the frescoes were seriously damaged during Allied bombings on the Nazi-occupied structure in 1944. In recent decades, great pains have been taken to restore the artwork.

There's a room where you can see historic photographs of the frescoes both before and after the bombing, and a few of the damaged pieces are still on view. Also, some of the funerary monuments in the cloisters are worth seeing because they inspired some of Pisa's Medieval sculptures.

Siena

Siena was a powerful Medieval city, and most of its architectural gems were built in the fourteenth century. The Black Death and frequent clashes with nearby Florence decimated its strength, and in 1559, Siena was annexed by the grand duchy of Tuscany.

Piazza del Campo

Siena's main city square, Piazza del Campo, is its political center. Dominated by the Palazzo Pubblico, the town hall, the piazza is a good place to start a tour of the city. The square itself is shaped like a fan and is divided into nine slats, representing the nine magistrates who presided over Siena at the height of its power.

The Museo Civico in the Palazzo Pubblico and the adjoining bell tower, the Torre del Mangia, are open to the public. Most of the town hall dates back to the thirteenth and fourteenth centuries, but additions in the seventeenth century enlarged it. The Torre del Mangia was completed just before the plague devastated Siena in 1348.

The museum is open daily from November through mid-March from 10 A.M. to 6:30 P.M. and from mid-March through October from 10 A.M. to 7 P.M. Tickets are €7 for the museum only and €10 for a combination ticket that includes the Torre del Mangia. Visit *www .comunie.siena.it* for more information.

Duomo

Siena's Gothic cathedral is considered one of the most beautiful in Italy, thanks to its distinctive dark-and-light-striped interior. It was built in the thirteenth century when Siena was a dominant city, but an ambitious expansion project had to be abandoned after the plague of 1348. The entire cathedral is a work of art. Frescoes adorn the walls, and even the floors are decorated with marble panels that show scenes from classical mythology and the Old Testament. Observe the dress code—covered shoulders and knees.

The cathedral is open to the public from March 1 through May 31 and September 1 through November 1 from 10:30 A.M. to 7:30 P.M. Monday through Saturday and 1:30 P.M. to 5:30 P.M. on Sundays and holidays. From November 2 through February 28, it is open 10:30 A.M. to 6:30 P.M. from Monday through Saturday and 1:30 P.M. to 5:30 P.M. on Sundays and holidays. From June 1 to August 31, it is open 10:30 A.M. to 8 P.M. Monday through Saturday and 1:30 P.M. to 6 P.M. on Sundays and holidays. Admission to the cathedral is €3. Visit *www. operaduomo.siena.il* for more information.

The adjoining Museo dell'Opera Metropolitana contains additional artifacts and works of art. It is open March 1 through May 31 and September 1 through November 1 from 9:30 A.M. to 7 P.M. From June 1 through August 31, it is open from 9:30 A.M. to 8 P.M. From November 2 through February 28, it is open from 10 A.M. to 5 P.M. Admission is €6.

The Palio

The Palio has been a point of pride for the Sienese since the thirteenth century. Held twice a year, on July 2 and August 16, the Palio is a no-holds-barred horse race in Piazza del Campo. Ten horses, representing ten of the city's seventeen *contrade*, or districts, race three times around the square. (Seven of the *contrade* must sit out each race.) The horse that crosses the finish line first wins—regardless of whether its jockey managed to hang on for the entire ride. Grabbing the reins of another jockey's horse is forbidden, but everything else is fair game in the highly competitive race. Thousands of spectators pack themselves into the square to witness the event, while hundreds of others buy seats on temporary bleachers set up around the perimeter of the track.

The race is a unique spectacle for tourists, but the true celebrants are the Sienese. Raucous celebrations spread throughout the city, the most exuberant taking place in the winning *contrada*. For a tourist, the Palio is a magical time to visit the city. Each *contrada* displays its colors, and on the afternoon of the Palio, processions of men in Medieval garb wind through the city streets. The highlight is the skilled flag-bearers and their entertaining routines.

Elba

Elba, at eighteen miles long, is the third-largest island in Italy after Sicily and Sardinia. It's part of the National Park of the Tuscan Archipelago and is best known as the place where Napoleon was exiled—with a guard of 600 men to protect him—in 1814. He had barely stayed a year when he escaped back to France, after which he was defeated at Waterloo and exiled again, this time to the far more isolated South Atlantic island of St. Helena. The Germans briefly held Elba during World War II, until, ironically, it was liberated by French forces.

There's an airport on Elba, but the least expensive and most scenic way to arrive is by way of an hour-long ferry ride from the Tuscan port of Piombino. You can wander the shops and restaurants in the old city, as well as the two residences where Napoleon stayed (now museums), or you can hit the beaches for some fun in the sun. There are plenty of hotels if you want to stay a day or two on Elba, or you can take the ferry back to Piombino for the night.

Other Must-See Spots

Had enough of churches, towers, and historic hotspots? Take some time to view Tuscany's lesser-visited offerings, including the famous marble in the mountains of Carrara, the vineyards in Montalcino, and the thermal baths that have drawn people seeking relaxation for thousands of years.

 Fact

The Palio has its roots in the long history of Siena's contrade, who have raced horses since the 13th century. Early iterations of the race spanned the entire city, but when the Grand Duke of Tuscany banned bullfighting in 1590, the contrade moved their races into the Piazza del Campo to replace the outlawed entertainment, and the modern Palio was born.

Carrara

There are two ideal ways to see the world-famous marble that has been extracted from Carrara for centuries. One is by driving along the highways A12 and SS1 Via Aurelia, from which you can see the mountainsides full of the stuff. The other is paying a few euro to tour the Museo del Marmo, halfway between Carrara and Marina di Carrara, where you'll find not just samples of the good stuff, but also legends written in English to help you understand how it has been extracted since the days of chisels and hammers, when artists like Michelangelo needed slabs for their sculptures.

The museum was founded in 1982 and usually draws fewer than 10,000 tourists a year, making it an interesting diversion away from the crowds of Tuscany's main attractions in Florence and Pisa. Guided tours are available, and there are special tours for people who use wheelchairs. Information about hours, admission fees, and more is available in English at the museum's website, *http://urano .isti.cnr.it:8880/museo/home.en.php*.

✪ Essential

Unless you plan to buy an entire case of wine and ship it back home, prepare to choose only your two favorite bottles. U.S. Customs regulations limit the number of bottles you can bring with you to the States. Also note that they must be packed in your checked baggage. If you put your $100 bottle of Brunello into your carry-on bag, it will be confiscated.

Montalcino

This countryside landscape is where the grapes are grown to create world-famous Brunello wines (hence the name Brunello di Montalcino on the labels). If you're a fan of rich Italian reds, then a day trip to Montalcino is a must.

Many of the vineyards here are family-owned and do not offer regular tours, but the largest producer, Banfi, offers tours as well as a restaurant with a gourmet tasting menu. Its manicured grounds are a vision of agricultural bliss—it even has a restored castle with a museum—and its store contains vintages that can be impossible to find at home. Bottles of Brunello that you might see on a Chicago restaurant's wine list for $300 are available here for less than $100.

The Banfi website, *www.castellobanfi.com*, provides details about restaurant reservations, on-site accommodations, and more.

Thermal Baths

Natural hot springs and thermal baths dot the Tuscan countryside and have long been considered a good location for balneotherapy—the treatment of disease by bathing. Pope Pius II was a believer who came to bathe in the "sacred water," as did countless wealthy settlers in the countryside even before it was part of Italy. Today, many of the springs and baths are part of spas that offer massages, mud baths, and more on site. Two good websites that list the various thermal bath locations with contact information in English are *www.vercenni.com* and *www.traveltuscany.net*.

Where to Stay

There are plenty of hotels at varying price points in the main Tuscan cities such as Florence and Pisa, but other interesting options for lodging in this part of Italy are rental farmhouses and villas.

The price code for the hotel listings below is $=€100 or less; $$=€100 to €150; $$$=€150 to €200; $$$$=€200 or more per night, per room.

Hotel Davanzati
$–$$$$

The Hotel Davanzati, within walking distance of many Florence sites as well as the Arno River, has single rooms, double rooms, double superior rooms, and suites. Rates vary widely depending on the season, with a standard double ranging from €120 to nearly €200. There are twenty-one rooms in all, each restored with Tuscan furnishings reminiscent of the building's original construction in the 1400s, but also offering air conditioning, satellite television, WiFi, private telephone lines, and other modern conveniences.

www.hoteldavanzati.it.

Hotel Romagna
$–$$$

Hotel Romagna is also in the heart of Florence, and rates change along with the seasons. Double rooms, for instance, can be anywhere from €58 to €125. This hotel has twenty-three rooms, all with en suite bathrooms, satellite television, and private telephones. Some rooms offer views of the Florentine rooftops.

www.hotelromagna.it.

Hotel Novocento
$–$$

Located in the historic center of Pisa, Hotel Novocento is within walking distance of the Leaning Tower and other attractions. There are just ten rooms here for an intimate at-home feeling, along with an on-site dining room, reading room, and garden. A photo gallery of the property and the guest rooms is online, along with booking information in English.

www.hotelnovocento.pisa.it.

Frances' Lodge
$$$–$$$$

This cozy bed-and-breakfast just outside Siena's city walls is a great place to get a feel for the Tuscan countryside and the city itself. The proprietors can arrange horseback riding tours and other guided sightseeing tours. Breakfast is included, and there is a swimming pool on the property. There are six double rooms, all of which have private bathrooms and satellite TV. Air conditioning is available at an extra cost.

www.franceslodge.it.

Hotel Ilio
$-$$

This boutique hotel is on the island of Elba, offering just twenty rooms. It was the island's first "all-nature" hotel, meaning it aims to treat the surroundings as well as the guests. Rates vary from room to room and change with the season, but do not go above about €130 for the most expensive room during the summer. Breakfast and dinner are served on-site.

www.en.hotelilo.com.

Farmhouses and Villas
$$$$

Countryside farmhouses and bed-and-breakfast-style villas can be a real bargain if you're traveling with a family or a group of adults. Some can even be booked by the room just like hotels. They'll also get you away from the tourist-swamped cities, so you can enjoy local restaurants and sights the way, well, the locals do. A good website that offers a wide selection of farmhouses and villas alike is:

www.discovertuscany.com.

Where to Eat

Tuscany is renowned for its cuisine. Be sure you order a nice Super Tuscan with your meal. Chianti and Brunello di Montalcino also are native to this part of Italy.

The price code for the restaurant entrees below is $=€25 or less; $$=€26 to €50; $$$=€51 to €75; $$$$=€100 or more.

Ristorante La Giostra
$$–$$$

This warmly lit restaurant in the heart of Florence offers a menu of countless Tuscan favorites, including pastas, meats, and fish. All the wines on the menu have matured in the restaurant's wine cellar for at least six months before being offered to patrons, and they feature selections from Tuscany as well as broader Italy.

www.ristorantelagiostra.com.

Ristorante Enoteca Pinchiorri
$$$$

If you want to blow big bucks on a killer meal in Florence, consider the Ristorante Enoteca, where pasta dishes start around €70. Main courses, such as monkfish filled with chopped capers, run about €110. Don't miss the "chocolate three ways" dessert, which comes with blueberry compote and mint yogurt, at a price of €40

www.enotecapinchiorri.com.

Enotria
$$-$$$$

This wine bar and restaurant in Florence has three floors. On the ground floor is the restaurant, which serves lunches and dinners designed to complement wine tastings. The lower floor is the wine cellar, which boasts bottlings from large and small producers alike. The upper floor is the office of the Florence Wine Society, which should give you an idea of just how delicious some of the reds and whites will be at this place.

www.enotriawine.it.

Da Bruno
$-$$

Within walking distance of the Leaning Tower, this Pisa trattoria is famous for its salt cod cooked with leeks and tomatoes, a dish the proprietor has been serving for three decades now. The menu changes with the season and typically includes a good number of fresh fish dishes, as well as mushroom dishes when the time of year is right.

www.pisaonline.it/trattoriadabruno.

CHAPTER 9

Central Italy

Most visitors who travel to Italy's mid-section stick to well-known hotspots from Tuscany to Rome, but there is far more to see and do if you have some extra time and are willing to explore beyond the tour groups. Cathedrals, palaces, and museums abound, while port towns large and small on the Adriatic coast offer countless opportunities for sightseeing, ferry trips, and, of course, deliciously fresh seafood. Beach resorts are an option in this part of Italy, as are long hikes, bicycle rides, and winter snow skiing up and over the beautiful countryside hills and mountains.

Lay of the Land

For the purposes of this book, Central Italy includes the regions of Umbria, Marche, and Abruzzo—basically the areas from Rome's immediate northeast to its immediate southeast. Each of the three regions in Central Italy has its own history, but because of their close geographic proximity, they share similar timelines and were all ruled by the Roman Empire, Charlemagne, Napoleon, and the Papal States at various points. Much of the land in this part of Italy is hilly or mountainous, with sloping plains that run along the coast of the Adriatic Sea. Thus, tourism here includes ski resorts as well as sandy beaches, each with its own season for you to enjoy. Medieval cities and towns also draw countless tourists, all of whom can sample the locally produced wines and olive oils.

 Fact

The Appenine Mountains run through Abruzzo, Umbria, and Marche and are believed to have been created by the same tectonic shift from which the Alps emerged. The region continues to suffer from earthquakes today, especially Abruzzo, where the most recent fatal shake, in April 2009, killed 307 people and damaged many historic buildings.

Getting Here and Around

Major highways and train lines connect this region to nearby Rome, which means you can easily fly into the capital city and then take a rental car, bus, or train to the region's smaller cities. From Rome to Ancona, which is about the farthest possible distance within this region, the train ride takes three to four hours, depending on whether you catch an express or local line. The views of the hillsides are lovely and make the train ride as picturesque as it is efficient. In the Marche region, there are highways and train lines running north-south right along the Adriatic coast, with spectacular views of the waterfront.

There is also a regional airport called Aeroporto di Ancona Falconara in the city of Ancona. It welcomes regional flights from Italian cities including Rome and Milan, as well as flights from other parts of Europe. The airport's website, which has an English version, is at *www.aeroportomarche.com.*

No matter how you get to this region, if you plan to stick to the cities and towns, then you should be able to get by with public buses and trains as opposed to a rental car. Bus and train routes become less accessible if you want to explore some of the more rural areas in this part of the country.

A Different Tourism Style

While this part of Italy includes Medieval towns, historic churches, and similar attractions that you can find elsewhere around the country, it is also relatively untouched by the masses, who tend to gravitate toward Tuscany when they want to escape Rome for a few days. The locals consider much of this land a beautiful place to travel through, so you can enjoy the solid network of roads and train routes without having to worry about following gigantic tour groups all the livelong day. In other words, if you want to combine your historic sightseeing with out-of-the-way restaurants, park trails, and working local ports, then Central Italy is a good place to be.

Ancona

The Adriatic port city of Ancona, home to about 100,000 people, is the capital of the Marche region. It's about 125 miles from either Bologna or Rome, which means you can tour one of those cities during the day, hop on a train, and reach Ancona by nightfall. Ancona is also accessible by ferry; lines run on regular schedules not just between Italian ports, but also from across the Adriatic Sea and cities such as Split, Croatia, and Igoumenitsa, Greece. The Greeks, in fact, first turned Ancona into a port city upon discovering it, and it remains the Adriatic's largest port city today. It also has become a major center for yacht building, and some of the world's largest private vessels are launched from its shipyards in multimillion-dollar style.

Ancona has an old town along its waterfront, as well as the modern city that you'll encounter immediately if you arrive by train. There are a good number of hotels in the newer area near the train station, but most of the sights that appeal to tourists are near the waterfront. Buses and taxis are available to get you from one area to the other.

Cathedral of St. Ciriaco

This structure dates to at least the twelfth century and is Romanesque, the Medieval style of architecture that eventually evolved into Gothic. The cathedral itself is worth seeing, but so is the view on the way to it. As you walk up and along Via Giovanni XXIII, you will be treated to a lovely view of both the waterfront and the city. This is a good first stop, both because it gives you a bird's-eye view and because the cathedral is set off by itself, away from most of the other sights.

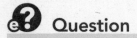 **Question**

Does the word Ancona come from the Italian language?
No, it comes from Greek. It's a modification of a Greek word that means elbow, and refers to a time when a harbor near the modern-day city was protected by a stretch of land that had a bend in it, like a human elbow.

Archaeology Museum

The Museo Archeologico Nazionale delle Marche is home to the earliest known artifacts from the Marche region. There are also works here from the Bronze Age, including some of the earliest examples of ceramics, weaving, and metallurgy.

A map of the museum's various rooms and collections is online at *www.archeomarche.it/museoanc.htm*, but the descriptions on the site itself are in Italian only. The page is translatable by Google, if you want to use that function to get the gist of what is available for viewing at the museum.

Parco Naturale del Monte Cònero

The Parco Naturale del Monte Cònero is technically outside the city limits, but it's nearby and worth a visit. You can spend a day at the 14,000-plus-acre park taking nature walks, birdwatching, sailing, bicycling, or simply lounging on the beach. It's possible to extend your stay for a few days by camping. Archaeological sites are within the park's boundaries, as are spectacular views of the rocky Adriatic coastline. There also are local eateries on site that prepare fresh regional cuisine. The visitor's center inside the park itself is the best place to get information in English, as the park's website, *www .parcodelconero.eu*, is currently available only in Italian.

Essential

If you're a fan of jazz, then be sure to visit Ancona during its annual summer jazz festival, which takes place in July. You can hear jazz (and opera, symphony orchestral music, and more) year-round at the Teatro delle Muse, which, with 1,000 seats, is the city's main theater. Its website, which lists upcoming acts, is *www .teatrodellemuse.org.*

Perugia

Perugia is the capital of the Umbria region and is home to about 170,000 people. It is famous for its chocolates, produced by the Perugina company, which was founded in 1907 and today is part of the Nestle corporation. Much like Hershey has its Kisses, Perugina has its Baci, which are kiss-like treats filled with hazelnut. They come with love notes written in many languages, including English. You can spot them at the city's annual chocolate festival, held each October, and they're also available in countless local shops year-round.

Like so many cities that date back centuries, Perugia has a historical heart that's at the top of a hill (all the better for lookouts to be positioned). The city is no longer completely walled, but it is nicely preserved despite the modern additions of trains, buses, and cable cars. They're typically packed with tourists during the summer—particularly during the Umbria Jazz Festival in July.

Piazza IV Novembre

This piazza was the main square in days gone by, and it is where you will find the Perugia Cathedral. The side of the cathedral that faces the piazza is marked by the Fontana Maggiore, a fantastic circular fountain whose design dates to the 1270s. The cathedral itself dates to the fourteenth century on this site, though other city cathedrals have been in different locations since at least the tenth century. The first chapel inside the cathedral is dedicated to the Virgin Mary's wedding ring, known as the Holy Ring, which is kept here. There is a museum, too. Admission is free.

Also in this piazza is the Galleria Nazionale dell'Umbria, a museum that houses the most comprehensive and complete collection of works from the Umbrian School of Painting, from the the thirteenth century to the nineteenth century. Some of the more unusual sections include artifacts from the history of law, graphics, and ancient topography. For hours and exhibit information, go to *www.gallerianazionaleumbria.it,* which offers an English translation.

Language Instruction

Perugia is known for schools that teach Italian to foreigners. You can enjoy a single private lesson or enroll in intensive courses that combine bookwork, conversation practice, and historic tours given in the native language. The length of the courses vary.

Comitato Linguistico is one such school, offering two- and four-week courses at beginner, intermediate, and advanced levels in addition to individual lessons of all lengths. There are also courses that focus on business, art, literature, and cooking, if you want to specialize right away to enhance your travel or work experience in the country. Prices range from €75 per week to €300 per week, depending on what type of class you choose (and whether you want group or individual instruction). Learn more at *www .comitatolinguistico.com.*

 Fact

> If you decide to study Italian at a school such as Comitato Linguistico, you will be given a student identification card—which, like all such cards, entitles you to student discounts at local shops, restaurants, museums, and the like. Hopefully, by the end of your class, you'll even be able to ask for your discount in Italian.

Pescara

Pescara is an Adriatic coast city in the Abruzzo region. It is home to about 120,000 people and more than its fair share of tourists, who come to enjoy the beaches every summer. The city has long been considered a strategic location for development not only because of its sea access, but also because it sits at the mouth of the Aterno-Pescara River. It's easy to understand where the name Pescara originates; the location formerly was known as Piscaria, or "abounding with fish." Though the city itself is centuries old, it has a newer look and feel to it than some others in Italy because of major reconstruction that was required after World War II. This is not the place to find great cultural artifacts, but if you're looking for hopping nightclubs and bikinis, you're in luck.

The shoreline in Pescara stretches for about twelve miles, all of it lined with hotels, bed-and-breakfast inns, restaurants, and discotheques overlooking the sea. Think of the string of high-rise hotels along Collins Avenue in Miami Beach (a sister city to Pescara), and you'll get the idea.

Alert

> You may see advertisements for ski resorts in Pescara, but the city really is a summertime destination. The ski resorts in the vicinity are to the west, typically beyond Pescara's borders and in fact closer to other cities including L'Aquila. You would be just as close to many of them if you traveled from Rome instead of Pescara.

Casa Natale di Gabriele D'Annunzio

One of the historical landmarks you can visit in Pescara is the birthplace home of Gabriele d'Annunzio, a poet who became a figurehead of fascism and mentor to Benito Mussolini. He never did participate in Mussolini's rule, having been crippled during an assassination attempt when he was pushed out a window, but the dictator did order a state funeral when d'Annunzio died of a stroke in 1938, at the height of Mussolini's power. The house in Pescara, which today includes a museum, is known as Casa Natale di Gabriele d'Annunzio. Its website, *www.casadannunzio.beneculturali.it*, offers an English section, but only for certain pages.

Museo Archeologico Nazionale

For a look back at history through a broader lens, consider taking a short day trip about ten miles south of Pescara to the nearby town of Chieti, which is home to the Museo Archeologico Nazionale. This archaeological museum documents the history of the Abruzzo region from ancient times and includes countless artifacts, including a superb collection of some 15,000 coins that date to the fourth century B.C.

The museum itself is a neoclassical villa that dates to 1830. It didn't become a museum until 1959, and it took its present form after a restructuring in the 1980s to accommodate recent acquisitions and donations.

Parco Nazionale d'Abruzzo

The Parco Nazionale d'Abruzzo is the oldest park in the Apennines, founded in 1923. It was small in the beginning years but continued to expand until the fascist government abolished it in 1933. The park was re-established in 1950 and continued its expansion beginning in the 1970s, after a period of massive tree destruction during the post–World War II building boom. Today, the park is nearly 200 square miles in size, about 100 times bigger than it was at its founding just after World War I.

Parco Nazionale d'Abruzzo is a wildlife lover's dream, with all the foxes, hares, and other mammals you would expect, along with Marsican brown bears and Italian wolves. The Marsican bear is an endangered species; by some estimates, the population may number as few as thirty bears. The bears can stand more than six feet tall and weigh nearly 300 pounds. Other interesting species that can be seen in the park include the golden eagle, wild boar, and polecat, which is a species of weasel.

There are also more than 2,000 plant species here, including a rare yellow-and-black orchid species of lady's slipper. In the United States, you might know this orchid by the name "moccasin flower."

The park is a year-round destination, with activities ranging from horse riding and hiking to canoeing and snow-skiing. You can find rental equipment at shops in the three provinces the park crosses: L'Aquila, Frosinone, and Isemia. L'Aquila, a college town full of energetic young adults, is arguably the place where you'll find the best selection of sporting goods.

Other Must-See Spots

Beyond these major cities in the Umbria, Marche, and Abruzzo regions are other metropolitan areas worth visiting for their preserved sites, cultural histories, and annual festivals. Five in particular are worth a closer look, and their offerings range from an early Renaissance palace to a Medieval jousting tournament.

Palazzo Ducale

Located in the walled city of Urbino in Marche—whose historic center was named a UNESCO World Heritage site in 1998—the Palazzo Ducale is a spectacular Renaissance structure designed to serve as both a residence and a fortress, with more than 250 rooms surrounding its courtyard. Today, the site is home to a Renaissance art gallery, an archaeological museum, a ceramics museum, and an underground level that showcases life as it was for kitchen, stable, and laundry staff during the palace's heyday.

 Essential

> If you tour the *studiolo* inside Palazzo Ducale, be sure to take a moment to appreciate the wood inlay work designed to surround the room's occupant in style. Many people consider the woodwork to be Italy's most famous example of the craft of inlays. Some of the shelves don't just hold books, but also display fine representations of them.

Construction on the palace began in the mid-1400s for Duke Federico da Montefeltro, who, while lord of Urbino, commissioned what was perhaps the largest library in modern-day Italy outside of the Vatican. Montefeltro's love of Greek literature is the reason the palace has a *studiolo*, or small reading room facing the countryside—an interior space that's highly unusual in Medieval palaces.

Palazzo Ducale eventually became a government building and served as such until the 1900s. Be sure to visit the Galleria Nazionale delle Marche that is housed inside today, with collections of

Renaissance art that include pieces by Titian and Raphael—the latter having been supported in his early training by Montefeltro himself.

Rossini's Birthplace, Museum, and Opera Festival

The Italian composer Gioacchino Rossini, who created thirty-nine operas during the 1800s, is best known for his works *The Barber of Seville* and *William Tell*. He inherited his musical background from his parents, and you can tour his birthplace, explore a museum created in his honor, or attend the annual Rossini Opera Festival each August in his hometown of Pesaro.

Rossini's birthplace is, as you might expect, small, but it does include a museum that contains personal items. The Museo Rossini is within Pesaro's Conservatorio di Musica, which hosts concerts and tours. The Rossini Opera Festival has been held since 1980 and takes great measure to host performances of Rossini's little-known and even unknown works in addition to those that are considered his masterpieces.

Fact

Piceno isn't the only Italian town that holds an annual festival that includes jousting. Folignio, in Umbria, has a tournament dating to 1613 in which participants must spear a ring. Arezzo, in the province of Tuscany, has a tournament that dates to the Crusades in which jousters aim for a target attached to an effigy of a king.

Of all the Rossini-themed tourism opportunities in Pesaro, only the opera festival has a website that is available in English. You can find it at *www.rossinioperafestival.it*.

Tourneo della Quintana

Translated as "joust of the Quintana," this annual event held each August in Piceno attracts about 1,500 people dressed in Medieval garb, all participating as characters in a three-day living history event that ends with a joust on the festival's final day, typically a Sunday.

You can watch games that date to the thirteenth century, such as flag-throwing contests and archery, or simply wander the streets enjoying the musical presentations and festival atmosphere. Of course, you'll also want to choose your favorite horseman before the joust begins, and then cheer as he attempts to strike a dummy that represents a Moorish soldier.

Skiing Hot Spots

Given the fact that the Appenine Mountains run like a thoroughfare through Central Italy, there are a good number of snow-skiing locations that you can enjoy during the winter months. Two of the more interesting options are Campo di Giove and Roccaraso.

Campo di Giove

Campo di Giove is a small resort ski area near Sulmona, about halfway between L'Aquila and Pescara, but to the south. It has just one cableway and three T-bars—but a vertical range of more than 4,000 feet. Thus, the hotels and guest houses here get plenty of business during the prime downhill skiing months. You must be an expert-level skier to attempt the full vertical run, but there are some beginner-level trails near the bottom of the mountainside. A good website that offers English versions of snow reports and resort availability is *www.onthesnow.com*.

Roccaraso

The skiing village of Roccaraso is to the south of Campo di Giove, offering excellent runs for intermediate-level skiers in addition to some trails for experts and beginners alike. The longest run is a bit over three miles, and the tallest vertical drop is 2,800 feet. Roccaraso is a far more developed resort area than Campo di Giove, with about two dozen ski lifts that can carry more than 30,000 skiers and snowboarders each hour. As with Campi di Giove, try the English version of *www.onthesnow.com* for up-to-date snow reports and other information.

ⓔ✳ Essential

If you want to honor the beginnings of the lesbian, gay, bisexual, and transgender movements, then you can visit the local cemetery in L'Aquilia where the movements' father, Karl Heinrich Ulrichs, is buried. He wrote a great deal during the late 1800s about what would come to be known as gay rights, including authoring the first gay vampire story, "Manor."

L'Aquila

The 70,000-strong city of L'Aquila is inland in the Abruzzo region, almost due west of the coastal city Pescara and about a ninety-minute drive east of Rome. It is home to the impressive Forte Spagnolo, a Renaissance-era castle whose construction cost local residents so much in taxes that construction eventually had to be halted. Although the castle was built for battle, it was never used in one. Not a single one of the expensive cannons was ever fired—a good thing, since the canons were pointed at the local citizenry, to keep it from rebelling, instead of at potential invaders from afar.

Today, Forte Spagnolo is best known for the views it offers of L'Aquila, as well as for being the home of the Museo Nazionale d'Abruzzo. Unfortunately, however, the third floor of the three-story museum collapsed during the devastating April 2009 earthquake whose epicenter was near L'Aquila. Priceless pieces of Medieval and modern art were left in tatters and rubble. As of this writing, reconstruction efforts were focused not on historic buildings and artifacts, but instead on basic shelter for the more than 40,000 people left homeless by both the initial tremor and the dozens of serious aftershocks that followed.

If you decide to tour this region, first take a look at *www .comune.laquila.it*, the city's official website. You will have to translate the latest news from Italian (you can use a free service like the Google translator), but the resource is essential for determining where tourism is rightly taking a backseat to recovery.

Where to Stay

Central Italy is not nearly as popular for tourism as other areas such as Rome and Tuscany, so there are bargains to be had both in the cities and the countryside.

The price code for the hotel listings below is $=€100 or less; $$=€100 to €150; $$$=€150 to €200; $$$$=€200 or more per night, per room.

Jolly Hotel Ancona
$$

The Jolly Hotel Ancona is part of a popular chain and is located in the heart of the city's shopping district, near the cathedral and train station. It's a short distance from the regional airport, so it makes for a convenient overnight stop either the day you arrive or the day before you depart Central Italy. Standard rooms come with air conditioning, cable television, private telephones, hairdryers, and more.

www.jollyhotels.it.

Hotel Sporting
$

This five-story, ocean-view hotel in Ancona offers ninety-nine guest rooms, a conference room for business events, and an on-site restaurant that specializes in fresh fish dishes. Breakfast is complementary, and there is laundry service available. Rooms come with satellite television, wireless Internet access, private bathrooms, and more. The website is in Italian only at:

www.sporting-hotel.it.

Sangallo Palace Hotel
$$–$$$

Located in the heart of Perugia (and offering special deals for the annual Eurochocolate Festival), the Sangallo Palace Hotel is within walking distance of virtually all the city-center tourist attractions. A swimming pool and gymnasium are on site, and all guest rooms have air conditioning, satellite television, high-speed Internet, direct telephone lines, and hair dryers. Some rooms have hot tubs for an extra charge, and wheelchair-accessible rooms are available.

www.sangallo.it.

Hotel Iris
$–$$$

Also in the city center of Perugia is the Hotel Iris, a building that dates to the seventeenth century and is famous for its fresco-decorated ceilings. Rooms include private showers and televisions, and there is a public terrace that surrounds the hotel as a relaxation area during the warmer months. Rooms come in single-, double-, and triple-bed configurations, and prices change depending on the season. Breakfast is available for an additional €5 per person.

www.hotelirispg.com.

Hotel Ambra
$–$$

This family-run hotel in Pescara was built in 1950 and completely renovated in 2000. It's within walking distance of the Adriatic coast and offers an on-site restaurant, meeting room, and laundry in addition to traditional guest services. Each of the sixty-one rooms has a private bathroom, satellite television, air conditioning, free WiFi, and private telephones. Some rooms have balconies.

www.hotelambrapalace.it.

Where to Eat

Central Italy's plethora of Adriatic Sea port towns means a constant supply of fresh fish that you can look for on the local menus.

The price code for the restaurant entrees below is $=€25 or less; $$=€26 to €50; $$$=€51 to €75; $$$$=€100 or more.

Ristorante Il Falchetto
$–$$

Located in the heart of Perugia, this restaurant has been specializing in local cuisine since it opened in 1954. The dining rooms are typical of what you'd find in a Medieval tavern, making them a good choice after a day of historic sightseeing. Try the goose breast with Barolo wine sauce, and save room for a dessert of banana flambé.

www.ilfalchetto.it.

Osteria del Gambero
$$–$$$

Also in Perugia is Osteria del Gambero, which offers regional dishes such as pheasant tortellini, umbricelli with duck meat sauce, and rabbit loin with pistachios and foie gras. You can order à la carte or enjoy a tasting menu with wine pairings selected by the chef. The wine list is fairly extensive and includes a good number of regional as well as international bottlings.

www.osteriadelgambero.it.

Taverna 58
$$–$$$

Taverna 58 is in Pescara, offering traditional dishes such as stuffed veal roll, braised mutton, and brook trout. House specialties include poached wild boar, the recipe for which is available in English on the restaurant's website. The restaurant has been in business for a quarter-century, receiving good reviews not only for its food, but also for its wine list.

www.taverna58.it.

CHAPTER 10

The Southeast Coast

Southeastern Italy—the "heel and instep of the boot," as it were—includes the regions of Basilicata and Apulia (also known as Puglia). This is where the Adriatic meets the Ionian Sea, where the base of the Apennine Mountain range collides with low-lying farmland and beaches. The steep mountains of Basilicata have prevented the Southeast Coast from developing its tourism industry the way Naples and the Amalfi Coast have to the west, and a good bit of the historic sites in this region have been destroyed by earthquakes and World War II fighting. But Italy's Southeast Coast strives to offer year-round activities for the increasing number of tourists who choose to visit.

Lay of the Land

Both the Basilicata and Apulia regions have histories that date back centuries, but because of the challenging, mountainous, and forested terrain in Basilicata, its past is filled far more with stories of wild wolves and boars than major cities and warring factions. Apulia, on the other hand, tends to be a region rich in archaeological discoveries, despite the fact that its coastal position never helped it rise in strategic prominence alongside cities such as Genoa and Venice. Ancient Greek and Roman civilizations both called Apulia home in their days, and in more recent times, before the unification of Italy, the French and Turks each had a turn at ruling here. Throughout it all, the terrain has made for a mostly agrarian economy, though today the traditional olive and grape farms are giving way to tourism.

Each of the major cities in these regions is reachable today via highway or train from other Italian hubs such as Rome, or you can fly here directly on a national flight or via one of a handful of internationally operating airline routes.

 Fact

Apulia is frequently referred to as "the Florida of Italy" because of the way tourism continues to encroach on the traditional, agrarian way of life. There's no Epcot Center or Disney World here yet, but the spas, golf resorts, and seaside hotels certainly could be a harbinger of more development to come.

Arriving by Air

Apulia has four airports, located in Bari, Taranto, Foggia, and Brindisi. Bari is the most international of the hubs and, given its proximity to the Basilicata region, serves it in addition to Apulia itself. Flights to the Bari airport originate in New York, Madrid, London, Athens, Paris, Amsterdam, and Dusseldorf (as well as in Italian cities such as Rome, Milan, Genoa, and Venice). The other three airports in Apulia, while they have some international flight schedules, are more regional in nature. Some offer only short itineraries entirely within Italy's borders.

Interestingly, the airport in Bari started out as a military facility. It opened to civilian use relatively recently, in the 1960s, and upgrades have continued in passenger areas. Most recently, a new terminal opened in 2005. Planning began in 2007 for additional extension of passenger areas after the airport saw a 20 percent increase in traffic over 2006—again, a sign of the region's increasingly dominant tourism sector. All four of the Apulia airports share a single website (with English translation available) where you can check airlines, flight schedules, and more. It's at *www .aeroportidipuglia.it*.

Arriving by Train

Trenitalia (*www.trenitalia.com*) offers service into the Apulia region from major cities including Rome, Naples, and Venice. Most of the lines feed or connect into the terminal at Bari. The trip from Rome to Bari takes four and a half to six and a half hours, depending on whether your line makes all local stops. From Naples, the shortest possible time to Bari via train is just under four hours.

❶ Alert

In the southern part of Italy, the major train lines run north to south, hugging the east and west coastlines until they get to Rome or Bologna and then splinter in all directions across the northern part of the country. Thus, the majority of trains that can get you to Bari by going west to east (say, from Rome or Naples) are smaller and slower, and transfers en route are likely.

Once you are in the Apulia region, you can take local train and bus lines if you want to travel without a rental car. Some of the lines cross over into the Basilicata region. Look for schedules and fares at *www.fal.srl.it*, *www.ferrovienordbarese.it*, *www.fseonline.it*, and *ferroviedelgargano.com*.

Bari

Bari, the capital of the Apulia region, is home to about 330,000 people. An additional 170,000 people live in the surrounding metropolitan region. It's not a major destination in terms of tourism, but it is a major place of arrival, which means you are likely to find yourself here, seeking things to do, for at least an afternoon before you move on to the rest of the Southeast Coast.

The city is divided into districts. The most popular among tourists are the old town to the north and the modern center to the south. The old town, in addition to housing most of the historic sites, is also a hub of go-go nightlife activity. The modern center offers shopping.

 Fact

Bari was the only European city to suffer from chemical warfare during World War II. German bombers attacked U.S. ships in Bari's harbor in 1943. The ships were carrying mustard gas, but its presence was classified, so doctors didn't know how to treat victims for exposure. The estimated number of resulting deaths ranges from 100 to 2,000.

Basilica di San Nicola

Orthodox Christians from all over Eastern Europe come to Bari on pilgrimages to the Basilica of St. Nicholas. Construction began on the basilica in 1087 after Nicholas asked to be buried in Bari, and work was completed in 1197. It's an interesting sight both in religious and architectural terms. The basilica looks squarish, almost like a castle. In fact, it was used as a model for other churches later built in what came to be known as the Puglian-Romanesque style.

There is a museum on site, and hours vary depending on the season. You can try the basilica's website (*www.basilicasannicola .it*) for up-to-date information after you plan your travel dates, but as of this writing, the site's English section was "coming soon."

Castello Svevo

Castello Svevo is a fortress on the edge of Bari's old town. It is believed to date back to the 1100s and has been destroyed and rebuilt several times over throughout history. Today, it's used as a display area for rotating exhibitions—and it's worth a look if only for your chance to cross an actual moat as you make your way inside. Admission is just a few euro.

Taranto

The coastal city of Taranto is home to about 200,000 people and is Italy's main naval base. Its origins date to the Greeks of the eighth century B.C., and legend has it that the city was founded by Taras, a son of Poseidon. The history to be unearthed here is likely exquisite—but is largely inaccessible because the modern city was built atop the old. Not as much attention has been paid here as elsewhere in Italy to preservation of historic sites, but there are a couple of locations worth visiting.

If you're a collector of gold jewelry, the National Archaeological Museum in Taranto is the one site that is not to be missed. It is home to the Ori di Taranto, "the gold of Taranto," a collection that dates back to the time of Magna Grecia, when the Greeks ruled what is now southern Italy all the way to Sicily.

Because of seemingly endless renovations, only the first floor of the museum is open to the public. It features Greek and Roman artifacts dating back to the fourth century B.C. You can take a look at some of the pieces at the museum's official website, *www.museotaranto.it*, though it does not offer an English translation.

Essential

After a trip to the National Archaeological Museum in Taranto, where you'll gain an appreciation for the era of Greek dominance in this part of Italy, keep your ears open for the sounds of people speaking Griko. It's a modern Greek dialect still spoken by about 30,000 people in the region, and its origins have been traced back to the days of Magna Grecia.

Foggia

The city of Foggia, home to about 150,000 people, was a key strategic stronghold during World War II. The city evolved during the late 1800s and early 1900s as a connection point for commerce between northern and southern Italy, and thus was bombed heavily by Allied troops before they invaded and took control in 1943. That intensive, manmade destruction—along with earthquakes that struck the city in 1456, 1534, 1627, and 1731—has all but destroyed the historic sites that otherwise might make Foggia an archaeological windfall today. For instance, only a single arch remains from the imperial palace of Frederick II, who was the Holy Roman Emperor beginning in 1220.

If you find yourself in this city on the way to others in the region, be sure to stop for a look at the city's cathedral, which offers an interesting look at architectural history. It was built in the 1100s, but then underwent extensive renovation in the 1600s and today boasts an eighteenth-century interior.

Matera

Matera is a small city of less than 60,000 people within the Basilicata region, just over the Apulia border. There has been civilization here since at least the third century B.C., and the sites that draw most tourists to visit here are at least that old. They're called the Sassi di Matera—and are perhaps the first human settlements ever in the land that is modern-day Italy.

Sassi di Matera

Sassi di Matera means "stones of Matera" and refers to houses dug right into rock, looking sort of like above-ground caves lined up side by side. When the sassi became a UNESCO World Heritage Site in 1993, they were described as "the most outstanding, intact example of a troglodyte settlement in the Mediterranean." (Troglodyte means primitive or cave-dwelling.)

People without means to go elsewhere lived in the sassi right up until the 1950s, when the government forced them out and decreed the roughly 9,000-year-old residences uninhabitable. Today, Hollywood scouts are often out and about, as the sassi resemble sites in and around Jerusalem. They were used as a backdrop for Mel Gibson's 2004 *Passion of the Christ.* The more tourism-minded of the current local officials are promoting the pubs and hotels nearby.

You can find the sassi from several parts of the city center where signs are posted. Look for the names Barisano and Caveoso, which are essentially sassi neighborhoods. Caveoso is a little bit prettier and offers a couple of rock churches in addition to the sassi dwellings themselves. Don't fall prey to the hucksters who descend upon out-of-towners to offer sassi tours; instead, grab a guide map at the tourism office in the heart of town.

Fact

The fictional television character Archie Bunker was said to have been stationed at Foggia during World War II. His service time was apparently unremarkable, though. He tells his doctor during one of the *All in the Family* episodes that he never saw combat and served only on the ground despite being a member of the U.S. Army Air Corps.

Tramontano Castle

Unfortunately, what's left of the early-sixteenth-century Tramontano Castle is viewable only from its exterior. The castle was begun by His Excellency Giovanni Carlo Tramontano, Baron of Sorrento, Count of Matera—a man whose tyranny, like his name, apparently knew no bounds. The idea of the castle was to protect the town while, of course, allowing Tramontano to live in the luxury he felt he deserved. On a December night in 1514, after construction had begun, he demanded that the people pay a hefty fine so that he would be free of debts. He didn't live another twenty-four hours; he was ambushed and beaten to death while leaving church the very next day. His castle was never completed, hence the fact that it offers only an exterior photo opportunity today.

Question

How did cave-dwelling people dig their homes out of the rock in Matera?
Tuff rock, which is actually consolidated volcanic ash, is much softer and easier to penetrate than, say, granite. In the fourth century B.C., for instance, tuff rock was used to build the entire Servian Wall to defend Rome.

Other Must-See Spots

What's interesting about the Basilicata and Apulia regions is that many of the most interesting places to visit are beyond the borders of the major cities. From the coastline to the mountains, you can poke around in a rental car and make your own unforgettable memories.

Lecce Baroque

The 100,000-strong city of Lecce is about as far down the heel of Italy's boot as you can get. Lecce is nicknamed "the Florence of the South" because it is so replete with baroque buildings. The stonework is truly over-the-top, thanks to "Lecce stone" (a form of limestone found here), which is very malleable. In fact, when architecture students discuss the baroque style, they call the ostentatious form found here "Lecce baroque."

✅ Fact

The term "baroque," in addition to describing a seventeenth- and eighteenth-century style of art and architecture, is used nowadays as a synonym for "Byzantine"—meaning anything thought to be excessively complex to the point that its meaning is lost. The word also can be used to describe an item decorated so ornately that it becomes tacky.

Perhaps the most significant example of ornate decoration in Lecce is Chiesa di Santa Croce, or Church of the Holy Cross. Its earliest portions date to the mid-1350s, though work on it was incomplete until 1695. The façade is a veritable mélange of carvings including animals, vegetables, and figurines. You could spend all day looking at the façade and still feel as though you'd gotten your money's worth at this site (which, being a church, is actually free to enter).

Vieste Beaches

Vieste is a town in the Apulia region that continually wins awards for the purity of its local waters. Stone grottos and arches dot the landscape within stretches of golden sand beaches, meaning that even though your beach chair might be propped up fairly close to another tourist's, you'll at least enjoy a terrific view in the distance. Some of the beachfront resorts are actually located within national parkland here, so you get surrounding trees in addition to waterfront access.

The town is home to fewer than 15,000 permanent residents, although it provides some of the best tourist access of all the seaside resorts in this part of Italy. Should your vacation here occur during the winter months, though, don't expect to find much open along the waterfront. Like beach towns all over the world, the locals lock up and go into warm cocoons until spring.

Grottaglie Ceramics

This tiny town outside of Taranto is known as the "city of ceramics." The first documentation of ceramics being produced here is in the post–Medieval period. Since then, styles have changed from era to era, leaving Grottaglie ceramics without a trademark look or design. But the town is still known for its ceramics today—and has an entire quarter where artisans will let you into their workshops to watch while they create new pieces. If you're lucky, you might get an eyeball on a "master potter" from Grottaglie's Art College.

Essential

When judging one piece of Grottaglie pottery against the next, remember that imperfections can add to a handmade item's quality, not detract from it. Any pottery created on a wheel is, by definition, far from being mass produced, and sometimes the most intriguing touches are the indents, swivels, and swirls created by the potter's fingers.

Part of what makes Grottaglie's ceramics unique is that they are, for the most part, made from locally extracted clay, but the true way to tell whether a local potter is schooled in the old ways is by watching him work the clay on his wheel. Local potters here still use the kind of wheel invented by the Greeks, though they've traded the foot pedal for an electric motor that makes the wheel spin. You can learn more about the history of Grottaglie ceramics, or see selections from the collections of local artisans, in English at *www.ceramistidigrottaglie.it.*

Sanctuary of Monte Sant'Angelo

This is the oldest Western European shrine to the archangel Michael, who is one of the primary angels in both the Christian and Islamic faiths. Michael is said to have left his own footprint here, and it is said that his statue covers the site of that impression. Countless believers have left traces of their own footprints here through graffiti, which you can see as you walk up toward the sanctuary itself.

There is no entry fee, but keep an eye on your wallet here. Plenty of shysters will try to get you to give them money for everything from fake tours to rental car parking.

Isole Tremiti

Arguably the epitome of rocky seascape beauty in this part of Italy, the three Tremiti Islands offer a single sandy beach and so many photo opportunities that you might as well toss your lens cap into the sea. San Domino has the most to offer tourists (including that aforementioned beach), Capraia is uninhabited, and San Nicola is home to a monastery from whence, it is said, the dead monk who resides there tousles up a vicious storm anytime anyone tries to move his corpse.

The main draw here, though, is the crystal-blue waters surrounded by those magnificent rock formations. You can access them by taking a ferry ride from Peschici between April and September. Tickets are usually cheap, no more than a few euro even in the busiest summer months.

Where to Stay

There are some good values for hotels in this part of Italy, where tourism has not yet come to dominate the local economies. You can also find top-dollar luxury, if that's what you want, both in the cities and along the shoreline.

The price code for the hotel listings below is $=€100 or less; $$=€100 to €150; $$$=€150 to €200; $$$$=€200 or more per night, per room.

Hotel Pugnochiuso Resort
$$–$$$$

Located on Gargano Promontory on the Apulia coast, this waterfront property in the town of Vieste includes four hotel options ranging from the four-star Hotel Faro to the Residence del Belvedere. The resort, completed in 2004 and the largest in the area, has two swimming pools and two beaches, and some of the rooms are "apartment villettes" with small kitchens and washing machines. Handicapped-accessible rooms are also available, and weekly rates are sometimes an option.

www.pugnochiuso.com

Hotel Parco Carabella
$

Also located in Vieste within short walking distance of the beaches is the Hotel Parco Carabella, a family-run, three-star hotel that has twenty-four rooms. Each room has a private terrace and private bathroom, plus air conditioning, television, and private telephones. There is a swimming pool on site, and guests enjoy discounts at a handful of local restaurants.

www.vieste.net/parcocarabella

Sassi Hotel
$-$$

This hotel is in Matera, carved right out of the rock like the sassi domiciles that draw tourists from around the world. Believe it or not, the hotel includes a bar, conference room, and breakfast area, and each room has air conditioning, a private bathroom, a private telephone, a television, and a small refrigerator. Because of the way the rooms are created, each one is different. Ask when making your reservation about which one will best suit your needs.

www.hotelsassi.it

Hotel Costa
$

This Bari hotel offers single- and double-bed rooms, some with private bathrooms and others without (you pay €10–20 extra per night for a private bathroom). The location is close to the train station, within walking distance of sights including Castello Svevo and Basilica di San Nicolo. Rooms are simple, with no bells and whistles, though there is a small bar on site.

www.hotelcostabari.com

Hotel President
$$-$$$

Located in Lecce, this modern hotel is in the business district and close to the old town. There are 150 rooms marketed toward businesspeople and families alike, with a restaurant on site as well as a banquet hall that can serve buffets for as many as 450 people. Free WiFi is available in the common areas, and laundry and babysitting services are offered. There are also safety-deposit boxes in the lobby.

www.vestas-hotels-lecce.com

Hotel Mercure Cicolella
$$–$$$

This hotel is in Foggia, with easy access to the train station and airport—and a fifteen-minute helicopter ride away from the Tremiti Islands. There are 200 rooms, each with air conditioning, television, and electrically controlled blinds. The hotel also caters to business travelers; fax and translation services are available.
www.hotelcicolella.it

Where to Eat

Given Apulia's long coastline, it's no surprise that fresh seafood plays a large role in the local cuisine. Also look for locally harvested olive oils and locally bottled wines.

The price code for the restaurant entrees below is $=€25 or less; $$=€26 to €50; $$$=€51 to €75; $$$$=€100 or more.

Pizzosteria Delirio
$–$$

This family-friendly pizza restaurant in Foggia offers some mighty tasty pies made with the freshest of local ingredients. You can find all the traditional toppings here, in addition to modern menu additions such as gluten-free crust. Charming tablecloths and wooden chairs create an ambience that will make you feel like a local in this part of Italy.
www.pizzeriadelirio.it

Ristorante Rivelli
$–$$

Located in Matera, this restaurant features traditional cuisine including fresh vegetables, homemade pastas, and fantastic antipasti. The vaulted, stone-carved ceilings are done in true Matera sassi fashion, with warm lighting that will let you linger for hours over your favorite bottle of local wine.

www.ristoranterivelli.com

Don Matteo Ristorante
$–$$

Also carved out of the stone in Matera is Don Matteo Ristorante, where the elegance of presentation on the plate is a surprisingly nice touch within the literally down-to-earth décor. The menu tends to be simple but made with the freshest ingredients, so even though there may be fewer selections here than at more touristy locations, the taste will be terrific.

www.donmateoristorante.com

Il Giardino Ristorante
$–$$

Located in Lecce, this restaurant specializes in fresh seafood and fish prepared in a style that it calls "creative cuisine." The wine list is filled with local favorites, and the décor is billed as simple, modern, and comfortable. Small groups are welcome. The restaurant is conveniently located in the center of town, near Piazza Mazzini.

www.ilgiardino-ristorante.it

Zio Giglio
$–$$

Also in Lecce is Pizzeria Zio Giglio, which proudly declares that its chefs are trained in "the art of pizza." More than two dozen types of pizza are on the menu, some traditional and others more exotic. You'll also find calzones, focaccia, Panini, and other eat-on-the-go favorites at this tourist-friendly restaurant.

www.pizzeriaziogiglio.it

Naples

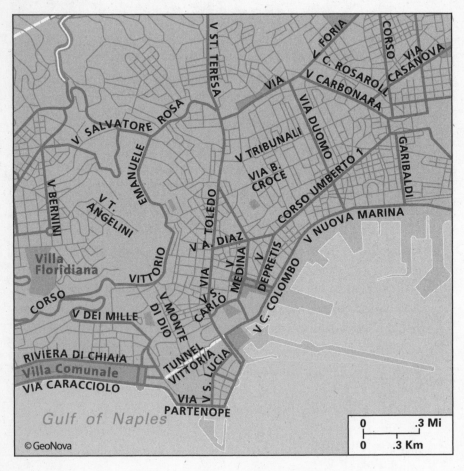

CHAPTER 11

Campania

The Romans used to call this part of southwestern Italy *Campania felix*, which means "fertile countryside." And it has been fertile indeed, producing centuries' worth of history, culture, and gastronomic delights. Naples, the birthplace of pizza, boasts a historic center that is a UNESCO World Heritage site. The remains of Pompeii continue to enlighten the modern world about day-to-day life during the Roman Empire. The Amalfi Coast is chock-a-block with seaside resorts, as is the island of Capri, which has been a beloved vacation destination since around 500 B.C.

Lay of the Land

Campania is on the southwestern coast of Italy, where the front of the ankle would be within "the boot." Nearly 6 million people live here, making Campania the most densely populated region in the country. That's nothing new; people have been flocking to the fertile country lands and sweeping seaside hills since the end of the fourth century B.C., when the area gave birth to much of what is associated today with ancient Greco-Roman culture.

Naples is by far the region's biggest city, with about 1 million residents, and it is the region's transportation gateway. You can arrive by train or airplane, and it is from Naples where you can most easily step aboard hydrofoils and ferries that will take you to the nearby islands—including Capri—as well as various ports along the Amalfi Coast.

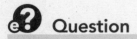

Question

Is pizza the most famous food to originate in Campania?
Possibly, but you also have to give Neapolitan residents credit for the highly popular spaghetti with tomato sauce. They were among the first people in all of Europe to use tomatoes not just as decorative plants, but also as ingredients in sauces and garnishes.

Travel by Air

Naples International Airport is less than five miles from the heart of the city center. About 140 flights come in and out of the airport daily, with more than 4 million people being served each year. There are no direct flights here from the United States, but you can pick up connecting flights in England, France, Spain, Greece, Germany, Belgium, the Netherlands, Hungary, Switzerland, and, of course, Rome. Better-known airlines with routes into Naples International Airport include Alitalia, Air France, British Airways, Lufthansa, Virgin Express, and EasyJet. The airport's website, *www.gesac.it*, offers a wealth of helpful information about traveling in the region.

Travel by Train

Napoli Centrale, sometimes noted on maps as Stazione Centrale, is the hub. As many as thirty trains arrive from and depart to Rome daily. You can also pick up trains from here to other locations, including many within the Campania region, such as Pompeii.

⊛ Essential

If you plan to travel by train within Campania or throughout greater Italy, then consider purchasing a Eurail Italy Pass from Rail Europe (*www.raileurope.com*). Passes at different price points will allow you unlimited travel on the national rail network for as many as ten days within two months' time, whether you use those days consecutively or not.

There is a tourism office in the train station, in the main hall on the ground floor. You can go there from 7 A.M. until 9 P.M. to get local maps, tourism suggestions, and help with additional transit plans.

Travel by Boat

Ferries depart from two ports in Naples: Molo Beverello and Mergellina. There is train service into Mergellina, but to reach Molo Beverello, you'll have to transfer from the Naples airport or train Stazione Centrale via bus or taxi. Expect a fifteen- to thirty-minute ride depending on traffic.

Four companies provide the bulk of fast- and slow-ferry service from Naples, with their boats typically operating in both ports, depending on the final destination. Each company's website offers route maps, timetables, and prices, along with descriptions of services, including car transport should you have a rental vehicle:

- Alilauro: *www.alilauro.it*
- Caremar: *www.caremar.it*
- SNAV: *www.snav.it*
- MedMar: *www.viamare.com*

Naples

The city of Naples is nearly 3,000 years old. It was founded by the ancient Greeks and served as the capital of the Kingdom of Naples from the late 1200s until the early 1800s. You can find architecture here from the Medieval, Renaissance, and Baroque periods, as well as more than 400 churches and multiple noteworthy castles. Museums here have collections that include artifacts from Pompeii and the Roman Empire, as well as crystals and rocks collected from in and around Mount Vesuvius.

Tourism is one of the city's primary industries, and as with any area that attracts a lot of tourists, Naples has its share of petty criminals. Most travel agents warn against walking alone at night in the Stazione Centrale area, and it's good common-sense advice to avoid dark side streets in the evenings, too.

 Fact

Foods such as pizza and tomato sauce are not the only things the city of Naples has contributed to worldwide culture over the years. Naples is also the birthplace of several string instruments including the mandolin (a type of lute) and the six-string romantic guitar (a precursor to the modern classical guitar).

Naples Cathedral

In a city dominated by hundreds of churches, the Naples Cathedral ranks first in order of importance. Dedicated to San Gennaro, the saint who is the patron of Naples itself, Naples Cathedral was built in the 1300s. It sits on land that previously housed two other basilicas and that, when excavated today, reveals Greek and Roman artifacts.

The original façade was almost entirely destroyed in a 1349 earthquake, and the façade that stands about 165 feet tall today was constructed in the late 1800s. Inside, the area that draws most visitors is the Chapel of the Treasure of St. Gennaro, whose walls and dome are decorated with frescoes. You can get inside to see it seven days a week, though Monday through Saturday the cathedral closes between 12:30 P.M. and 4:30 P.M. (on Sunday, the cathedral is closed from 1:30 P.M. until 5 P.M.). Much historical information is available in English at the official cathedral website, *www .duomodinapoli.it.*

Museo Archeologico Nazionale

The Naples National Archaeological Museum is considered the most important archaeological museum in all of Europe, boasting a large collection of Greek and Roman antiquities, including some found during excavations of Pompeii and Herculaneum. You can also see the Farnese Collection here. It features marble sculptures and gemstones found in Rome, including the Farnese Bull, which is believed to be the largest existing sculpture from ancient times. Bronzes and mosaics are also on display, along with the third-largest collection of Egyptian artifacts in Italy. There is also a 200,000-piece collection of coins and metals, some from ancient Greece and imperial Roman times.

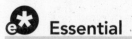 **Essential**

If you plan to visit the Naples Cathedral on the first Saturday in May, on September 19, or on December 16, be sure to ask what happens when the blood of San Gennaro is brought out to liquefy. Legend states that if the blood fails to liquefy, then the city of Naples will fall victim to some kind of tragedy.

The museum is open daily from 9 A.M. until 8 P.M., with last admissions at 7 P.M. You can pay a €6.50 entrance fee, or gain entry with a €13 ArteCard, which also gets you admission to other Naples museums and forms of public transportation (a good bargain depending on your travel plans). Feel free to bring your camera, as long as you can disable the flash. Non-flash photography is permitted throughout the museum. Learn more at *www.marketplace.it/museo.nazionale*.

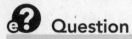 **Question**

What is the Secret Museum?
A section of the Naples National Archaeological Museum that houses sexually explicit objects unearthed at Pompeii has been dubbed the Secret Museum. The objects range from frescoes to inscriptions to phallic oil lamps. The room, because of its erotic contents, has been opened and closed "for the public good" multiple times during the past century.

Castel Nuovo

The "New Castle" is the main symbol of architecture in Naples. Its original three-year construction began in 1279 at the order of Charles I of Anjou after the Kingdom of Naples moved its capital to the city from Palermo. Later kings enlarged and embellished the castle, including ordering modifications to withstand attacks by new weapons that evolved during the passage of centuries.

The castle contains a civic museum filled with frescoes and sculptures from the 1300 and 1400s. Admission is €5, and the castle is open Monday through Saturday from 9 A.M. till 7 P.M. There is no website, but you can try to reach someone who speaks English by calling +81 795 5877.

Ancient Sites

Pompeii is the best known of the ancient sites in the Campania region. However, it isn't the only one. Pompeii's sister city, Herculaneum, and the remains of the Greco-Roman city known as Paestum also have beautifully preserved structures.

Pompeii

The Roman city of Pompeii thrived until the two-day-long eruption of the 4,200-foot-tall Mount Vesuvius in the year A.D. 79. The suffocating black blanket of earthen innards that spewed from the volcano's mouth buried the city beneath the equivalent of six stories of rubble. It was lost for some 1,700 years until it was rediscovered during excavation work in the mid-1700s.

Because no oxygen could reach the virtually entombed buildings and bodies beneath the ground, decomposition was kept relatively at bay. Many of the locations where residents undertook day-to-day activities remain well preserved, including the city's forum, baths, and houses. The remains draw more than 2 million visitors each year, and the area has been named a UNESCO World Heritage Site.

ⓔ✔ Fact

The eruption of Mount Vesuvius occurred the day after Vulcanalia, the festival of the Roman god of fire. The volcano had been dormant for 800 years. Some sixty feet of lava, dirt, and ash buried the people and the city. One of those killed was the philosopher Pliny the Elder, who reportedly perished while trying to rescue others who were stranded.

Pompeii's ruins are part of Vesuvius National Park and are easily accessible if you walk to one of the multiple entrances from the modern-day city of Pompeii, which is served by trains daily. Allow yourself at least half a day to look around; most people find the ruins so vast and interesting that they wander and explore for a good four hours.

Herculaneum

Herculaneum, a neighboring city to ancient Pompeii that also perished in the Mount Vesuvius eruption, was actually the first of the two cities to be rediscovered in the mid-1700s. Herculaneum was smaller yet wealthier than Pompeii, and some of the structures that have been unearthed are believed to be large private houses and luxurious villas. One is even said to have been used as a seaside retreat by Julius Caesar's father-in-law.

 Fact

It was not a volcanic eruption but the development of marshy conditions that led citizens to abandon the ancient city of Paestum. It is believed that the direction of water flow changed, leading to a swamp-like environment. The area was infested with malaria-carrying mosquitoes, which made it uninhabitable.

The ruins at Herculaneum are just as well preserved as those of Pompeii, and the crowds tend to be smaller at Herculaneum. You can get there by taking a train to the Ercolano Scavi station, then walking or taking a taxi about a mile downhill to the ruin entrance.

Paestum

The Greco-Roman city of Paestum was originally known as Poseidonia, a reference to Poseidon, the Greek god of the sea. It is believed to have been founded during the seventh century B.C., and archaeological evidence shows that as the city developed throughout the centuries, it included a system of roads, temples, and coins used for trade. Civilization in the city was abandoned sometime during the Middle Ages, and its ruins remained unknown until the mid-1700s, when other excavations in the region began to unearth the cities of Pompeii and Herculaneum.

You can still see the remains of three temples and parts of defensive walls that include round towers. There are also painted tombs, including the Tomb of the Diver, which depicts a human being jumping off what in modern days would be called a form of diving board. This tomb is believed to be the only example of Greek painting with a human figure to have survived in its entirety from its time period.

An archaeological museum is located right next door to the ruins, and it's in that museum that you can view the Tomb of the Diver. The modern town of Paestum, a seaside resort offering many places to stay and dine, is to the north of the archaeological ruins.

Mount Vesuvius

The previous section makes the power of Mount Vesuvius all too frighteningly clear—and the eruption that buried Pompeii and Herculaneum was just the beginning. The volcano has since erupted more than forty recorded times, most recently in 1944, when it destroyed several villages and dozens of U.S. bomber planes that were staged nearby as part of World War II battle preparations.

Question

How long would it take to evacuate the people who live near Mount Vesuvius?
The emergency plan calls for a seven-day evacuation of about 600,000 people in the *zona rossa*—the red zone. One reason the upper part of the volcano was named a national park was to prevent further structures from being built, which kept the number of people in the red zone from growing.

Mount Vesuvius is most definitely still classified as an active volcano. Scientists constantly monitor a substantial array of instruments intended to provide advance warning if magma collects and begins to rise underground. It is currently estimated that those instruments would provide a warning time of two weeks before the next eruption—a fact that no doubt helps to ease the minds of the estimated 3 million people who now live within the potential blast radius.

In 1995, the area around Mount Vesuvius was named a national park, and as such it is open to the public with walking trails. You can take a bus from the Ercolano train station and then walk about a half-hour to the rim of the crater. While at the park, you also can visit the Museo dell'Osservatorio Vesuviano, whose website, *www .ov.ingv.it*, offers not just information about the observatory and museum offerings, but also the latest news about earthquakes and eruptions.

Amalfi Coast

If you're interested in spectacularly rugged coastal views, charming towns climbing along seaside cliffs, boats and yachts plying crystal-blue waters, and some of the highest prices ever to be seen at summertime resorts, then the Amalfi Coast should be your first destination within Campania.

Amalfi is just one of the picturesque towns along this thirty-mile stretch, which also includes the popular vacation spots of Positano and Ravello. There is a small airport here, called Aeroporto di Salerno, which receives a limited number of flights from the northern Italy cities of Turin, Milan, and Verona, as well as from international cities.

The prettiest way to arrive at the Amalfi coast is by automobile, though the breathtaking, cliff-top turns can be as scary to navigate—and as jam-packed with summer traffic—as any along California's famous Highway 1. Easier arrival routes can be found by way of ferries from Naples or SITA buses that connect to the Sorrento and Salerno train stations. The SITA website (*www.sita-bus.it*) does offer schedules, but the information is available only in Italian.

ⓔ✱ Essential

If you plan to savor a few sips of the favorite local drink, Limoncello, be sure to do so after dinner—the time when the lemon liqueur is typically served. Expect a small, chilled ceramic glass instead of a more modern cup, and be sure to sip instead of gulp even though the size of the ceramic glass will sometimes be no bigger than that of an American shot glass.

Amalfi

Amalfi, now a town of about 5,500 permanent residents, has a history that dates back to the sixth century. It was once a prominent city with some 70,000 dwellers. Long before tourism became a primary economic underpinning, Amalfi served as a strategic port for traders wanting to bargain for grain from inland, salt from nearby islands, and silks from the Byzantine empire. Today, the town is part of the UNESCO World Heritage Site that encompasses the entire Amalfi Coast, and it draws visitors who want to linger in the resorts, taste the locally made Limoncello liqueur, and purchase some of the elegant paper for which the region is known. There is a paper museum in town—Il Museo della Carta—where you can not only learn the centuries-old techniques of making fine paper, but where you can buy everything from writing tablets to wedding invitations. (Some information is available in English at *www.museodellacarta.it*.)

On the architectural front, an interesting stop is the Sant'Andrea cathedral, with an imposing, ornate façade that blends Byzantine style with other movements. Bring your best aerobic mindset here:

The cathedral sits atop a steep staircase that has left many an out-of-shape tourist's knees wobbling.

Positano

The seaside town of Positano is, like the cathedral in Amalfi, accessible only to those willing to navigate steep staircases. They're seemingly everywhere in this picture-perfect enclave, which brims with pricey shops and boutique restaurants—most of which make getting around worth the effort.

While tourism is the main industry in Positano today, the town's popularity is a relatively recent development, having been spurred by a glowing article about the place that John Steinbeck wrote for *Harper's Bazaar* in 1953. Positano's beauty was again put on the world stage in the 2003 film *Under the Tuscan Sun*.

The best way to enjoy Positano on a budget is by simply walking around with your photographer's eye at the ready. Look for lunch on-the-go from a vendor, and savor your keepsake photographs instead of splurging on meals that can easily cost more than your camera.

Ravello

The thing to do in Ravello, after you're done gawking at the spectacular seaside views offered all over the small town, is visit Villa Rufolo. Constructed in the 1200s and once having served as a watchtower, the villa was built on such a grand scale that it has served as a home to several popes over the centuries. The gardens are world renowned and are said to have been the natural landscape that inspired German composer Richard Wagner to write the third act of his final opera, *Parsifal*, on site.

❗ Alert

The hotels in Positano tend to be among the priciest along the entire Amalfi Coast, and some regularly make the lists of the best places to stay in the entire world. A standard room at Il San Pietro di Positano, for instance, will set you back at least €550 a night. If you want a top-notch room, the nightly rate is around €1,300.

Villa Rufolo is also the setting for Ravello Festival, which typically begins in late June and runs straight through until the end of October, featuring classical music, ballets, films, and more. The town may be small, but the talent is not; recent participants have included legendary choreographer Bill T. Jones and the Prague Philharmonic Orchestra. You can order tickets online and learn more about the festival at *www.ravellofestival.com*.

Capri

Capri is an island in the Gulf of Naples, easily accessible by ferry from multiple Campania locations including the city of Naples. As many as 5,000 people a day make day trips to Capri from the mainland during the popular summer months. That's a lot of bodies on an island that's less than four miles long and less than two miles wide, and it's something to keep in mind if your schedule allows you the option of visiting during the shoulder seasons in spring or autumn.

All the ferries arrive at Marina Grande, where you can connect to buses and cable cars that will take you to Capri town. But there is also worthwhile sightseeing in the sea itself, at the legendary Blue Grotto.

The Blue Grotto

Known locally as *Grotta Azzura*, the Blue Grotto once was used by the emperor Tiberius as a private swimming pool. Today, the sea cave is a must-see destination for swimmers from all over the world who want to enjoy the way sunbeams pass through an underwater space and fill the cave with rich, blue reflections.

You can only swim inside before 9 A.M. and after 5 P.M.; during the prime hours of the day, tour boats dominate. They, like the ferries from the mainland, are based at Marina Grande. Just follow the crowds and the signs.

Villa Jovis

If you would prefer to do your exploring on terra firma, then consider a long walk or short taxi ride to Villa Jovis, which is east of Capri town. The emperor Tiberius is said to have built this Roman palace sometime between A.D. 27 and 37, when it spanned nearly two acres.

 Fact

Local rowboats are often the transportation of choice for visiting the Blue Grotto at Capri. Don't be surprised to pay good money for a two-seat variety that looks like it would be more at home in a backyard swimming pool. Also, it is common for the tour guides to ask you to lie down in the boat's bottom so that you don't whack your head as the boat moves into the cave.

It is believed that Tiberius chose the location because it was difficult to reach, and thus a safe haven from potential assassins. Bring plenty of bottled water to stay hydrated if you choose to walk from town and back.

Where to Stay

The Campania region is a tourist magnet, one that typically lures many of the world's richest and most famous travelers. There are bargains to be had, but don't expect to find many during the jam-packed summer months. If you prepare mentally to splurge a bit on the high life in Italy, then you will likely fare better when looking at hotel and restaurant rates.

The price code for the hotel listings below is $=€100 or less; $$=€100 to €150; $$$=€150 to €200; $$$$=€200 or more per night, per room.

Hotel Miramare
$$$-$$$$

Located in the Naples seafront area known as Santa Lucia, the Hotel Miramare offers standard, superior, and luxury rooms, each with private bathrooms and some with tubs in addition to showers. All of the rooms have balconies, and the views include not just the coastline, but also Mount Vesuvius. Interestingly, the building once housed the U.S. Consulate.

www.hotelmiramare.com.

Hotel Il Convento
$-$$$

This restored seventeenth-century palace in Naples offers a breakfast room, a bar, and handicapped access in one room. Some of the rooms are designed as adjoining "cells" that can accommodate multiple family members. All rooms have their own bathrooms, some with bathtubs and others with shower only. Air conditioning is in each room, as well.

www.hotelilconvento.it.

Caravaggio Hotel
$$–$$$$

The Caravaggio Hotel is the self-proclaimed "only four-star hotel in the historic center of Naples." It is within a restored sixteenth-century palace and offers rooms with air conditioning, whirlpool bathtubs, satellite television, private telephones, soundproofing, and more. There is a meeting room for small business gatherings, if you are combining work with pleasure.

www.caravaggiohotel.it.

Hotel Amalfi
$

The rates at the Hotel Amalfi, in the town of Amalfi, look low, but that's because they are per person and not per room. Double that dollar sign if you are traveling as a couple. The hotel is right off the main piazza and within easy walking distance of the beach. It's also a good location if you plan to catch a nearby boat from the local pier out to Capri for the day.

www.hamalfi.it.

Grand Hotel Quisisana,
$$$$

This top-dollar luxury hotel on the island of Capri has been welcoming the wealthiest of vacationers since 1845. Regular rooms start around €350, while some suites are more than €1,000 per night. A spa and three restaurants are on site, including one that offers fresh sushi along with traditional Italian specialties during the high-season summer months.

www.quisisana.com.

Where to Eat

Pizza. Mozzarella cheese. Spaghetti with tomato sauce. These foods aren't just modern favorites in Campania; they were *born* here. Failing to order a little of each during a visit to the region should be illegal.

The price code for the restaurant entrees below is $=€25 or less; $$=€26 to €50; $$$=€51 to €75; $$$$=€100 or more.

Umberto
$

This enticingly priced restaurant is in the Chiaia section of Naples, west of Stazione Centrale and Centro Storico on the Gulf of Naples. You'll find a classic menu, a pizza menu, and even a gluten-free menu here. Favored recommendations from the chef include marinated fish with apple vinegar, pumpkin cannelloni, local squid and potatoes, and Neapolitan meatloaf.

www.umberto.it.

Don Salvatore
$-$$

Also in Naples, right on the coast, is this restaurant, whose location is a good one if you're returning to the mainland at dinnertime on a ferry from Capri. Fresh fish and vegetables are the heart of the menu, and the wine list is both high quality and reasonably priced.

www.donsalvatore.it.

La Capannina
$$

Located in Pogerola, a small town a few miles from Amalfi, La Capannina serves fresh, locally caught fish along with vegetables plucked from the restaurant's own garden. Meats are grilled in a large, open fireplace for an added stagecraft flair. If you order a steak, be sure to get the local porcini mushrooms on the side.
www.ristorantelacapannina.com.

Da Gelsomina
$$–$$$$

This inland restaurant on the island of Capri offers wines from its own vines, along with other labels from throughout the Campania region. The restaurant's ravioli caprese is called "legendary" by the local media, and a lot of the produce used in the seasonal dishes comes straight from the restaurant's own garden.
www.dagelsomina.com.

CHAPTER 12

The Southwest Coast

C alabria is the southwestern-most region in Italy, the "toe of the boot." Its western shore is defined by the Tyrrhenian Sea, while its southern shore lies against the Ionian Sea. There is less development here than in other coastal areas, which means you can enjoy views of pristine cliff sides far from the main throngs of tourists. There are also fantastic mountains lying inland, where skiing is a popular activity during the winter months. You can also find remnants of Greek rule here, including the town of Scilla, the mythological home of the sea monster Scylla from Homer's *Odyssey*.

Lay of the Land

Some of the cities in the Calabria region date back to the Magna Grecia era of the sixth and fifth centuries B.C., when Greeks created settlements that later would become one with modern-day Italian lands conquered by the Romans. Eventually, Calabria became part of the kingdom of Naples, where it remained until the unification of Italy. The region was one of the poorest in Italy until the 1970s, when improvements in agriculture and tourism slowly began to buttress local economies. Today, a lot of tourists simply pass through Calabria on their way from Naples to the nearby island of Sicily. What those through-travelers miss out on are some lovely beaches, fun ski resorts, and a great deal of Greek history and mythology.

A small, two-runway airport called Reggio Calabria Airport, or sometimes Aeroporto dello Stretto, serves the area if you would prefer to take a flight from Rome or Milan to Calabria instead of a train or bus from elsewhere in Italy, such as Naples. Three airlines operate here: Alitalia, Air Malta, and MyAir. You can get information about them all in English at the airport's website, *www.sogas.it*.

 Alert

> The planes that fly in and out of Reggio Calabria Airport are on the smaller side, and thus have strict weight limitations. If your checked baggage weighs more than the maximum amount indicated on your ticket, you will be forced to purchase an "excess weight ticket" or, in some instances, have your luggage checked onto a later flight.

There is also an airport to the north of Reggio Calabria Airport, due west of Catanzaro, called Lamezia Terme. A new terminal that is expected to be able to serve as many as 3.5 million passengers per year is currently under construction. You can find out the status of that construction, as well as its effects on airlines and timetables, by visiting the airport's official website, *www.sacal.it*.

Catanzaro

Catanzaro is the region's capital, home to about 100,000 people. It is an interesting mountaintop city in that it sits on a rock split in two by a valley, and thus a concrete-steel bridge connects city sections. Though the city is centuries old, most of its ancient sites are gone, having succumbed to earthquakes in 1783 and 1832 and bombings during World War II. What's left today is less than spectacular, though the city does remain a transportation hub from which you can explore this part of Italy.

You aren't going to miss much if you skip the historic sightseeing in town, though if you have time to spare, there is the town cathedral, which was entirely rebuilt after Allied bombings in 1943. Several other historic churches are also spread around the city, some with Renaissance and Byzantine architecture on a smaller scale than you will find when touring other regions in Italy.

 Fact

One of Catanzaro's claims to fame is that it was the birthplace of artist Domenico "Mimmo" Rotella, a leader of the Decollage movement until his death in 2006. Decollage is the opposite of collage, which is the creation of artwork by layering. In Decollage, you strip away—as Rotella did famously with advertising posters torn from outdoor walls in Rome.

A better bet in this part of Calabria is to head straight to Catanzaro Lido, a resort area on the Ionian Coast. The beaches here are less spectacular than those to the north on the Amalfi Coast, but they're a perfectly respectable choice if you want to spend a night or two at a local hotel while exploring small towns along the Ionian Sea. You can use Catanzaro as a hub for your travels, as opposed to a destination unto itself.

Reggio di Calabria

This city of nearly 200,000 people is some 2,700 years old, having been settled initially by the Greeks as part of Magna Grecia. It served as the capital of Calabria for many years, and it has produced multiple famous sons over the centuries. Pythagoras, of mathematical and Pythagorean theorem fame, is said to have lived here during the fifth century. More modern local names that you might know include Gianni and Donatella Versace of the fashion world.

Unfortunately, the city today has fallen into a state of tourist-unfriendly disrepair in many respects. Most people who come here use Reggio di Calabria as a stepping-off point to get aboard ferries bound for the island of Sicily, which is well within view across the Strait of Messina. Still, before you travel onward, there are a few things worth seeing in Reggio di Calabria, including the Museo Nazionale and its famous Bronzi di Riace statues.

The Bronzi di Riace

In August 1972, a Roman chemist named Stefano Mariottini was enjoying a scuba diving vacation at a presumed shipwreck off the coast of Riace when he found two bronze sculptures. They are now widely regarded as major additions to the world's known pieces of surviving Greek sculpture from the fifth century B.C.

Each of the two pieces depicts a nude, bearded warrior; their spears and shields have been lost to time, likely beneath the sea. What did survive were the inlays that make the statues so striking and memorable: eyes featuring bone and glass, teeth done in silver, and lips and nipples shaped in copper. Experts are unsure whether the statues represent specific warriors; for now, they are known simply as "A" and "B." Many serious students of sculpture consider the statues so significant that they trek all the way down to Reggio di Calabria just to see them.

Restoration of the statues took place in Reggio di Calabria from 1975 until 1980, after which the statues went on display in Rome and Florence to great acclaim before being returned to specially constructed, air-conditioned rooms at the Museo Nazionale in Reggio di Calabria. You can learn more before your visit at the museum's website, *www.museonazionalerc.it.*

Waterfront Promenade

Before you leave Reggio di Calabria, take some time to enjoy a walk along the waterfront, from which you can see the lights of the world-famous island glimmering in the distance. There isn't much else to do here along the promenade, but a stroll can be a nice, leisurely diversion after a day of travel.

Cosenza

Cosenza is home to the University of Calabria and is as much a college town as anything else—albeit one with an interesting heart of Medieval architecture and a history that dates back to the time of antiquity. There are lots of museums here along with a half-dozen or so annual festivals. Three of the more interesting sights are the town's cathedral, Hohenstaufen Castle, and the Museo All'aperto Bilotti.

Cosenza Cathedral

Most likely constructed in the eleventh or twelfth century, the cathedral in Cosenza has seen its share of rebuilding and modification over the years. An earthquake in the 1180s destroyed so much of the original church that reconstruction was not completed until the 1220s. In the early 1700s, a new Baroque superstructure was created, destroying the original. In the early 1800s, the façade was changed to neo-Gothic style.

What stands today is thus a hodgepodge of various men's visions. It's worth seeing if you have even the slightest interest in architectural history and how periods of design can be brought together (effectively or ineffectively) into one structure. And the fact that the cathedral stands in the center of Cosenza's old city makes it an easy landmark for touring the rest of the area.

Hohenstaufen Castle

Believed to have been built around the year 1000, the Castello Svevo, also known as Hohenstaufen Castle, lost its original looks at the command of Roman Emperor Frederick II, who is said to have restored it in the early thirteenth century so that it could serve as a prison for one of his sons, Henry. (Henry was the name of Frederick's first child by his first wife, as well as the name of his third child by his third wife. There were mistresses, as well, but none of those known children were named Henry.)

 Fact

> There is also a ruin in Germany called Hohenstaufen Castle, named for a dynasty of Germanic kings who ruled from the 1130s until the 1250s. At one point in history, the dynasty also ruled over the Kingdom of Sicily, which is how their name came to grace the castle that today remains in the Italian city of Cosenza.

You can still see some of the modifications that were made for imprisonment if you tour the castle today. Interestingly, Frederick II was a great patron of science and the arts during his time in power, so the castle at one time may have held some impressive treasures from those arenas.

Museo All'aperto Bilotti

Museo All'aperto Bilotti, also known as Museo MAB, is Cosenza's open-air sculpture museum. It's literally a sculpture garden in a street, named for collector Carlo Bilotti, an Italian-American cosmetics and perfume entrepreneur who donated the pieces to the city for the good and enjoyment of residents and tourists alike.

The works are not insignificant; some of the artists represented include Surrealist masters Salvador Dali and Giorgio de Chirico. Those artists had become friends of Bilotti's over the years, as had other prominent artists including Roy Lichtenstein and Andy Warhol. As Bilotti neared his death in 2006, he decided to release a good deal of his private collection for public use in Rome and Cosenza, which was his birthplace. (There is a Museo

Carlo Bilotti in Rome, housed in what used to be a sixteenth-century palace. Bilotti paid for its renovations in order to create the museum to showcase his collected artworks, and the doors opened in 2006.)

 Fact

Art collector Carlo Bilotti enjoyed mixing business with pleasure. As the head of a European cosmetics company that managed brands including Pierre Cardin and Geoffrey Beane, he commissioned his friend Andy Warhol to create a series of flower paintings that he then used to promote his company's fragrances.

Soverato

Soverato is a small fishing village of about 10,000 people whose deliciously white sand beaches have become a magnet for summertime tourists from northern Italy. You won't find much here by way of culture, but the beaches are nice enough that a few days at a bed-and-breakfast along the coast might be just what you are seeking in terms of away-from-it-all relaxation.

A couple of summertime festivals provide welcome diversions. There's the Feast of Maria Santissima di Porto Salvo, patron saint of sailors, which naturally includes a parade of boats.

Also look for the festival of fried sardines and peppers, as well as the festival of aubergines. "Aubergine" is another word for eggplant, a name you will rarely see on menus in Italy. The word aubergine developed French, while the term eggplant came into being in the United States, Canada, Australia, and New Zealand because plant fruits are yellow and white, and thus resemble hen's eggs.

Other Must-See Spots

There is a good bit of Greek history in the Calabria region, especially in the towns of Sybaris and Scilla. Also worth a visit before you leave Calabria are the town of Crotone, for its archaeological museum, and a couple of wintertime snow-skiing resorts where you can rest your brain cells and work your thigh muscles a bit.

Sybaris

What remains today of the wealthy Magna Grecia city of Sybaris sits in ruins near the modern-day town of Sibari. It is believed that Sybaris was the first of the Greek colonies in this part of Italy, and perhaps the first to develop a system of streetlights—as early as the fifth century B.C. The people of Sybaris, like their counterparts in Milan today, knew a thing or two about fashion. They are said to have dressed in fine wools, which they purchased using coins minted in town.

Their decadence and luxurious lifestyle was eventually their undoing, but their legacy continues today: the word sybaritic is derived from the city's name and refers to something or someone that is defined by its opulence.

 Fact

It is said that the Sybarites went so far as to try to plan a competing version of the Olympic Games, offering fineries and financing to top athletes of the day if they would go to Sybaris to compete instead of taking part in the primary Olympic festivities.

Despite attempts at excavation, the Italian people have never been able to unearth very many remains from Sybaris.

Scilla

If you are a fan of Greek mythology, then you know the phrase "between Scylla and Charybdis"—which is the equivalent of today's saying "between a rock and a hard place." The phrase refers to the sea monsters Scylla and Charybdis, which were said to have lived on either side of a channel of water, ready to destroy any sailor who strayed too far from the channel's center. A lot of historians say this channel is in fact the Strait of Messina, which separates Calabria from Sicily. It's a waterway that can develop a ripping current so strong it could easily pound sailboats into the rocks or shore on either side. In Homer's *Odyssey*, Odysseus loses six of his shipmates to Scylla—who devours them alive.

⊛ Essential

One of the great things about places like Scilla is small-town charm, as compared with the highly developed resort areas along other coastlines in Italy. If you truly want to feel like one of the locals, then consider a bed-and-breakfast instead of a room in hotel. In Scilla, bed-and-breakfast spots with air conditioning can be found for as little as €40 per night.

The modern-day Calabria town of Scilla takes its name from this creature, which is unfortunate, really, because Scilla is a charming summertime getaway with cliffs that offer fantastic views of Sicily. There is also good swimming to be enjoyed on the beaches here, and no known dangers from sea monsters of any kind.

Museo Archeologico Statale

In the 60,000-strong port town of Crotone, you can visit the Museo Archeologico Statale, which houses artifacts from around the region of Calabria. The collections include coins, ceramics, vases, bronze miniatures, and other artifacts that literally trace the development of human civilization from its origins in this part of the world.

That includes the history of the people of Crotone itself, a city that has evolved from the ancient town of Croton, which was founded in 710 B.C., and then the town of Cotrone, which is how the area was known until 1928. The people who lived here were renowned for their physical strength and sober lifestyle, and athletes often made it to the competitions of the Olympics.

Snow-Skiing Retreats

Of course, the region of Calabria is not nearly as well known for wintertime activity as other Italian cities that have access to pristine white powder from the Alps. But if you are visiting during the winter months and want to enjoy a bit of downhill or cross-country fun, there are a few small resort areas that would be delighted to host you.

Aspromonte

The name Aspromonte means "rough mountains," a moniker given to this region's peaks by farmers who had a difficult time plowing and planting along the steep, rocky mountainsides. They didn't complain about the view, though, which includes the Strait of Messina below—giving today's snow skiers the rare chance to fly downhill while enjoying a look at the sea.

Gambarie d'Aspromonte is the resort area of choice, offering the highest peaks in the area. There aren't a lot of advanced or expert runs here, but beginner- and intermediate-level snow skiers will have plenty of trails to enjoy. The longest run is just over a half mile, and there are about a half-dozen lifts available. More information is available at *www.onthesnow.com*.

La Sila

The La Sila mountain plateau crosses through the geographic boundaries of Crotone, Cosenza, and Cantazaro. It is the home of Parco Nazionale della Silla, which offers "easy tracks" for cross-country and downhill skiers between December and February.

If your visit doesn't coincide with snowfall, you can enjoy the park's horse trails, walking trails, mountain biking trails, sailboat rentals, and more. Full details about recreational opportunities are available in English at the park's official website, *www.parcosila.it*.

Question

What is canyoning?
It's a recreational activity offered at Parco Nazionale della Silla. Essentially, it means that you go hiking through canyons, combining easy-to moderate-level rock climbing with walks along riverbeds and into the whirlpools of waterfalls. The park's website colorfully describes the experience as "gymnastic living in contact with nature."

Lorica

Lorica is about equidistant from the Ionian and Tyrrhenian seas, making it about an hour's drive from some of the beach towns on either coast. Its ski slopes include Valle dell'Inferno—the Hell Valley—that are used for national skiing competitions in Italy. No need to fear if you're not in prime downhill condition; there are easier slopes, too, along with a good number of cross-country trails. And the trails typically aren't that crowded. There are only two lifts and most vacationers choose more developed areas. You can find up-to-date information about Lorica ski conditions and offerings, as well as visitor-posted reviews, at *www.snow-forecast.com*.

Where to Stay

Calabria isn't considered one of the primary tourism regions in Italy, and as such it offers a good number of great deals, even along the waterfront.

The price code for the hotel listings below is $=€100 or less; $$=€100 to €150; $$$=€150 to €200; $$$$=€200 or more per night, per room.

Hotel Palace
$–$$$$

The Hotel Palace is on the Catanzaro Lido promenade, just a few minutes' drive from the downtown and the local resort areas. Among the facility's recent awards is the Certificazione di Qualita Ambientale, an environmental quality certificate. There is a restaurant on site, and pets are welcome with a deposit. All the rooms are air conditioned.

www.hotel-palace.it.

La Residenza de Nobili
$–$$

This Catanzaro bed and breakfast is housed on the first floor of a seventeenth-century palace in the town center. Each room has a private bathroom along with heating, air conditioning, and a television. Rates change with the seasons, sometimes by as much as €30 per night.

www.residenzadenobili.com.

Hotel Savant
$-$$$

Located in the town of Nicastro, west of Catanzaro, the Hotel Savant was restored in late 2004. Each guest room has a hydromassage shower, air conditioning, direct telephones, satellite television, and soundproof walls. There is a restaurant on site, along with a separate bar and tea room.

www.hotelsavant.it.

Holiday Inn Cosenza
$-$$

Located near the business center in Cosenza, this Holiday Inn property has high-speed Internet access, satellite television, air conditioning, and an on-site restaurant that serves Italian as well as international cuisine. If you need to do some business during your travels, this hotel also offers five multifunctional rooms that can host videoconferencing and other amenities.

www.ichotelsgroup.com.

Hotel San Francesco
$-$$

This hotel is in the town of Rende, which is near Cosenza. It is a favorite with business travelers because of its conference facilities and its 110 "business rooms," which are different from regular rooms and designed for longer stays. There is a restaurant as well as a business center on site, and WiFi is available for free throughout the property.

www.hsf.it.

Where to Eat

Since the region of Calabria is bordered on two sides by the sea, you can expect excellent fish and seafood dishes to be among the entrée suggestions at countless restaurants.

The price code for the restaurant entrees below is $=€25 or less; $$=€26 to €50; $$$=€51 to €75; $$$$=€100 or more.

La Sosta
$$–$$$

Located in Crotone, this traditional Italian restaurant offers everything from mushroom risotto to shrimp scampi to cuts of filet. The wine menu features local as well as regional favorites, and the fact that Diners Club International cards are welcome should give you an idea about just how well this staff is trained to please visitors from outside Italy.

www.lasostamarcello.it.

Ristorante L'Approdo
$$–$$$$

Ristorante L'Approdo, located at Vibo Valentia Marina just north of Reggio di Calabria, specializes in homemade pasta and just-caught fish from the very sea that its restaurant overlooks. The chef prides himself on using only the freshest ingredients, and the eatery's sophisticated nautical décor is anything but touristy or tacky.

www.lapprodo.com.

La Locanda di Alia
$$–$$$$

Located in Cosenza, this restaurant offers traditional, local foods presented with an original and often elegant flair. There are traditional as well as "traditional reinvented" menus suggested by the chef, and there is a wine-tasting room in addition to an extensive wine list from which you can choose during your meal.

www.alia.it.

Ristorante Il Ducale
$–$$

This Reggio di Calabria restaurant is on the waterfront promenade, right next to the museum that houses the Bronzi di Riace statues. Seafood is the specialty, with menu items including pasta with squid, mixed grilled fish, and peppery mussels. The wine list is small but wide-ranging in terms of both quality and price. (Several bottles cost less than €15.) Save room for traditional desserts such as lemon sorbet and nut truffles.

www.ristoranteilducale.com.

Sicily

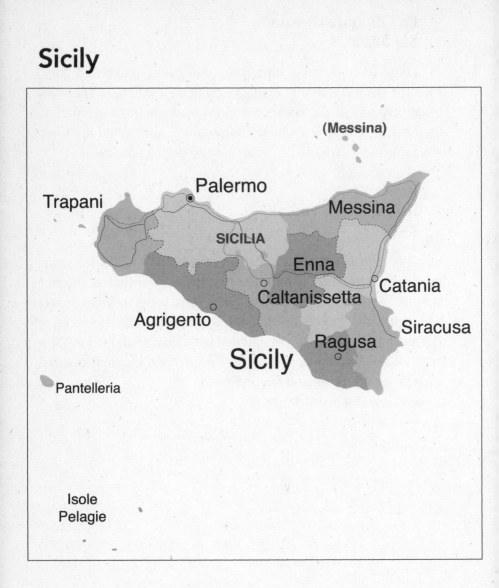

CHAPTER 13

Sicily

Sicily—land of thick pizza, rich cannoli, and Mafia legends—is the island that Italy appears to be kicking with the toe of its boot. Its strategic location in the early years of seafaring Mediterranean trade helped it to develop based on multiple cultures. You will find ancient Greek archaeology here, as well as Arab-influenced ceramics and jewelry. Orange and lemon orchards dominate the natural landscape, which also literally breathes fire in the form of the lava-spitting Stromboli—one of the only active volcanoes on Earth where it is considered relatively safe for tourists to hike to the summit.

Lay of the Land

Sicily is actually the largest island in the entire Mediterranean Sea and has a population of about 5 million people. The island's history is believed to date back to about 8,000 B.C., based on scientific dating of cave drawings. Greek settlers arrived around 750 B.C., and as they incorporated Sicily (and present-day southern mainland Italy) into Magna Grecia, they erected many temples to the gods. The Romans took over around 242 B.C., making Sicily the first Roman province beyond the mainland of modern Italy and building settlements with amphitheaters much like those on the other side of the Strait of Messina.

Years of war and various rulers followed, with Byzantine emperors, Arabs from Tunisia, the Norman dynasty, Austrian and Spanish leaders, and Napoleon Bonaparte all taking a turn at calling Sicily their own. Finally, the island joined the Kingdom of Italy in 1860, and after a short-lived attempt at independence and the rise of the Mafia crime network in the late 1800s, Sicily eventually became a republic in 1946 after being invaded by World War II Allied forces. According to the Constitution of Italy, the island is one of just five "autonomous regions" that are part of modern-day Italy. (The other four are Sardinia, Trentino-Alto Adige, the Aosta Valley, and Friuli-Venezia Giulia. The government gave them autonomy because of cultural and linguistic differences following World War II. However, there were strings attached. For example, the autonomous regions have to finance much of their own public infrastructure.)

Today, tourism is a major part of Sicily's economy, though agriculture still offers key financial support as well. Many visitors to Italy believe that Sicily is as "must-see" as Rome or Naples, both because of its ruins and because of its enduring natural beauty.

 Fact

Many people saw the rise of Sicily's Mafia in the late 1800s as a good thing. The Pope was fighting with state officials in Rome over general regional leadership, and the Mafia sought to fill the resulting lack of attention to local residents' needs. The secret society's work may not have been legal, but someone had to maintain order and protect property on the island.

Arriving by Air

Three airports welcome visitors to Sicily. The busiest is Catania-Fontanarossa, which is just south of Catania on the island's eastern shore. The airport's most recent upgrade occurred in 2007, when a passenger terminal with twenty new gates was opened to help accommodate the estimated 6 million people who travel through the airport each year.

Multiple regional airlines offer flights here, as do international brands including Air France, British Airways, Delta Air Lines, KLM/Northwest Airlines, Lufthansa, and Virgin Express. You can pick up a connecting flight to Catania from pretty much any major city in Europe, as well as from farther-away cities including Casablanca and Moscow. Details are available in English at the airport's official website, *www.aeroporto.catania.it*.

ⓔ✔ Fact

Palermo International Airport is also known locally as Falcone-Borsellino Airport, in honor of two anti-Mafia judges who were killed by the organized crime syndicate in 1992. There is a plaque at the airport featuring their portraits along with the words, "The Pride of New Sicily."

The second-biggest airport on Sicily is Palermo International Airport, on the island's northwest coast. It is in Punta Raisi, about twenty miles west of Sicily's capital city of Palermo. About 4.5 million people transit through this airport each year, with Alitalia being the largest major carrier that offers flights. Other international airlines that serve Palermo include EasyJet. Your best bet getting here will often include a connection from the international airport in Rome. More details are online in English at the airport's website, *www.gesap.it*.

Last of Sicily's three airports is Trapani-Birgi, located on the island's far western coast. It is a combined civilian and military facility that serves about 500,000 travelers each year. Only a handful of airlines operate here, including AirBee, Avanti Air, RyanAir, and Meridiana. Most connections are from Italian cities, though you can find flights on RyanAir from major European cities such as Barcelona, Dublin, Dusseldorf, Frankfurt, and Stockholm. The airport's official website offers some information in English at *www.airgest.it.*

 Alert

Ferry routes to Sicily book up quickly between June and September. It's ideal to have your ticket several weeks in advance. Whether you book directly through a ferry company or with a travel agent or a self-service website, be sure to have your confirmation number handy. There will be many other potential customers for your space if your paperwork is not in order.

Arriving by Boat

It is virtually as easy—though not always as quick—to arrive in Sicily by ferry as it is by airplane. Ferries run regularly from nearby Reggio di Calabria on the mainland. There also are ferries available from large mainland cities including Genoa, Livorno, and Naples.

Different ferry routes arrive at different points on the island of Sicily. Messina is just across the strait from Reggio di Calabria, on Sicily's eastern shore, while ferries from Naples and Genoa arrive at Palermo, on the island's northwest shore. Some of the ferry rides can be mini-cruises unto themselves. The trip from Naples to Palermo, for instance, can be a little more than ten hours long with the major carrier Tirrenia (*www.tirrenia.it*). From Genoa to Palermo with Grandi Navi Veloci (*www.gnv.it*), some of the eight-hour transits are offered only on an overnight basis, with sleeping cars available.

Expect to pay at least €120 per person, round-trip, for a room with a bed during one of these extended ferry rides. Rates go up if you want to bring a rental car onboard with you, and as with everything tourist-oriented in Italy, prices also rise with the peak summer travel season. The website *www.aferry.to* is a helpful tool that offers route and price information about most of the ferry lines that service Sicily year-round.

Palermo

More than 1 million people live in Palermo and its immediate suburbs, a region that is believed to have been first settled as early as 8,000 B.C. Early Greek settlers dubbed the area Panormus, meaning "all port," in honor of the natural harbor where so many boats and ferries still ply the waters today. Unfortunately, the architecture and monuments of Sicily's first people suffered remarkable damage during Allied bombing raids during World War II. Not much has been rebuilt or restored since troops invaded the island during the summer of 1943, so the island's beauty is now visible only through its weathered scars. Main sights include the town cathedral, another church called Chiesa di Santa Maria dell'Ammiraglio, the royal chapel Cappella Paletina, and the Teatro Massimo opera house.

✅ Fact

The people who used the heliometer in the Cathedral of Sicily believed that every twenty-four-hour day began at sunrise, which of course meant that days began at different true times throughout the year. Always happy to stand apart, the Sicilians had no problem with the fact that their days had different times than those in Rome, including at St. Peter's Basilica.

Cathedral of Palermo

The Cathedral of Palermo dates back to 1185, but renovations changed its appearance to reflect the architectural periods from the 1300s to the early 1800s. There is an interesting feature inside, called a heliometer, a word that derives from the Greek for "sun" and "measure." Essentially, the cathedral's heliometer—believed to have first been used in the late 1600s—is a hole in a dome that lets a sunbeam through so that it can shine onto the floor. The ends of a north-south line on the floor indicate the summer and winter solstices, and various points represent other dates throughout the year. The tool helped the church figure out when it was time to celebrate Easter, among other things.

The cathedral is open daily from 7 A.M. until 7 P.M. Its official website, *www.cattedrale.palermo.it*, offers more information, though only in Italian.

Chiesa di Santa Maria dell'Ammiraglio

The stunning mosaic interior of Chiesa di Santa Maria dell'Ammiraglio, also known as La Martorana, makes it one of Palermo's most oft-visited churches (and premier wedding sites). Construction appears to have begun in the 1140s, and the interior mosaics also date back to that time, having been created by Byzantine artisans. Many of the mosaics are heavy with gold, which makes the interior positively sparkle when sunlight flows through the windows.

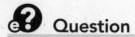 **Question**

Is the sweet treat *frutta di Martorana* related to La Martorana church?
Yes indeed. A convent of Benedictine nuns, founded by a woman named Eloisa Martorana, absorbed the church in the 1430s. The nuns were well known for their marzipan molds shaped like various fruits— hence the enduring name *frutta di Martorana*, which you can buy in Palermo today.

The church is open daily, but the best time to see the light glint on the mosaics is early morning. Doors usually open at 9:30 A.M. from Monday through Saturday, and at 8:30 A.M. on Sunday.

Cappella Paletina

Cappella Paletina, which translates as the Palatine Chapel, is the royal chapel of the Norman Kings of Sicily. Its shimmering interior mosaics, like those at La Martorana, are exceptionally memorable, adorning virtually every inch of the walls, arches, and dome. Historians believe that most, if not all, of the mosaics date to the 1100s, and the scenes depicting Acts of the Apostles are renowned for their Byzantine beauty. The chapel is located within Palazzo dei Normanni, a palace that once served as the seat of the Kings of Sicily.

Teatro Massimo

Palermo's Teatro Massimo is the biggest opera house in Italy, and the third-biggest in Europe after those in Paris and Vienna. It took more than twenty years to build, finally opening in 1897 with a performance of Giuseppe Verdi's *Falstaff*. Originally, the theater was to have seated 3,000 people, but today, it holds just shy of 1,400. If you're one of the lucky visitors who gets a seat inside, then you might recognize some of the locations where director Francis Ford Coppola filmed scenes from *The Godfather III*.

Twenty-five-minute guided tours in multiple languages are available for €5 Tuesday through Sunday from 10 A.M. until 2:30 P.M. A cafeteria and bookstore are on site. Scheduled performances change with the seasons; check the official website, *www.teatromassimo.it*, for up-to-date ticket listings during the dates of your trip.

Catania

Catania, like Palermo, is one of Sicily's main cities and is located alongside a natural harbor. It sits at the foot of Mount Etna, which towers nearly 11,000 feet tall and is the largest active volcano in Europe. And it is *active*: Mount Etna's most recent eruption began in May 2008, accompanied by about 200 earthquakes, and continued throughout the rest of the year. But despite such protestations from Mother Nature, the city continues to thrive, albeit without the benefit of wholly complete ancient monuments, many of which have succumbed to lava, ash, and earthquakes over the years.

 Fact

Legend has it that Fontana dell'Elefante, the elephant statue that stands in Piazza del Duomo as a symbol of the city of Catania, was originally assembled as a neutered beast—an insult to the virility of the town's men. Legend goes on to say that the sculptor had to add the appropriate appendage to ease the locals' minds.

You can still see a great deal, though, including the historic city center, which is part of a group of southeastern Sicily towns that were named a collective UNESCO World Heritage Site in 2002. In adding the areas to the list, the committee stated that the buildings pay "outstanding testimony to the exuberant genius of late Baroque art and architecture." There is no better place to stand in the center of that exuberant genius than Piazza del Duomo, a square surrounded by the building facades that so enchanted the UNESCO judges.

St. Agatha of Sicily

Agatha is the patron saint of Catania. She suffered many tortures—including the amputation of her breasts—as punishment for her Christian faith after she spurned the romantic advances of a Roman prefect. Her cathedral in Catania boasts a marble façade, and its interior is said to house her remains.

Question

Is Agatha the patron saint of anything else besides Catania?
Yes. She is also the patron saint of Malta and—because of the way her amputated breasts have been portrayed in paintings throughout the centuries—she is also the patron saint of bell-founders and bakers.

Each February 3–5, a massive festival takes place in her honor, drawing hundreds of thousands of locals and visitors. Lights adorn the city center, much as they would during a holiday parade, and a large mosaic of colored lights is created to display a scene from Agatha's life. Songs and fireworks delight the crowds, as do sweet cakes made in the shape of breasts and served on platters—a reference to the way Agatha is often depicted in paintings with her amputated breasts on a tray.

La Pescheria

Whether you are hungry or not, be sure to allow some time for a stroll through La Pescheria—the fish market of Catania. It bursts at the seams with so much fresh filet, cheese, beef, and the like that it is often compared to the Vucciria, a market in Palermo whose name literally translates from Sicilian as "confusion."

This is a free show on the highest order of entertainment, especially if you have rented an apartment with a kitchen and can find some freshly iced treasures to take home for dinner. It's hard to go wrong with your cooking when the ingredients—and the experience of shopping for them—are so fantastic.

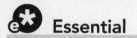

Essential

Need a history lesson about the civil and religious history of the city of Messina? Stop by the city's cathedral any day at noon, when mechanical statues offer details of important events. It's not exactly a Disney World-level production, but it is perhaps the only place in Italy where you can see an animatronic lion and cockerel paired with Norman architecture.

Messina

Messina is the eastern Sicily town that gives its name to the Strait of Messina, the mythical home of the dueling sea dragons Charbydis and Scylla. This is the city where you are likely to arrive on Sicily if you take the ferry from Reggio di Calabria on the mainland. Messina is more of a waypoint than a tourism hotspot, but there are a handful of sights worth a look if you have time in your schedule to spare.

The city's cathedral is interesting, though it no longer stands in its original form. Built in the 1100s, it suffered massive damage in a 1908 earthquake and was nearly entirely rebuilt around 1920. Much of that work was again destroyed during World War II, when Allied planes dropped bombs on the historic building. Bits of the original Norman architecture are still visible, but many parts of the cathedral, including its mosaics, are reconstructions.

Also allow a moment to stop and reflect at the impressive Fountain of Neptune, built in the mid-1500s. It looks out toward the sea, reminding visitors of just how important the adjacent waters have been to Messina's development throughout the centuries.

Syracuse

Historians believe that Syracuse, today a city of about 125,000 people, was founded by Greek settlers around 730 B.C. Much of the ancient city was on the island Ortygia, which connects so closely to the mainland today that you might not realize you have crossed a bridge to get to it. This is where you will find the historic city cathedral, which once served as a Greek temple, as well as the Fontana Aretusa, which served as the ancients' supply of fresh water.

✅ Fact

Paradise Quarry, which is located inside Parco Archeologico della Neapolis, is one of the most famous ancient quarries in all of Italy. It was from here, as well as three or four other primary quarries, that great stones were hauled and then carved into some of the grandest statues in the history of Syracuse.

Perhaps more interesting because of its unique presence on Sicily, Syracuse is also home to Parco Archeologico della Neapolis, an archaeological park that features the remains of a fifth-century B.C. amphitheater once believed to have held more than 15,000 people. The stage is still somewhat intact, and you can stand atop it, just as performers did in the days of Euripedes.

Also still standing in the park—and perhaps just as theatrical in its day, albeit in a gruesome way—is the Altar of Heron. It is believed to have once included the longest altar base ever built, which allowed the Greeks to sacrifice the lives of hundreds of animals simultaneously.

Aeolian Islands

Some 200,000 people visit the volcanic archipelago off Italy's northeastern shore each year. Known as the Aeolians, these eight islands offer particularly terrific scuba diving and nature hikes, thanks to their crystal-clear waters and their multitude of flora onshore.

You can catch ferries several times a day during the summer months from Milazzo and Messina to the Aeolians, with most routes arriving at Lipari, the largest of the islands. Your visit can stop there if you are simply looking for a place to get your water sports fix, or you can travel onward to other Aeolian islands including Stromboli, which is home to an active volcano.

Lipari

Lipari is the name of both the largest of the Aeolian islands and the main town on that island, with about 11,000 residents. That number tends to double during the summer months, and most of the tourists head straight to the snorkeling and scuba diving centers along the coastline, as well as to the island's beaches.

❓ Question

What is obsidian?
Obsidian is a naturally occurring form of glass that is created when lava cools without any accompanying growth of crystals. Lipari, a volcanic island, is covered in the stuff, which Stone Age cultures broke apart to use as spearheads and mirrors. Today, obsidian is used not just as a gemstone, but also in creating sharp, thin scalpels for use by heart surgeons.

Even if that is your primary plan, consider setting an hour or two aside for a look around the Museo Archeologico Eoliano, which not only will teach you about artifacts from the islands, but which also discusses its geological history. As with lava and eruptions elsewhere throughout history, the tales rarely fail to disappoint in terms of excitement.

Vulcano

What beaches are to Lipari, steaming mud baths are to Vulcano. This Aeolian island has fewer than 1,000 year-round residents, most of them earning their living from the tourists who arrive by ferry and hydrofoil to visit the natural hot springs and mud baths.

 Alert

Leave your silver jewelry behind when climbing into the mud baths at Laghetto di Fanghi. The naturally occurring chemical properties in the mud will tarnish your favorite rings and necklaces. They will also stink up any fabric that they touch, so consider wearing an old bathing suit that you wouldn't mind parting with after your day trip is done.

Laghetto di Fanghi is the mud bath that for centuries has been rumored to heal everything from arthritis to skin ailments. It's an easy walk from the pier where you ferry will deposit you, and it's pretty much the only thing to do on Vulcano. Just follow the crowds. You can squirm around in the "medicinal mud" for as long as the sulfuric smell doesn't choke your nostrils (it is reminiscent of rotten eggs, like any good ointment), and then cool and clean yourself off at the nearby beach.

Stromboli

Stromboli is the Aeolian island that houses an active volcano— one whose minor eruptions are so consistent that they have become a tourist attraction. You can visit by day for a look around, but it is considerably more memorable to visit at night, when yellow and red plumes of heat pierce the black sky like a fireworks display.

There is hiking on Stromboli, but only when the volcano is not erupting. The last eruption was in late 2007, when two new craters opened up, one of which sent lava flowing down into the sea.

Other Must-See Spots

Sicily's main cities and surrounding islands certainly offer plenty to see and do, but if you have even more time to spend touring, you can enjoy still more archeological and cultural sites. The Necropolis of Pantalica, for instance, boasts more than 5,000 tombs cut into the rock quarries, while the town of Taormina offers chances to see and be seen with the most glamorous of Sicily's visitors.

Necropolis of Pantalica

The Necropolis of Pantalica became a UNESCO World Heritage Site in 2005. The tombs carved out of its rocky hillsides reportedly date from the thirteenth to the seventh centuries B.C. These tombs, which are essentially gutted stone caves, were a way of life for many of Sicily's original inhabitants, who fled the easier life along the coast and plains when the Siculi tribe entered the island. All of this was before Greek colonization, and thus the tombs stand as a timeless reminder of just how long human beings have struggled to control the island.

Taormina

The small town of Taormina is the playground of ritzy resort-goers, the place where tourists go to attend summertime film festivals instead of archaeological museums. Taormina Arte is the summertime arts festival, which includes music and dance as well as theater. Events run throughout June, July, and August, with individual as well as package ticket prices available. Full details, including a schedule of events, are available online in English at *www.taormina-arte.com.*

Where to Stay

You can go inexpensive or completely over-the-top in terms of accommodations on Sicily, but keep in mind that the island is just that—a fixed amount of space with no suburbs for sprawling—and as such books up quickly during the prime summer months.

The price code for the hotel listings below is $=€100 or less; $$=€100 to €150; $$$=€150 to €200; $$$$=€200 or more per night, per room.

Hotel Villa Romeo
$-$$$$

This Catania hotel offers virtually every type of room you might want, from an inexpensive single to quadruple rooms and suites. It is housed in a restored nineteenth-century palace with inner courtyards, a feature you don't often find elsewhere. Rooms have air conditioning, satellite television, WiFi, safes, and additional amenities.
www.hotelvillaromeo.it

Hotel Savona
$$$$

Also in Catania, the Hotel Savona is a three-star hotel less than 100 feet from the city's cathedral and other main sights. A buffet breakfast is available, and there is a bar that stays open until midnight. Special rates and package deals are often promoted exclusively on the hotel's website.
www.hotelsavona.it

Villa Ducale Taormina
$$–$$$$

Villa Ducale is about a fifteen-minute walk (or a free shuttle ride) away from the hustle and bustle of the main town. It is a small hotel, an actual Sicilian villa, and as such offers a more elegant environment than typical hotels on the island. Traditional Sicilian breakfast is served daily, and rooms have private terraces with views of Mount Etna.

www.villaducale.com

Hotel del Centro
$–$$$

Located in Palermo, Hotel del Centro is within walking distance of the city's central transportation terminal, should you want to be close to the bus station for touring farther afield. Rooms are air conditioned and have soundproof windows, a must in the center of the city. WiFi is available, and continental breakfast is served.

www.hoteldelcentro.it.

Where to Eat

Sicily's history of food is just as long as its history of civilization. Some recipes have been handed down from family member to family member not just for generations, but for centuries. Relax, linger, and enjoy.

The price code for the restaurant entrees below is $=€25 or less; $$=€26 to €50; $$$=€51 to €75; $$$$=€100 euro or more.

Il Mirto e la Rosa
$-$$

This Palermo restaurant opened in 1987 under the stewardship of vegetarians. It added meat and fish to the menu in 1994, and today the chefs bring the same level of organic-mindedness from the early days to the selection of all raw ingredients.

www.ilmirtoelarosa.com.

Principe Cerami Restaurant
$$$-$$$$

Chef Massimo Mantarro earned this Taormina restaurant its Michelin star by offering traditional Sicilian food with an elegant, modern twist. The restaurant is one of several on the grounds of the San Domenico Palace Hotel, a five-star resort built on the site of a fifteenth-century monastery.

www.thi-hotels.com.

La Grotta Azzurra
$-$

Located in the historic center of Taormina, this family-friendly restaurant specializes in traditional Sicilian food, primarily fresh fish and crustaceans. A buffet option lets you sample various local dishes without committing to any single one from the menu, a nice option if you're new to, say, chewing on steamed squid.

www.ristorantegrottaazzurrataormina.com.

Sardinia

CHAPTER 14

Sardinia

Sardinia is the second-biggest island in the Mediterranean, after Sicily, yet it lies much farther to the west of the Italian mainland than its sister island. With its northern tip due west of Naples, Sardinia is actually geographically closer to Tunisia, in Africa, and the French island of Corsica, than it is to Italy. No matter: The island remains culturally connected to its mother nation, albeit with a spirit of independence and a special statute of regional autonomy. Its restaurants, beaches, and resorts woo everyday travelers along with the world's richest and most famous, all of whom are seeking to "get away" without leaving too much of Italy behind.

Lay of the Land

Scientists have found human remains on Sardinia that they say date back to 250,000 B.C. Nobody is sure what life might have been like on the island so many years ago, but more recent ancient history indicates a well-developed system of trading obsidian, the volcanic glass you read about in Chapter 13. Sharp spear points were apparently a big commodity in the early days of humankind, and Sardinia was awash in one of the best materials for creating them.

The business that developed seems to have drawn people to the island from all over northern Africa and present-day Europe. Each group left its own cultural imprint for future generations. Conquerors, too, have left their stamp on the island, with Sardinia having been ruled at various points in history by Roman, Byzantine, and Spanish leaders.

🅴❗ Alert

For practical purposes, especially in high-tourism areas, Italian is the language you will hear spoken on Sardinia. Yet the island does have a language of its own, Sardinian, which is full of Spanish and Catalan influences. If you venture into the island's more rural areas, your Italian vocabulary will get you only so far in terms of communication.

Today, one particular remnant of these early cultures draws a lot of interest on Sardinia: the nuraghe. Nuraghi are stone towers that look a bit like beehives, some standing more than sixty feet tall. They have no foundations or other supports, but are held up simply by the multi-ton weight of the stones that comprise them. Scientists estimate that they were built during the Bronze Age, from the eighteenth century to the fifteenth century B.C., and more than 8,000 nuraghi still stand on Sardinia today. The purpose of the nuraghi has been lost to time, but they certainly make for an interesting tourism adventure today.

Arriving by Air

Four airports on Sardinia—at Cagliari, Olbia, Alghero, and Arbatax—offer you the option of flying to the island from multiple cities within mainland Italy and greater Europe.

About 2.7 million people fly into Cagliari-Elmas Airport each year; a new terminal opened in 2003 to allow an expansion of capacity to 4 million travelers. About a dozen airlines have routes here. The major carriers include Alitalia, British Airways, and Lufthansa. This airport is on Sardinia's southern shore. More information is available in English at *www.sogaer.it*.

Olbia Costa Smeralda Airport has services with some fifty different operators, many of them small, regional airlines. The major players that offer flights here include Alitalia, Iberia, and Lufthansa. This airport is on Sardinia's northeastern shore. You can learn more in English at *www.geasar.it*.

The airport at Alghero is called Fertilia Airport. It handles about 1 million passengers a year. Only a handful of operators advertise services here, though; they include AirOne, RyanAir, and Volare-Web. This airport is on Sardinia's northwestern shore. More information is online in English at *www.aeroportodialghero.it*.

Tortoli-Arbatax Airport is your fourth option on Sardinia. It's located about halfway up Sardinia's eastern shore, just south of the popular beaches of Golfo di Orosei. The airport does not have a website of its own, but you can find information about flights by plugging its international code, TTB, into any travel reservations site.

❓ Question

Can you get a better ticket price by choosing one Sardinia airport over another?
Prices probably won't differ much between airports during the high season, in the summer, when most flights are jam-packed. Your best option is simply to choose the airport closest to your final destination on the island and pay the going rate before all the seats are gone.

Arriving by Boat

The same general locations where Sardinia's airports are located also serve ferries. There is Porto Torres in the northwest, near Alghero airport; Golfo Aranci in the northeast, near Olbia airport; Tortoli on the central eastern shore, near Arbatax; and Cagliari, on the southern coast, near the Cagliari airport.

You have multiple departure options. Ferries leave from various cities on the Italian mainland, including Civitavecchia (Rome), Genoa, La Spezia, Livorno, Naples, Palermo, Piombino, and Trapani. The fast ferries typically take four to six hours one-way, while the crossing on regular ferries can last seventeen hours. Rates vary widely depending on what kind of ferry you book, and then what kind of seat or cabin you request onboard. There are also additional fees if you plan to bring a vehicle aboard.

A couple of good online resources for ferry tickets include *www.aferry.to* and *www.directferries.co.uk*. Both websites let you book directly on multiple ferry lines from all the key operators.

Cagliari

Cagliari is Sardinia's capital, a city of about 160,000 people with a history that dates back to at least the seventh century B.C. Like many other cities of strategic importance in modern-day Italy, Cagliari was heavily bombed by the Allied Forces during World War II. Thus, today, the city combines a long, rich history of culture with battered and restored remains of the years gone by. There is a lot to see and do here, even if your only intentions are to enjoy a few days on the beach with some fine dining at seafront restaurants.

Four tourism purposes, think of Cagliari as being divided into two primary areas: the old town and the waterfront. The old town is known as Il Castello and includes several noteworthy museums, while the waterfront is known as Marina and boasts lots of places to eat, sleep, and play.

Il Castello

Il Castello means "the castle," a name derived from this hill-top area's former life as a walled-in fortress of a town. The views from here are fantastic of the Gulf of Cagliari, and there are some sights worth seeing in addition to the handful of museums that offer unique displays.

 Fact

> Cagliari is a large city, but it also happens to have some special beaches—including Poetto Beach, which by day is family-friendly and by night transforms into a waterfront paradise of bars and nightclubs. Boating and surfing are based at the Marina section of the city, so the waters nearest the beach itself are quiet and filled with leisurely swimmers.

Cagliari Cathedral, also known as Cattedrale di Santa Maria, dates to the 1200s but has been rebuilt and modified so many times over the years that few remnants of the original construction remain. At one point, the cathedral had a Baroque façade, but even it has been changed so much that it's hard to appreciate what once was there. The bell tower is the only part of the cathedral that is virtually unchanged, and it's worth a quick look as you make your way around the area.

The most interesting museum in this area is the Museo Archeologico Nazionale, which houses finds from the pre-Nuragic period. There also is a series of sculptures on site that dates to the Bronze Age, with each sculpture offering a small clue as to how people lived and worshiped during that time. A visit to this museum teaches you about more than the history of Sardinia; it offers details about the history of human civilization itself.

Marina

Cagliari's Marina area is, among other things, one of the best places in all of Sardinia where you can go to eat. Its waterfront location means a bevy of fresh fish and seafood being brought to market, and, then, to your plate. There are a couple of hotels here as well, but the primary sensory experience to be had is dining, not sleeping. You could spend a week just trying out the various eateries at lunch and dinnertime, never having to return to the same table unless you so desire.

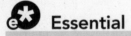 **Essential**

> The Museo Archeologico Nazionale does not have a website with information available in English, so be sure to ask your travel agent about current operating times, fees, and the like. If your hotel in Cagliari has a concierge, that's probably the best place to get up-to-date information about the museum's offerings.

This is a good place to snack as well, with gelato and various confectionary treats on offer to help you get a little sugar rush as you make your way around the city. Enjoying a double scoop of anything while you walk along the waterfront is a downright decadent experience.

Iglesias

Iglesias has just 30,000 residents and is perched in Sardinia's southwestern hills, about 600 feet above sea level. It was once an important mining district, producing large quantities of zinc, lead, and silver. The mining went on for about 200 years. The skills and tools were passed down from generation to generation. Now, tools from as early as the late 1700s are set out for display at the Museo dell'Arte Mineraria, which opened in 1998.

This museum is actually part of a local mining school, and some of the displays are used to educate future miners about the realities of the dangerous job. As such, the museum has limited hours of operation. From April through June, you can get inside between 6 P.M. and 8 P.M. on Saturday and Sunday. From July through September, entry is allowed between 7 P.M. and 9 P.M. Friday through Sunday. If your travel times don't jibe with those allowances, you can request a personal reservation by e-mailing *apimmg@tiscali.it*. The museum's website, available only in Italian, is *www.museoartemineraria.it*.

If you plan to stay in Iglesias for any significant length of time, bring a rental car. Public transportation is less than ideal. The town's mining economy has faltered, and about half the local residents who remain are unemployed and don't need extensive public transportation on frequent schedules.

Oristano

About 30,000 people live in Oristano, whose economy is based on fishing, not tourism. That makes this western Sardinia town achingly endearing as a place to "live like the locals" for a few days, as well as a place to see some archaeological relics and sites without the massive crowds that you will find in more popular spots such as Cagliari. The best of the nearby sites is Tharros, which is close enough to town that you can make a day trip of visiting.

Tharros

Tharros is essentially an open-air museum where excavations are continuing, but what has been unearthed so far reveals that the town was likely founded by the Phoenicians during the eighth century B.C. The scholar Ptolemy, who died around 168 A.D., mentions the location in his writings, and Tharros was for a time a Roman settlement as well. It is believed that the city's final inhabitants were forced to flee around 1070 because of raids by the Saracen people.

 Fact

"Saracen" was a word used in the Middle Ages to describe believers in the religion of Islam, also known today as Muslims. Various etymologies suggest, among other things, that the word originally translated as "not well founded." It also may mean "those empty of Sarah," a reference to the wife of Abraham as described in the Hebrew Bible.

Italian, English, and French excavators have all contributed to unearthing what remains of Tharros, which is why you can see relics from the site not only in Italian museums, but also in museums in London and Marseille. During your visit to Oristano, the place to see artifacts after your visit to Tharros itself is at the Antiquarium Arborense.

Antiquarium Arborense

The Antiquarium Arborense museum has a collection that ranges from pre-Nuraghic to early Medieval. Here you can see bronze sculptures, ceramics, and tools believed to have been used by the people of Sardinia's earliest civilizations. One room inside offers a reconstructed look at the Phoenecian tomb of Tharros, while another area details the thirteenth-century construction of the city walls in Oristano.

There is no website for the museum, but a travel agent or local tour operator can help you get any additional information you may need. In general, the museum is open on Tuesday, Thursday, and Saturday.

Alghero

Alghero is a popular city on the northwestern Sardinian coast whose population of about 42,000 souls tends to double during the summer months. The area dates back to ancient and even prehistoric times. More than 100 nuraghe remains are spread throughout Alghero proper and the immediately surrounding suburbs. The historic town center dates to Medieval times and is still surrounded by the sea walls that have protected its people for centuries.

There is a lot of Spanish influence here because Spain controlled the city until the early 1700s. Nearly a quarter of the local residents still learn Algherese Catalan as their first language, and you can regularly hear the dialect spoken along the city streets.

eV Fact

Allied warplanes did a good bit of damage to the historic sites in Alghero during World War II. Rebuilding efforts have focused not on reconstruction but on improving the city's infrastructure for tourism. Demand is so high for hotel rooms that the city becomes fully booked every July and August, and most reservations are made months in advance.

The best way to tour Alghero is not to visit a specific church or monument, but instead simply to walk around. The historic town walls are now dotted with restaurants, bars, and shops, making for an unparalleled experience in modern shopping with a historic ambience. You also will see a good bit of Romanesque and Gothic architecture as you walk along the historic town's main streets, and you can gaze up at the remaining defensive towers to get a good idea of what life might have been like in the days of seagoing raiders.

Sassari

Sassari is also in Sardinia's northwest quadrant, just inland and to the northeast of Alghero. In terms of population, Sassari is second only to Cagliari among Sardinian cities, with about 122,000 residents. The city is believed to date back to the early Middle Ages, when coastal people fled inland to escape repeated Saracen attacks from the sea.

There is an important library at the university here that holds what are believed to be the first documents ever written in the Sardinian language. The main sights to see, though, are a pair of churches and an archaeological museum.

Sassari's Churches

The city's cathedral, known as Duomo di San Nicola, dates to the 1200s and was enlarged in 1480, in Gothic style. The façade was created between the mid-1600s and early 1700s, and it has a Baroque architecture. The cathedral's bell tower, adding yet another layer of interest, is Romanesque. Duomo di San Nicola is in the center of the historic section of town, so it's a good place to start your touring.

Also worth a look is the nearby Chiesa di Santa Maria di Betlem, which dates to the 1100s with major expansions in the 1400s, 1600s, and 1800s.

Museo Nazionale G.A. Sanna

This museum is named for Giovanni Antonio Sanna of Sassari, an Italian senator who donated his personal collections so that the facility could open its doors in 1931. The collections have of course been updated over the years, most recently in 2000, when a new "Medieval and Modern" section was inaugurated. You can view artifacts and more throughout this museum, as Sanna was also a collector of historic artworks.

❓ Question

> **Is there historic jewelry to be seen at Museo Nazionale G.A. Sanna?**
> Indeed, but it's not called jewelry. It's called "history della'ornamento," meaning the history of ornaments, or personal jewelry. Examples on display include shells and metals used as necklaces and bracelets throughout history, along with pieces created from animal bone.

The museum is open Tuesday to Sunday from 9 A.M. until 8 P.M., though the ticket office closes at 7:30 P.M. The entrance fee for adults is €2. There is more information available at the museum's website, though it is only in Italian: *www.museosannasassari.it*.

Other Must-See Spots

As you can tell by now, Sardinia is awash not just in beaches and natural beauty, but also in history. There are still more places for you to enjoy both, starting with the Costa Smeralda—the Emerald Coast.

Costa Smeralda

Costa Smeralda is on Sardinia's northeastern cost, comprising a stretch of land about thirty-five miles long and filled with beaches and modern towns. It is known as a getaway spot for the rich and famous; limousines and private helicopters are as regular a sight as the beautiful, white-sand beaches. Polo matches and sailing regattas are held seasonally, as is a vintage car show that lets collectors show off their antique roadsters and sportscars.

Porto Cervo is the place to go if you want to gawk at some of the world's largest and most impressive megayachts, which cruise these waters trying to outdo one another in size and grandeur throughout the months of July and August. The Yacht Club Costa Smeralda is in Porto Cervo, too, and is a regular challenger to the America's Cup.

 Alert

Hotels and restaurants along the Costa Smeralda are breathtakingly designed to lure the wealthiest of travelers not just from Europe, but also from Russia and the Middle East. They are exceptional to see, but they're perhaps not ideal for your pocketbook as an overnight location.

Su Nuraxi di Barumini

Su Nuraxi di Barumini ("the nuraghi of Barumini," in Sardinian) is the island's most important nuraghic archaeolocial site, recognized by its 1997 addition to the list of UNESCO World Heritage Sites. As the committee noted in adding the site to its list, "The complex at Barumini, which was extended and reinforced in the first half of the first millennium under Carthaginian pressure, is the finest and most complete example of this remarkable form of prehistoric architecture."

Alert

You can walk into and around Su Nuraxi di Barumini to explore, but only with a guide—and English-speaking guides are not always available on demand to help you understand what you are seeing. If you plan to tour this site, work with a travel agent in advance to hire a local guide who speaks English.

Cala Cartoe

Not known to as many vacationers as the more popular beaches on Sardinia's central eastern shore, Cala Cartoe is a gem of white sand and crystal-blue water. It's just north of the popular Cala Gonone, which sits atop a string of a half-dozen or so prime tourist-magnet beaches.

If you're looking for a place to kick back in the sand without a line of restaurants and bars in the background, then this is the beach for you. There is a kiosk that sells ice cream, sodas, and the like, but don't expect any major luncheons or dinners here.

Where to Stay

The key to booking a great hotel room on Sardinia is making your reservation early. Nightly rates don't matter so much on this island, which is so popular during the summer months that some hotels literally turn visitors away.

The price code for the hotel listings below is $=€100 or less; $$=€100 to €150; $$$=€150 to €200; $$$$=€200 or more per night, per room.

Hotel Sa Pischedda
$–$$

Located in the Medieval town of Bosa in Sardinia's northwestern section, the Hotel Sa Pischedda is housed in a late nineteenth-century palace. There are just twenty rooms, and the hotel is within walking distance of the sea. The on-site restaurant/pizzeria has been mentioned favorably in the Michelin guides to the area.

www.hotelsapischedda.it.

Hotel Il Querceto Dorgali
$–$$

This twenty-room hotel is in Dorgali, close to Cala Gonone in the middle of Sardinia's eastern shore. It offers inclusive packages such as half-board (continental breakfast with four-course dinner daily); "room and canyon" (a room plus an English-speaking guided tour of the nearby canyon); and the self-explanatory "stay seven, pay six" or "stay fourteen, pay eleven."

www.ilquerceto.com.

Hotel Villa Selene
$

Also on Sardinia's eastern coast, in a town called Ogliastra, is the Hotel Villa Selene. The hotel is actually four separate, partly connected, private houses with a total of seventy-seven rooms. The on-site restaurant promises "the flavor of grandmother's recipes," and there are billiards and television rooms if you want to relax outside your own room for a few hours.

www.hotelvillaselene.net.

Hotel La Bitta
$$–$$$$

Hotel La Bitta is also in Ogliastra, offering a more upscale beachfront option with waterfront-view rooms and suites. The highest-end rooms have private terraces with swimming pools sized to accommodate two people, along with private hot tubs. There are multiple bars and restaurants on site, as well as a spa and a private yacht that you can rent for excursions.

www.hotellabitta.it.

Euro Hotel
$–$$

This hotel is in Nuoro, an inland town in central Sardinia that offers access to great nature walks and hiking as well as relatively nearby beaches (they're about a half-hour drive). There are fifty-four rooms, all with private bathrooms and some remodeled to accommodate handicapped access.

www.eurohotelnuoro.it.

Where to Eat

You can spend a little or a lot of money when dining out in Sardinia, but no matter your price point, it's always a good idea to stick with fresh fish and seafood. This island is world-renowned for the freshness of its daily catch.

The price code for the restaurant entrees below is $=€25 or less; $$=€26 to €50; $$$=€51 to €75; $$$$=€100 or more.

Ristorante Cocus
$-$$

Located in Cagliari, the Ristorante Cocus offers a traditional menu as well as multiple prix fixe options that range from about €20 to €30 apiece. The traditional menu is heavy on fish and seafood, but there are enough meat dishes available to keep any serious carnivores content.

www.ristorantecocus.it.

Angedras
$$-$$$

This waterfront restaurant in Alghero offers elegantly presented fish and more, with outdoor tables that overlook a waterfront promenade. There are prix fixe menus along with à la carte offerings, and the soothing, upscale interior is a nice break for the senses of any weary or overburdened traveler.

www.angedrasrestaurant.it.

Andreini
$$–$$$

Also in Alghero, Andreini is a Michelin-reviewed eatery with a menu that includes pasta, fish, meat—and a tasting menu if you want to try them all. Dishes are simple in terms of ingredients and bursting with complexity in terms of flavor. The wine list is not primarily regional, but instead is regularly rearranged to accompany the specials from the chef.

www.ristorantiandreini.it.

CHAPTER 15

Italian Food

*M*angi, mangi! It's impossible to think of Italy without salivating. You can literally eat your way through the country's various regions, sampling everything from pizza to pesto in the land where they originated. From pasta with spicy Bolognese sauce to sweet, cream-filled cannoli on Sicily, the delicious offerings of Italy virtually demand that you travel with elastic-waistband pants. This chapter offers a look at the traditional foods and cooking experiences that will whet your appetite throughout Italy.

Cooking Vacations

Eating, of course, starts with cooking, and you can enjoy both during a vacation in Italy. Yes, there are more than enough restaurants to satisfy your desire for true regional food, but if you're the type who loves to be in the kitchen, then you can have just as much fun learning how to make a traditional dish from a local expert. Some tour packages incorporate cooking classes and tastings everywhere from major cities to rustic farms, letting you create the gastronomic itinerary of your dreams.

One English-speaking agency that has spent nearly a decade specializing in food-oriented tours of Italy is Delicious Italy, *www.deliciousitaly.com*. Another good English-speaking resource is Cooking Vacations, *www.cooking-vacations.com*, which has offices in Boston, Massachusetts, as well as in Italy. These and other agencies offer everything from single cooking classes to multiday tours with tastings and instruction around an entire region.

Here's a brief look at just a few of the cooking-oriented vacation packages that are available.

Bologna Cooking School

This school offers lessons that go well beyond the stove—specifically, to the local markets and specialty food shops, where you can learn how to choose ingredients before dicing a single thing. Actual cooking demonstrations include handmade egg pasta, classic Bolognese sauce, traditional *bolliti misti* (mixed boiled meat), and dessert cakes often eaten during the carnival season. *www.bolognacookingschool.com.*

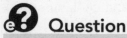 **Question**

Are cooking classes in Italy for adults only?
Cooking Vacations offers a week-long program on the Amalfi Coast that teaches children how to make antipasto, fresh pasta, risotto, fish, meat, pizza, and lemon gelato—that last one after picking their own lemons from a grove. Children as young as three can participate.

Hotel Gritti Gourmet Experience

The Hotel Gritti Palace is a luxury hotel on the Grand Canal in Venice, built in 1525 and still just as impressive as it was when the city's doge lived there. Chefs from the hotel's restaurant, including the on-site executive chef, offer cooking courses alongside visiting chefs and regional cookbook authors. The cuisine is classic Venetian, with tips on presentation for even the most elegant affairs. *www.venice-hotel-gritti.com.*

Renaissance Women

This eight-day tour on the Amalfi Coast is for independent women travelers, or groups of women including mothers, daughters, and grandmothers. It intermixes hands-on cooking classes with optional activities such as shopping tours and painting demonstrations. Tasting dinners and informative talks about important Renaissance women are also part of the package. *www.cookingvacations.com*.

Taormina Cooking Classes

There are multiple cooking itineraries available in and around Taormina, on the island of Sicily. Some include tours of local markets and cheese factories, while others focus on local wine cellars with instruction on wine-and-food pairings during exclusive tastings. Of course, there is also bound to be a thick, rich slice of Sicilian pizza along the way. *www.deliciousitaly.com*.

The Language of a Meal

In Italy, unlike in the United States, you don't typically order an appetizer, main course, and dessert. There are more courses available for each meal, usually smaller than the ones you would find in New York or Chicago. You could skip a course (or three) if you wanted to, but in general, a full meal will appear on the menu as follows:

- *Apertivo*, a pre-meal aperitif such as vermouth
- *Antipasto*, similar to an appetizer and always served before the meal
- *Primo*, your first course, typically carbohydrate-rich dishes such as pasta or risotto
- *Secondo*, your second course, almost always fish or meat
- *Contorno*, a side dish such as vegetables, especially if your *secondo* does not include a salad

- *Formaggio e frutta*, your first dessert, literally translated as "cheese and fruit"
- *Dolce*, your main dessert, such as gelato or tartufo
- *Caffé*, your post-dinner coffee or espresso
- *Digestivo*, a post-meal drink such as grappa or limoncello, intended to aid digestion

Note that restaurants in Italy don't all fall into the same category of "full service." A bar or *caffé*, for instance, will serve only drinks. An *osteria* typically serves local food, sometimes without a written menu and based solely on what is available in the daily markets. A *paninoteca* is a sandwich shop, while a *pizzeria* is the place to grab a slice with cheese. A *trattoria* is an informal restaurant, often family owned, while a *ristorante* is the full bore of upscale service and printed menus.

Pasta, Pasta, Pasta

Lest there be any confusion about just how important noodles are in Italy's culture, know that the word "pasta" is actually Italian for "dough." Nobody is sure exactly where pasta originated, in part because there are more than 350 shapes and styles of known pasta—thus making an original definition troublesome.

 **Essential**

If you plan to travel in Venice, you might skip the pasta altogether and instead devote your entire daily allotment of carbohydrates to risotto. Sure, you can find a bowl of spaghetti or a piece of pizza on the Grand Canal, but the Veneto region's specialty dishes favor rice instead of noodles. Risotto also is popular in the eastern Piedmont and western Lombardy regions.

The U.S. National Pasta Association (*www.ilovepasta.org*) says that pasta as we know it today originated in Sicily, after Arabs conquered the island centuries before the unification of Italy as a nation. The Chinese might argue, but either way, Italy continues to be known for its pasta today.

Types and Shapes of Pasta

Pasta can be made fresh or dried. Dried pasta typically doesn't include eggs as an ingredient and thus can be stored far longer than fresh pasta. It also has fewer milligrams of cholesterol, if you're reading labels. According to the written laws of Italy, dried pasta made within the country's borders may only be made using durum wheat flour or durum wheat semolina, both of which are high in protein and gluten. This is why pasta sometimes tastes differently in Italy and why a smaller dish will often leave you feeling fuller.

Alert

If you are following a gluten-free diet, then you need to avoid dried pasta in Italy. Stick to fresh pasta, but be sure to ask what is being used as the base flour. Different *trattorias* and *ristorantes* use different ingredients for their specialty pastas.

In general, types of pasta can be categorized as long noodles, short noodles, minute noodles, and *pasta all'uovo* (fresh egg pasta). Examples of long noodles would include *spaghetti*, *fettuccine*, and *vermicelli*, while examples of short noodles would include *penne*, *farfalle* (bowties), and *conchiglie* (shells). Many of the most common pasta shapes are shown with illustrations at *www.ilovepasta .org*, if you want to memorize a few new names before flying to Rome.

Pasta Sauces

Of course, one of the best things about any type or shape of pasta is the sauce that comes atop it. Most Americans think of tomato or marinara sauce as the classic Italian offering, but depending on the region, that's not always the case. In Genoa, for instance, it can be hard to find a red sauce on any *ristorante* menu. The city is the birthplace of pesto—made from olive oil, basil, and pine nuts—and that's often the chef's sauce of choice no matter what kind of noodles you order.

 Fact

Fettucine alfredo, made with a sauce of Parmesan cheese, butter, and heavy cream, is actually the American name for a dish in Italy known as *fettucine al burro e panna*. And don't expect to find shrimp or chicken alfredo, either. They are Americanized versions of the classic Italian recipe.

In general, thin noodles tend to be served with lighter sauces while thicker styles of pasta come with richer sauces. Bolognese sauce, for instance, is a meat-based *ragu* that is quite hearty and thus often served with thicker noodles. Indeed, in Bologna the sauce is traditionally served only with *tagliatelle* or *lasagne* noodles. Ordering the meat sauce atop *spaghetti* will instantly mark you as a tourist in Bologna, at least among the locals who are connoisseurs.

In southern Italy, you will more often find thinner noodles paired with sauces made from tomatoes, olive oil, and garlic. Fresh vegetables or fish can be added, too, for sauces such as *pasta con le sarde* (which includes fresh sardines).

Pizza

Pizza has been cooked throughout the world since at least the 1800s and may have existed in multiple forms even earlier than that. The dish as you know it nowadays was born in Naples when poor people started using tomatoes as a topping to increase the nutritional value of flat bread. The city's Antica Pizzeria Port'Alba is believed to be the world's first pizzeria. It opened in 1738 and is still serving up slices today.

Marinara and Margherita

The people of Naples believe that true pizza comes in only two varieties: marinara and margherita. Marinara includes toppings of tomato, oregano, garlic, olive oil, and basil, while margherita includes tomato, mozzarella, and basil. Marinara gets its name from fishermen in the Bay of Naples, who used to eat pizza after a long day of working at sea, while margherita takes its name from Queen Margherita of Savoy, who thought pizza should be made using the colors of the Italian flag (red tomatoes, white cheese, and green basil).

Believe it or not, there's even a group called the True Neapolitan Pizza Association that recognizes only these two recipes and provides explicit instructions for cooking a purist pizza, right down to the temperature of the wood-fired oven and the proper technique for flattening the dough (use hands instead of a rolling pin). The pizza you will find in Naples is often different from that in other parts of the country, such as in Rome, where thin crust is all the rage.

Other Varieties

Of course, there are far more varieties of pizza available in Italy and the rest of the world today (just don't let your friends in Naples hear you call it pizza before you eat it). Toppings include all sorts of vegetables and meats, creative sauces, and even pasta

or chicken parmesan. White pizza is made with ricotta cheese instead of only mozzarella, and some restaurants get highly creative and offer versions such as taco pizza (with jalapeño peppers, nacho cheese, and chili). Breakfast pizza is also popular in some locations, with eggs and sausage replacing tomato sauce and pepperoni.

Question

Did Sicilian pizza really originate in Sicily?
Yes—but it's not the same Sicilian pizza that most Americans would recognize. A true Sicilian pizza is defined by its lack of mozzarella cheese; pecorino is used instead. The thick-dough, square pizzas so often called Sicilian in the United States are actually more like the square-baked *pizza al taglio* or *pizza rustica* in Italy.

In general, you will be able to find all kinds of pizza in Italy—even in the more tourist-oriented parts of Naples. The slices that are served from carts are often just as tasty as the more expensive pizzas in *ristorantes*. Follow your nose and you'll do just fine.

From the Sea

Italy's proximity to the sea makes it a natural home for fish and shellfish dishes. In the Puglia region, for instance, you are bound to see fresh-caught oysters and mussels on virtually every menu. The Calabria region is typically a gastronomic haven for lobster, shrimp, squid, and sea urchin. Islands such as Sardinia and Sicily, known for many types of cuisine, are also obvious locations to indulge in fresh fish (written as *pesce* on your menu) such as tuna, sea bass, and swordfish.

You can get fish everywhere in Italy, of course, but just as in any other country, the freshest ingredients are those available nearby. Stick to the coastal areas and islands when sampling fresh fish and seafood, and you will not be disappointed.

⊖! Alert

If you order fish as the main part of your meal, don't be startled to have it arrive at the table with its eyeballs looking up at you. The tradition in Italy is to serve fish whole, though you can usually request that the kitchen decapitate and debone it before you dine. With shellfish, you'll often have to remove shells and heads yourself.

Shellfish lovers will be interested to know that Italian *ristorantes* tend to offer more types of shrimp and prawns than you'll typically find at the seafood market in St. Louis or New Orleans. Each offers the taste of shrimp, of course, but with subtle variations. Some versions of shrimp and prawns that you might see on a menu in Italy include *canocchie* (mantis shrimp), *gamberoni* (jumbo prawns), *mazzancolle* (triple-grooved shrimp), and *scampi* (large prawns with claws).

That last type, *scampi*, is almost a cross between a shrimp and a lobster. The name confuses some Italian chefs who aren't used to the American tradition of ordering "shrimp scampi," meaning shrimp in a white butter sauce. In Italy, you have to order just that—shrimp with white butter sauce—because the phrase "shrimp scampi" is redundant to an Italian-speaker, meaning "shrimp with shrimp."

Meats

Carnivores, have no fear: Italy has plenty to offer you. Yes, the nation is largely surrounded by water, but its inland grazing areas make for some outstanding meats. There are hams, sausages, and steaks galore, each prepared to local tastes. Here's a look at some of the most popular meat dishes, and the regions where you can taste them at their best.

Sopressata

You are most likely to find this type of dry-cured salami in and around Venice. Most of the time, it's made from pork, but there are beef versions as well. It's seasoned with hot pepper and hung out to dry for as long as three months before being stored in jars full of olive oil. *Sopressata* is quite tasty atop crackers, or as one of several meats in a sandwich (as are most Italian salamis, and there is quite a variety depending on where you are traveling).

 Fact

Historically, salami has been a popular food among Italian peasants because it can be stored without refrigeration for as long as a year without going bad. Originally, the word salami was used to describe all kinds of cured meats, including pork, beef, venison, lamb, goat, and horse. Various styles of salami can still be found in the different regions of Italy.

The *sopressata* that you will find in Italy is similar to the supersada that some Italian immigrants make and sell in the northeastern United States. That's why it's so often sought out by American travelers.

Bistecca alla Fiorentina

This is the signature steak of Tuscany, a cut that, in American restaurants, you would likely see listed as a porterhouse or a T-bone. Cuts can be as thick as two finger widths, and they're served with the bone intact. Sauces are not traditionally used, only a seasoning of salt, pepper, and olive oil that lets the flavor of the meat dominate your palate. The steak is usually served rare, with red wine and a side dish of beans.

If you want the truest form of *bistecca alla Fiorentina,* look for a cut that comes from a farm in the Chiana Valley. The breed renowned for the finest taste is known as Maremma, which is also the name of an area in Italy that crosses the border between southern Tuscany and northern Lazio.

Essential

Can't get enough *prosciutto*? Attend the Festival del Prosciutto di Parma, a month-long celebration of the meat that typically begins in late August and runs during the weekends throughout September in the twelve municipalities of the Parma hills. Tastings, exhibitions, and entertainment are all part of the fun. The website for the festival is *www.festivaldelprosciuttodiparma.com.*

Prosciutto

Prosciutto is the Italian word for ham, and in Italy it refers to a specific cut of pork versus the way that pork is served, as is the case in the United States. You may think of *prosciutto* as ultra-thin slices served raw, often atop fresh melon as an appetizer. In Italy, there is both *prosciutto crudo* (served raw) and *prosciutto cotto* (cooked). The best *prosciutto* is typically found in the Tuscany and Emilia regions, with names you might recognize such as *prosciutto di Parma,* meaning from Parma. If you really want to learn the differences, companies such as Parma Golosa (*www.parmagolosa.it*)

specialize in gourmet tours that include the ham factories and local restaurants with tasting menus included.

Dishes in which you can enjoy *prosciutto* range from antipasto to pasta, and from mozzarella appetizers to pizza. If you love the stuff, you can literally enjoy it several meals a day in Italy without ever having it the same way twice.

Cheese

The mozzarella oozing off your pizza is just the beginning when it comes to sampling the cheeses of Italy. Parmesan, ricotta, mascarpone—this is the place where all these delicious options originate, and where you can taste them at the height of their local flavor. Cheese is such an important part of Italy's culinary tradition that after the global economic crisis hit in 2008, the government created a "cheese industry bailout plan" to buy 100,000 wheels of Parmigiano-Reggiano and donate them to charity.

The subtle textures and flavors of various cheeses are taken as seriously by Italian producers as are the variations in local wines. You could try fifteen types of parmesan, for instance, or a dozen styles of provolone, and never enjoy the exact same flavor twice. The art of cheese making in this part of the world dates back to the Roman Empire, and it is estimated that there are some 400 different cheese variations made within Italy's modern borders. With that in mind, here are some of the more popular cheeses that you might want to sample during your vacation in Italy.

- *Fontina Val d'Aosta*, often served during the dessert course, is also the primary ingredient in *fonduta*, or cheese fondue.
- *Gorgonzola*, which takes its name from a town near Milan, is often an ingredient in risotto and can make a tasty topping for salads or pizza.

- *Mascarpone*, a specialty of the Lombardy region, is the main ingredient in the popular dessert *tiramisu*. Sometimes, you can also find it in risotto dishes.
- *Mozzarella* is a generic term for several kinds of Italian cheeses. *Mozzarella di bufala* is made from water buffalo milk, while *mozzarella fior di latte* is made from cow's milk. The *mozzarella di bufala* from the Campania region is generally considered the best, and is often enjoyed in a *caprese* salad mixed with slices of tomatoes.
- *Parmigiano*, known in the United States as parmesan, is named after the town of Parma and by law in Italy must come from the Parmigiano-Reggiano region.
- *Pecorino*, all styles of which are made from sheep's milk, is a hard cheese often found in pasta dishes on the Italian island of Sardinia.
- *Provolone*, which originated in southern Italy, is produced mainly in the Lombardia and Veneto regions, making it ultra-fresh from sandwich vendors in Venice.
- *Ricotta*, often used in dishes such as American lasagna, is often used in Italian desserts such as cheesecake and cannoli. It is sometimes served on its own as a dessert, perhaps covered in chocolate shavings.
- *Romano*, named after the city of Rome, is a hard cheese typically served grated over a pasta or other dish. Purists say *romano* must be made from sheep's milk, though the romano you have likely tried in the United States probably came from cow's milk.

Note that in many parts of Italy, you will be served cheeses that are unpasteurized. United States law, since 1944, has required that all soft-milk cheeses—even those imported from places such as Italy—must be aged at least sixty days to avoid spreading diseases such as salmonella. The rules are different in Italy, and while the cheeses are often said to taste better if left unpasteurized, outbreaks do occasionally occur. Keep an eye on the local media to ensure your own safety depending on when and where you do your own cheese tasting.

Sweet Treats

Haven't packed on enough pounds with all that pasta, pizza, meat, and cheese? Rest assured; the desserts you'll find on local menus are just as delicious as the first and second courses. Whether you enjoy desserts that are crunchy or soft, frozen or filled, Italy's sweet treats are a delight.

Zeppole

Zeppole is also known as St. Joseph's Day cake, since Italians traditionally eat the pastry as part of the St. Joseph's Day celebration on March 19 every year. A *zeppole* is lighter-tasting than it sounds, made traditionally from fried dough rolled in powdered sugar and then topped and filled with cream, jelly, or a mixture of butter and honey.

Other variations you might see include savory *zeppole*, such as those filled with anchovies, which are popular in the Calabria region. Think of them as the Italian version of filled doughnuts, and let your imagination run wild. They're best enjoyed hot, as are many doughnuts fresh from the oven.

🅔❗ Alert

At many festivals in Italy, you will see signs offering "six *zeppole* for €3," or some such bulk-purchase discount. *Zeppole* may be small, but they are filling. Most people, even large men, can eat no more than two or three at a time. Don't waste your money on a huge bag of *zeppole* unless you have more than one mouth to feed.

Cannoli

Cannoli originated in Sicily, where it continues to be a popular sweet treat today. Each *cannolo* (the singular form of the word) is made from a tube-shaped pastry shell and a sweet filling. Historically, the fillings are made from a ricotta cheese base, but there are also *cannoli* filled with *mascarpone*.

In the United States, you can find *cannoli* filled with sweet custard, but that's not the case in Italy, where tradition still reigns. There is some leeway in the Old Country, though, for enhancements, as evidenced by *cannoli* shells being dipped in chocolate before they are filled.

Panna Cotta

Panna cotta means "cooked cream" in Italian. It's a dish made from milk, cream, sugar, and gelatin, and is typically served with a fruit sauce and mixed berries. It's custard-like in texture, and can be served either cold or lukewarm just after setting from a mold. If you want to go decadent, order *panna cotta* with a chocolate or fudge sauce topping. It's not traditional, but it sure is good.

Biscotti

Biscotti is Italian for "biscuit" and can actually refer to multiple types of the crunchy sweets, as opposed to the single type of long biscuit typically served with coffee in the United States. What Americans typically describe as *biscotti* is actually known as *cantucci*, which comes from Tuscany. In Italy, you will sometimes be offered *biscotti* for dipping in wine as well as in coffee.

Tartufo

Tartufo is the word for "truffle" in Italian, but it actually originated in France. In the United States, a truffle is a bite-sized chocolate, but in Italy *tartufo* means an ice cream dessert. Traditionally, there are two flavors of ice cream covered in a chocolate shell. Sometimes, there is fruit within the ice cream, and you also can enjoy *tartufo* that is coated in nuts, crushed cookies, or cocoa powder.

 Fact

Of all the Italian desserts, *tartufo* is probably the easiest to make at home. Line a baking sheet with waxed paper, plop a scoop of ice cream onto it, make an indent in the middle, drop in some fruit (such as a maraschino cherry), add a little more ice cream to cover the fruit, drop the ice cream ball briefly into a pot of melted chocolate, return to the wax paper and freeze.

Gelato

Gelato looks like ice cream and is served from stands that resemble Baskin-Robbins, but the taste is far richer and creamier than what you have experienced atop a cone in the United States. *Gelato*, when made properly, is blended so that it contains less than 55 percent air, which makes it denser and fuller in flavor than many types of ice cream.

As with ice cream, you can buy *gelato* in a cup or on a cone, one scoop or two, in countless flavors. Expect to find old standbys such as chocolate, vanilla, and pistachio, but also look for regional variations including hazelnut, peach, and *tiramisu*.

CHAPTER 16

Italian Wine

C hianti. Barolo. Brunello. Sangiovese. Pinot Grigio. Wine labels bearing these names are sold around the globe, making their way onto dinner tables and into wine cellars to be savored year after year. Italy rivals France in terms of wine production, and occasionally produces more bottles than the world-famous French regions of Bordeaux, Burgundy, and Champagne. What's different about Italian wines is that they are meant not to be the star of the day, but to complement the food from the region where they are cultivated.

Italy's Wine-Making History

Inland regions such as Tuscany are heralded today as the cradle of Italian wine making, but Italy's history of viticulture—the practice of growing grapes specifically to make wine—actually got its start in what is present-day Sicily. It was the Greeks who taught the ancestors of today's Sicilians how to ferment the good stuff, which spread to other parts of modern Italy during the second century B.C. Many of the grapes were grown and harvested by slaves, a dark blotch on an otherwise grand tradition.

It wasn't until 1963 that the Italian parliament created the wine classification system that is the basis for what exists today. The aim was to ensure that wines are actually produced in the regions their labels indicate. The system was modified in 1992 to make room for Super Tuscans—a blend made with grapes from different regions—which winemakers began producing in the 1970s despite the fact that they violated existing regulations.

 Fact

The Roman Empire knew it had a good monopoly when it outlawed the production of wine beyond Italy's borders. People from all over present-day Europe would pay handsomely for the intoxicating stuff, trading slaves in return. Today, Italy exports more wine to the United States than any other country.

Classification System

The Italian system puts all wine produced within the nation's borders into one of four classifications:

- **Vino da Tavola (VdT),** the lowest level of table wine. These may be made from grapes grown in various regions, and may indicate nothing more on their labels than whether the wine is red, white, or rosé.
- **Indicazione Geografia Tipica (IGT),** which generally means a more esteemed level of table wine. This category was created to recognize superb wines that previously were relegated to the VdT category, including Super Tuscans.
- **Denominazione di Origine Controllata (DOC),** meaning wines made from a specific and controlled area by following rules for permitted grape varieties, alcoholic content, and aging. There are several hundred DOCs, and wines that fall into this category will have the letters DOC plus their area listed on the label.

- **Denominazione di Origine Controllata e Garantita (DOCG),** the highest level. There are fewer than forty DOCG areas in existence as of this writing. These wines follow all DOC rules plus additional, stricter controls, including analytical testing of composition.

Which classification is the best? It depends on your personal taste buds. Many a wine lover will argue that a VdT from an outstanding producer is just as good with any given meal as a DOCG—and likely much less expensive. As you taste Italian wines, you will notice that those ranked at the same level of classification are often very different from one another, even if they're from neighboring vineyards. It all boils down to the angle at which the sun hits the grapes, how much sunlight they get each day, in what kind of soil they are grown, and how much water reaches the roots—variables that can substantially, at least to a practiced connoisseur, change the aroma and flavor of wines made from grapes that were grown just a few rows apart.

In many cases, Italian wines reflect the cuisines of their regions. Wines in Sicily taste very different from those in Venice or Genoa. If you want to enjoy tastings as you travel, then consider focusing on wines from regions as opposed to DOCs or DOCGs. Don't simply order a Chianti because you're in Italy; if you're in Tuscany, for instance, try a Super Tuscan.

Today's Wine Regions

It would take an entire book to describe every DOC and DOCG. It's far easier to consider wines as being from the northwest, northeast, central, and southern parts of Italy, each of which have their share of DOC and DOCG zones. Some areas, like central Italy, have more premier zones than other areas, but you will be able to find top-quality wines no matter what part of Italy is your vacation base.

In general, wines from each of these four geographic areas are grown in similar conditions, so the various wine styles, tastes, and characteristics will be relatively similar. You can't find a locally grown Super Tuscan in Sicily, for instance, nor would you look in Venice to find a locally bottled vintage from the foot of the Alps.

Of course, there will be good and bad wines in all four of the areas, and you'll have to do some taste testing to discover your personal preferences as well as the best of each region's better-known brands. But hey, that's the fun of exploring wine in Italy, right? You get to go where the grapes are grown and decide whether you prefer a €10 bottle of table wine to a fancier brand that would cost you five or even fifty times as much anywhere else in the world.

The Northwest

Italy's northwest, stretching from Milan to Genoa and the foot of the Alps, is not known for producing the largest quantity of wine in Italy—but it is the home of the Piedmont area, which is where grapes are grown for Barolo and Barbaresco reds, as well as Asti Spumante sparkling wine. Though parts of northwestern Italy share a border with France, the Italian growers stay true to their roots, literally. Don't expect any French influences here, but do expect some top-quality Italian wines. Piedmont alone boasts more DOC and DOCG zones than any other region in the nation.

If you're traveling in northwestern Italy with an eye toward sampling local wines, spend a few nights in Alba, on the Tanaro River. It's the nearest decent-size town to the local vineyards that produce Barolo and Barbaresco wines, and it's the home of the white truffle, a delicacy mushroom that's in season from September through December and costs about $1,000 per gram in American stores. Some tour operators, such as Arblaster & Clarke (*www.winetours.co.uk*), can organize a "truffle hunter" to take you into the woods between wine tastings during the autumn season.

❓ Question

Barolo

Barolo is often called "the king of wines, and the wine of kings." It is regularly renowned as the finest wine that one can get from Italy, and aficionados regularly clamor for cases at auctions from London to New York City. It's made from the Nebbiolo grape, which is grown only in the Piedmont, Aosta Valley, and Lombardy regions of Italy. That may have something to do with the weather, which typically includes a heavy fog in late October. Nebbiolo derives from the Piedmontese word *nebbia*, or fog.

More than 1,100 vineyards produce Barolo, which, at everyday wine stores in the United States, start at about $40 per bottle and go well into the hundreds of dollars. The vintages widely regarded as the finest of the past few decades are 1982, 1989, 1990, 1996, and 1997 (though 1998 and 1999 have many fans as well).

Barbaresco

Barbaresco, which takes its moniker from the 650-person Piedmont municipality of the same name, is also made from the nebbiolo grape. Though Barbarescos and Barolos are grown about ten miles apart, they do have differences. In general, a young

Barbaresco tastes better than a young Barolo, but a Barbaresco will not last as long in the bottle as a Barolo.

 **Alert**

In Piedmont, you may be asked which side you favor in the "Barolo Wars." This is a disagreement between classic producers, who let the wine ferment for at least three weeks and age in wooden casks for years, and modern producers, who prefer fermentation of less than two weeks and shorter aging periods in oak barrels. Neither is necessarily right.

In addition, Barolos tend to be more expensive than Barbarescos, even though there is more Barolo out there to be had. Each year, the production of Barbaresco is only about 35 percent that of Barolo. The best vintage years of Barbaresco tend to mirror those for Barolo.

Asti Spumante

Asti Spumante is a white, sparkling wine made near the town of Asti in Piedmont. It comes from the moscato bianco grape, which is also cultivated to make wine in France, Australia, and South Africa. Asti Spumante is primarily known as a dessert wine and has earned quite a following in the United States, where it has been aggressively marketed by the Italian company Martini & Rossi. Asti Spumante is often promoted as a good sparkling wine to serve in lieu of French Champagne for events such as New Year's Eve.

Because Asti Spumante is produced in mass quantities, you can often find a decent bottle, even in the United States, for less than $10. The trick when traveling in Italy is to look for the more expensive brands being sold at low prices.

The Northeast

Italy's northeastern wine producing region, easily accessible from Venice, is known primarily for white wines. The two best-known types are Soave and Pinot Grigio, both typically described as "light and fresh" versus "complex and rich." If all you know is California chardonnay, the white wines of northeastern Italy will surprise your palate—and are especially refreshing during the hottest months of July and August.

Essential

If you're traveling in Venice in April, be ready to explore the entire region of Veneto, home to the annual Vinitaly festival. It is Italy's most important wine fair, dating to 1967. Italian and international exhibitors bring their best vintages here, to promote alongside presentations that include food and wine pairings, technical tastings, and more. Check out *www.vinitaly.com* for more information.

Soave

Soave is described as a dry white wine, made primarily from the garganega grape. The wine takes its name from the town of Soave, home to about 6,800 people and a Medieval castle that's worth a look if you decide to go wine tasting. In fact, the third Sunday of May, Soave hosts a "Medieval White Wine Festival," combining the area's history with locally produced vintages.

Typically, Soave is served before dinner, ideally with hors d'oeuvres or a salad course. The bottles labeled as Soave DOC are typically the best value. Soave Classico DOC are grown in the original, traditional zone, while those labeled Recioto di Soave Superiore DOCG must follow the most stringent production rules. They often sell for more than $150 in the United States, sometimes more than $200 per bottle.

Pinot Grigio

Pinot grigio is a white wine made from the grape of the same name, which is known as pinot gris in France. Its use for wine is believed to have originated there, and today it is grown everywhere from Canada to New Zealand. In Italy, it is popular among vineyards in the Lombardy region, which is the easternmost of all regions in the northern part of the country.

 Fact

The brand of pinot grigio known as Santa Margherita, which has found countless loyal American followers in recent years (creating a price spike in the process), comes from the Trentino-Alto Adige region of Italy, just north of the Veneto region, which is home to Venice.

Though pinot grigio doesn't have a lot of fans in the wine aficionado clubs (they prefer heartier chardonnays), it is popular with the public, and is sometimes the most imported wine of the year in the United States. You can find countless brands below $10 per bottle, so your goal in Italy should be to look for pricier options offered at reasonable rates.

Central Italy

Just as with Italian food, central Italy's Tuscany is the heart of Italian wine. This is where you will find locally produced reds such as Chianti and Brunello di Montalcino. The former has been a favorite the world over for ages, while Brunello has only more recently become a premier offering.

The region of Umbria is also in central Italy, and is best known for the white wine called Orvieto. It has the same name as the place where it has been produced since the Middle Ages.

Chianti

Chianti is perhaps the best known of all of Italy's wines. It is mass produced, can be highly affordable, and is served in Italian restaurants globally. Even still, the "table" version of Chianti that you know from home is likely far less complex than the more sophisticated offerings you can find in Italy. In fact, if you look closely at labels, you will see that some wines sold as Chianti in the United States aren't from the region at all.

 **Question**

Why do some Chiantis come in odd-shaped bottles?
Traditionally, Chianti was bottled in a *fiasco*, the Italian word for a bottle with a long, thin neck and a wide, round bottom. The bottom was covered in a straw basket. Today, many producers favor Bordeaux-style bottles, making Chianti look, at least on store shelves, a lot like every other kind of red wine.

Since the mid-1990s, Italian law has stated that true Chianti must be made with at least 80 percent Sangiovese grapes, which are believed to have originated in Tuscany. However, these grapes also grow in the United States, Australia, Central America, and South America, which is why the word Chianti is sometimes used in a generic sense, referring to the grape instead of to the Chianti geographical region. The taste of Chianti in Italy may be far different from what you have experienced at home.

Brunello di Montalcino

Brunello di Montalcino, like Chianti, is made from Sangiovese grapes—but more specifically, from a clone of those grapes known as Brunello. Hence the name Brunello di Montalcino, meaning grapes from the area of Montalcino, which is about seventy miles southwest of Florence. This type of wine was considered rare as recently as World War II, but today there are more than 200 producers in the area. Collectors' demand for this much-sought-after red remain high, putting Brunello di Montalcino in the same price category as Barolo.

 Fact

In 2008, Italy endured *Brunellopoli*—a scandal in which several Brunello producers were accused of using unauthorized grapes to make their wines more popular on the international market. Laboratory tests revealed most of the charges to be false, but the widespread reaction to possible fraud shows just how seriously connoisseurs take the Brunello name.

What makes Brunello grapes different from Sangiovese grapes is their adaptation to growing in the Montalcino region's *terroir*—its earth. The grapes ripen with a more fleshy texture, which gives Brunello di Montalcino wine its distinctive taste. It's especially popular with Americans; about one in three bottles of Brunello di Montalcino are exported for sale in the United States. Sometimes, you will see these wines listed on American menus at more than $600 per bottle.

Orvieto

Umbria and Lazio are the regions in central Italy where Orvieto is produced, within the DOCs Orvieto and Orvieto Classico. The wine comes from a blend of grapes, primarily grechetto and trebbiano. Grechetto is believed to be of Greek origin and is often used in dessert wines, while trebbiano dates back to the Roman Empire and is key to the production of Cognac in France.

This primary combination of grapes makes Orvieto dry, but semi-sweet when compared with other white wines. It is often served with appetizers and cheeses, but also pairs nicely with some main courses of fish. As with Chianti, Orvieto is widely available at all price points, so when you are in Italy, look for unusual producers that you can't taste at home.

Southern Italy

The type of wine you will probably recognize from southern Italy is Marsala, from Sicily. In fact, southern Italy has long been noted primarily for its whites, though there are a few reds, including Taurasi from the Campagnia region, that are now gaining favor as well.

Marsala

Marsala wine shares a name with the Sicilian seaport city on the western side of the island. If you've ever enjoyed a dish of veal or chicken Marsala, you have the people of this city to thank. They fortified their local Marsala wine so that it would be able to withstand long shipping distances across the oceans, and that fortification made today's Marsala more like port than wine, ideal for an *aperitif* or use in cooking.

There are actually three styles of Marsala wine, each indicating a different level of sweetness. *Secco* is the lowest level, followed by *semisecco* and *sweet*. It's the sweetness that makes Marsala wine so popular as a cooking ingredient, because when the wine is reduced over heat, it becomes almost syrupy in texture.

Essential

The leading producer of Taurasi is Feudi di San Gregorio, which in 2004 opened a multimillion-dollar facility for winemaking and hospitality tours. The vintner also offers regional tours that include food and wine pairings, if you want to see how other forms of Taurasi compare to its brand. Learn more at *www.feudi.it,* which offers information in English.

Taurasi

Taurasi is a red wine named for a town in the Campania region. It has exploded in popularity recently, with only one exporting winemaker in the area as of the early 1990s—and about 300 today. The consensus in the area is that Taurasi, made from the local Aglianico grape, can be developed on par with wines made from the Sangiovese and Nebbiolo grapes that grow so well elsewhere. Aglianico grapes grow at higher altitudes, which is perfect for the volcanic topography in southern Italy.

Super Tuscans

Super Tuscans are an unofficial classification of Italian wine. The name evolved because some producers wanted to work in ways that violated existing classifications beginning in the 1970s. Knowing full well that their products would be classified as "lowly" VdT, they intentionally balked at DOC and DOCG regulations with the hopes of impressing the international market. They succeeded, primarily in Tuscany, where they created blends such as Sangiovese and the non-native Cabernet Sauvignon. Such blends are now known as Super Tuscans, and they have amassed loyal followers the world over.

❓ Question

Who coined the phrase Super Tuscans?
It's a matter of much debate. Some sources cite the noted wine connoisseur Robert Parker, while others attribute the first usage to writer Bruce Palling of *The Independent*, a British newspaper, which published an article about the search for a perfect Chianti in 1989.

The problem with Super Tuscans is that they follow no rules or standards, and thus can be anything from exquisite to disgusting.

For a time, any grower could call a blend a Super Tuscan and earn a hefty income, a trend that soured the concept in many wine lovers' minds.

Today, there are still many superb Super Tuscans, but the prices are usually stiff—well into the range of several hundred dollars. As with all wine, let your own taste buds be your guide.

Popular Reds

Obviously, it's impossible to say which wines are "the best" in Italy. However, it is quite possible to say which wines are among the most popular from Italy, as well as which popular wines regularly garner the highest ratings from experts in the international wine press.

Bartolo Mascarello Barolo

Within the rarefied air of the Barolo community, Bartolo Mascarello's Barolo consistently earns high marks. The man for whom the winery is named died in 2005, having held firmly to traditional methods of winemaking and always producing Barolo in its purest form. His Cantina Mascarello Barolo Estate is now run by his daughter Maria Teresa, who is continuing to produce fine Barolos in the same manner.

You can taste wines and take tours of the estate without reservations. It doesn't have a website, but Mascarello is a legend in the Barolo community, so all you need to do is tell a local taxi driver, "Please take me to 15 Via Roma."

Angelo Gaja Barbaresco

The Gaja Winery owns some 250 acres of vineyards in the Piedmont region, including the Barolo and Barbaresco areas. Its current owner is Angelo Gaja, the great-grandson of Giovanni Gaja, who founded the winery in 1859. Since the 1960s, Angelo has campaigned worldwide on behalf of Barbaresco and in turn has made the name Gaja synonymous with the highest-quality bottling from that village.

If you visit the address 36 Via Torino in Barbaresco, look for the 1999, 2000, and 2004 vintages of Gaja Barbaresco. Other recent years have also received high marks from aficionados, but those three years took top honors.

 Fact

Angelo Baja is nicknamed the "bishop of Barbaresco" for his dominance in producing local wines of the highest quality from that small village, but he has also branched out to purchase vineyards in other parts of Italy, including Barolo.

Isole e Olena Chianti

A good number of Chianti producers regularly receive high marks, including Marchesi de'Frescobaldi, La Massa, and Gruppo Italiano Vini. One current favorite is Isole e Olena, an estate run by Paolo de Marchi. His family has owned the estate only since the 1960s, and he is widely regarded as the man who brought quality Chianti back to this patch of *terroir*.

Frequently noted for excellence is Isole e Olena's Chianti Classico, which is produced in the Classico sub-area of the Chianti geographic area. You may recognize the black rooster on the label of any Chianti Classico that is produced here.

Casanova di Neri Brunello di Montalcino

Casanova di Neri took the *Wine Spectator* magazine "Wine of the Year" award in 2006 for its 2001 Brunello di Montalcino, which scored a rare 100 out of 100 points and was described as "one of the greatest Brunellos of all time." It runs about $160 per bottle in the United States, obviously with limited availability because of all the media buzz.

Other recent vintages of Brunello from Casanova di Neri have received marks in the nineties—still very good—and are available for half to less than half that price. Keep an eye out for the label as much as the year.

Feudi di San Gregorio Taurasi

Feudi di San Gregorio is widely regarded as the premier wine-making estate in the region of Campania—an interesting fact, given that it has only been in the village of Sorbo Serpico since 1986. Feudi di San Gregorio is not nearly the largest winemaker in the Taurasi area, but is more like the tiny mouse whose excellence roars louder than the largest lion's. Look for the 2003 vintage, which is typically offered at a price equivalent to the $20–$40 range in the United States.

 **Essential**

If you visit the Fattoria di Fèlsina estate, be sure to bring your imagination. Yes, it is a haven of wine making today, but history shows that it was once a roadside hospital where Benedictine monks cared for ailing pilgrims. There's no evidence, unfortunately, to indicate that the monks used wine of any kind for easing their patients' pain.

Fattoria di Fèlsina Maestro Raro

Maestro Raro, a Cabernet, is one of two well-regarded Super Tuscans from Fattoria di Fèlsina (the other is Fontalloro, a Sangiovese). The winemaking estate dates back to the 1100s, but it did not gain prominence in the international wine community until the 1960s. It's located in the Chianti Classico zone, and while its Felsina

Chianti Classico Reserva Rancia remains its flagship product, the Maestro Raro Super Tuscan enjoys many followers as well.

Popular Whites

Reds coming out of Italy continue to be the most highly regarded, but there are a handful of whites worth seeking out during your travels.

Soave

The 2004 Prà Soave Classico has been called an example that "will change your view of what Soave can do," while the 2007 vintage has been hailed as "dollar for dollar, one of northern Italy's premier white wines." Indeed, the Soaves being produced by this winery in the Veneto region near Venice continue to earn praise from connoisseurs worldwide. Beyond the wine itself, the winery run by brothers Sergio and Graziano Prà is also noteworthy for its use of organic fertilizers, which are shunned by many traditional growers.

Oscar Bosio La Bruciata Moscato

Moscato d'Asti is a lesser-known alternative to the widely produced Asti Spumanti in Italy's northwest. Oscar Bosio is the third-generation producer of the family who runs the La Bruciata vineyard in the town of Valdivilla, southwest of Asti. His Moscato d'Asti is a sweet white recommended as a post-meal drink or in place of Champagne at parties. Visitors are welcome at the winery, which is one of the few that has a website in English: *www.la-bruciata.com.*

Barberani Orvieto

Barberani Cantina is near the town of Baschi in the region of Umbria. It's a large estate with nearly 250 acres, though only about half is planted with vineyards (olive groves and woodlands dominate the rest). Among the 30,000 or so cases of wine that Barberani produces each year is its Orvieto, which can often be found at prices comparable to $12 or $15 even though, year after year, it earns four- or five-star reviews from various experts. The 2004 vintage is easiest to find in wine shops outside of Italy, so look for other years to sample while you are there.

CHAPTER 17

Visiting Italy by Boat

To look at a map of Italy is to understand the nation's longstanding ties to the water. Sicily and Sardinia are the largest islands in the whole of the Mediterranean Sea, and water surrounds Italy's mainland on three sides: the Ligurian and Tyrrhenian seas to the west, the Ionian Sea to the south, and the Adriatic Sea to the east. People have been coming by boat to the Italian Peninsula since the beginning of recorded history, and you can, too. Whether you want to cruise for a single day or for several weeks, options abound for coming ashore to Italy in much the same way that other people have for centuries.

A Tradition of Boating

Merchants have been arriving on the Italian peninsula by boat for more than 1,000 years, perhaps beginning with Chinese traders who forsook the land-based Silk Road and instead favored cruising across the Arabian Sea, up the Red Sea, and into the Mediterranean Sea to the ports of Magna Grecia and the Roman Empire. These were the days when ships followed trade routes that helped to develop entire cultures from Egypt to Turkey, forming the basis of Western civilization itself.

Italy's power flourished because of these trade routes throughout the Middle Ages, because the peninsula's location made it a strategic stopover for sailors moving goods between what today are known as Asia and Western Europe. Venice, Genoa, Amalfi, and Pisa were known as the *Repubbliche Marinare*—Maritime Republics—competing with one another to create the largest, wealthiest empires extending inland from their coastal ports. They were at the height of their power when the Renaissance began, with much of the wealth generated in the port cities funding the great architecture, art, and music for which Italy is still renowned today.

 Fact

The modern flag of the *Marina Militare*, or Italian Navy, includes three horizontal stripes of green, white, and red. In the center of the white stripe is an ensign that looks like a four-square checkerboard, with designs inside of each square. Those designs are actually the four coats of arms of the historic *Repubbliche Marinare*.

The eventual invention of stronger, more seaworthy boats made it possible for some traders to bypass Italy altogether, instead taking their ships from China through the rougher seas around the southern tip of Africa and beyond to the Americas. This is when the *Repubbliche Marinare* began to decline in power. By the time of Italy's unification as a nation in modern times, Venice, Genoa, the Amalfi Coast, and Pisa were no longer major world powers.

They do, however, continue to be fantastic areas of civilization, filled with history and ports that still welcome boats of all sizes and styles today. Trade does occur, on a smaller scale than it did a few centuries ago, and it's now intermixed with everything from day ferries to international cruise ships that make tourism an economic pillar in its own right.

Large, International Cruise Ships

Most international cruise ship companies offer Mediterranean itineraries that include at least one stop in Italy. You will often see the port of Civitavecchia on the schedule. This is the main port of Rome, from which countless day tours depart for the Colosseum, the Sistine Chapel, and the rest of the city's historic sites. The longer the Mediterranean itinerary, the more sites within Italy you are likely to see. On a ten-day cruise, you might see Civitavecchia alone, while on a twenty-day cruise, you might find an itinerary that also includes Sicily and Livorno (the latter is a port city on the western edge of Tuscany, within easy striking distance of Florence).

Some cruise lines incorporate Roman history into their itineraries. Holland America (*www.hollandamerica.com*), for instance, offers a ten-day "Roman Empire" option that begins in Civitavecchia and ends in Sicily, with ports of call that include Croatia, Greece, and Turkey.

Celebrity offers an "Ancient Empires" itinerary that cruises round-trip from Civitavecchia. It includes stops in Greece, Turkey, Egypt, and Israel before returning to Italy with a visit to Naples. Other itineraries from Celebrity incorporate the ports on Sicily, in Livorno, and in Venice. The "specials" tab at *www.celebrity.com* shows current deals being offered for onboard credits on itineraries of all kinds.

🅔❗ Alert

You don't always have to fly to Europe to board a cruise ship that makes stops in Italy. Some itineraries begin in Fort Lauderdale or Miami and cross the ocean as part of sixteen-day or longer journeys into Europe. Interestingly, these cruises can be about the same price as round-trip plane fares from the United States.

Different cruise lines go into different ports, so one company's Italy-based itinerary is likely to be different from the next. If you have your heart set on a specific port of call, such as Naples or Venice, be sure that your chosen cruise ship actually goes there. Some companies do not operate in certain ports, even though their ships do stop in Italy.

Costa Cruises

You might not be as familiar with this international cruise line as you are with, say, Carnival or Princess, but that's only because its marketing program in the United States is not as strong. Costa's tagline is "Cruising Italian Style," which makes it ideal for an itinerary that includes Italy. Even if you visit other parts of Europe along the way, you will get to enjoy Italian culture and hospitality the entire time on your ship.

Costa has ships that visit nine ports in Italy: Civitavecchia, Catania (at the foot of Mount Etna), Genoa, Livorno, Naples, Olbia (on Sardinia), Portoferraio (on the island Elba), Palermo (on Sicily), and Savona (near Genoa). No single itinerary includes them all, but various options let you choose the ports that most interest you as parts of broader schedules that can also include Spain, Portugal, Egypt, and Israel. There's a "hot deals" section on the company's website, *www.costacruise.com*, where Mediterranean cruises are sometimes offered at discounts of 50 to 60 percent over published fares.

Cunard

As an upscale cruising choice, Cunard is a line whose ships visit multiple Italian ports including Alghero and Cagliari (both on Sardinia), Livorno, Messina, Naples, Palermo, Civitavecchia, Trieste (near the Slovenia border), and Venice. Shore excursions include everything from walking tours of Rome to rides in Venetian gondolas. Details are online at *www.cunard.com*.

Norwegian Cruise Line

Norwegian Cruise Line offers seven- to twenty-one-day Mediterranean itineraries, and some of the shorter ones include multiple stops in Italy. Some of the seven-day schedules, for instance, include full days in Naples, Civitavecchia, and Livorno. Some ten-day itineraries add a day in Messina as well.

In either case, you would spend nearly half your time ashore in Italian ports—a good ratio compared with a lot of other cruise companies' Mediterranean itineraries. Learn more at *www.ncl.com.*

❓ Question

Do you have to take pre-arranged excursions from cruise ships?
Absolutely not. You can get off your ship, hop in a taxi, and go see anything you would like—as long as you are back at the ship in time for departure, often later the same day. If your chosen ship is going into Venice, for instance, but has no excursions of interest, then you can walk around on your own.

Princess Cruises

Princess Cruises offers multiple Mediterranean itineraries, some of which include several stops in Italy. The twelve-day "Greek Isles and Mediterranean" option, for instance, cruises up and down both sides of the Italian peninsula with stops in Civitavecchia, Livorno, Naples, and Venice. The twelve-day "Mediterranean Collection" itinerary stops in Venice, nearby Ravenna, Messina, Sorrento (near Capri), Portofino, and Civitavecchia.

Princess offers a land-based add-on called CruiseTours. You can extend your vacation in Italy beyond your stay on the ship by purchasing the "Classic Italy" CruiseTour in addition to a cruise departing from or ending in Italy. The package includes three nights in Rome and two in Florence, with group tours as well as time for exploring on your own. Details are online at *www .princess.com*.

Smaller-Scale
Cruise Tours

The idea of seeing Italy from the water may appeal to you, but you may be put off by the thought of being aboard an enormous ship with thousands of other passengers. Or, maybe you want to visit Italy by boat without being forced to "do Rome in a day."

Luckily, a handful of tour operators offer smaller-scale cruise vacations that help you enjoy a more in-depth cultural experience within certain regions of Italy. Some incorporate onboard educational lectures from local experts, while others help you arrange small-scale shore tours to places that most large cruise ship passengers don't even know exist.

CroisiEurope

CroisiEurope is a France-based company that has been offering boat tours in Europe since 1982. It has twenty-six boats in its fleet, each of which holds 100 to 180 passengers. They all cruise on Europe's rivers, including the Po, which runs eastward from the Alps in northern Italy and drains into the Adriatic Sea near Venice.

The company offers four-, five-, and six-night itineraries along the Po, including boat tours of the Venice Lagoon and local islands in addition to land-based excursions. The longer itineraries can include a stop in Verona, made so famous by William Shakespeare's *Romeo and Juliet*.

Prices are in euro, typically between €400 and €600 per person, and do not include drinks or optional excursions. More details about the various itineraries are available in English at *www.croisieurope.com*.

Travel Dynamics International

Travel Dynamics International is a New York City-based company that, for more than thirty-five years, has offered educational programs onboard small cruise ships. This is a high-end option, with guest lecturers ranging from bestselling authors to television personalities (Bill Moyers, who has won more than thirty Emmy Awards, was a 2008 speaker). Shore excursions tend to go beyond typical tourist offerings and include receptions in private homes with local officials, museum tours by curators, and other similar options that would be impossible with a larger group.

Question

What are *navigli*?
They are a system of interconnected canals that connect Milan to the Po River. Their design is credited in part to Leonardo da Vinci. At the time of their creation, the *navigli* were important in assuring boat traffic could maneuver goods from the river into the city, but over time, virtually all of the canals have become rundown and impossible to navigate.

The ship that offers cruises in Italy is the *Callisto*, which takes just thirty-four guests. At 165 feet long, the *Callisto* is about the same size as many of the world's private motoryachts, meaning it can get into places often reserved for more exclusive travel, where large cruise ships simply don't fit. Of course, you pay for the privilege of such intimacy, with rates for nine-day itineraries starting around $7,700 per person. That price doesn't include airfare, but it does include an open bar. If you're looking for an upscale Italian cruising option, Travel Dynamics International is a natural competitor to any luxury cabin that you will find on a large, less formal cruise ship.

Two itineraries are offered aboard the *Callisto* in Italy: a circumnavigation of Sicily, and a tour of the Cinque Terre and nearby islands. Details about these two itineraries, as well as others that include Italian ports as stops within broader Mediterranean schedules, are online at *www.traveldynamicsinternational.com.*

Sicily: Crossroads of Mediterranean Civilizations

This itinerary is generally offered in the spring, from mid-April until early May, while the wildflowers are still blooming and well in advance of the annual summer onslaught of tourists. It runs round-trip from Palermo, on the northwestern coast of Sicily, and includes stops at the island's ports in Riposto, Syracuse, Porto Empedocle, Marsala, and Trapani—with day trip options to additional inland towns and villages from each port.

The Islands of Italy and the Cinque Terre

This itinerary begins at Palermo, on Sicily, and ends at Genoa. Stops in between include Lipari (where you can see the active volcanic island Stromboli), Capri, Ponza (in the Pontine Islands), Porto Torres (on Sardinia), Elba (the island where Napoleon was exiled), and Portovenere (on the mainland, in the Cinque Terre region).

Affordable Private Yachts

Smaller-scale cruising options such as Travel Dynamics International are offered at a price point that makes it worthwhile to consider small private yachts. Italy is one of the premier yacht charter destinations in the world, luring some of the finest personal boats ever built and welcoming rich and famous guests at weekly rates that are well into six figures. Those boats are fun to look at and dream about, but their presence often overshadows the perfectly lovely smaller private yachts that are also available in Italy on a far more reasonable economic scale.

In many cases, a private yacht with a captain and chef can be had for the same total cost that you might spend for a group of four or six adults to spend a week on a cruise ship with separate, balcony-level cabins. You can book a private yacht either as one person's expense or as a cost split among your group, and you can control expenses such as food provisions and fuel usage, which are determined by the itinerary and menus you choose (instead of being predetermined by a cruise ship company). Private yacht vacations tend to be excellent for multigenerational families, or for groups of adult couples traveling together and sharing expenses.

ⓔ Alert

Any boat that takes by-the-cabin bookings is not, technically, operating as a private charter yacht. When you look to book a private yacht, you should expect to fill the entire boat with your own charter party, in addition to the yacht's captain and crew. Your party, by law on a true yacht, can be anywhere from two to twelve guests depending on the size of the yacht.

Finding a Reputable Charter Broker

The biggest mistake most people make when seeking to book a private charter yacht is looking online for pictures of the boats themselves. There are countless horror stories of small, affordably priced yachts with gorgeous websites that turn out to be massive rip-offs in real life.

To avoid this situation, your best bet is to book through a reputable charter broker—whose job it is to go from boat to boat in Italy, inspecting the yachts themselves and interviewing the crews to ensure that what's being promoted is actually what you'll get. Reputable charter brokers operate much like real estate agents, meaning any broker, anywhere in the world, can help you book a charter yacht in Italy. The best in the business visit Italy at least once a year to inspect yachts, typically in May, when a large charter boat show is held in Genoa.

Reputable charter brokers typically belong to at least one of the industry's four primary professional associations. Each broker's name and contact information is listed online as part of the Mediterranean Yacht Broker Association (*www.myba-association.com*), CYBA International (*www.cyba.net*), the American Yacht Charter Association (*www.ayca.net*), or the Florida Yacht Brokers Association (*www.fyba.org*). Other groups do exist, based in places such as Greece, but have less-stringent requirements for entry than the internationally minded groups listed here.

Question

Are there any independent resources for finding a charter broker?
The leading resource is *www.charterwave.com*, an online magazine founded in 2006 by this book's author. The site is free to use, has more than 50,000 readers, and offers interviews with charter brokers who discuss their areas of expertise, including Italy vacations.

Choosing the Right Yacht for You

After you discuss your budget, type of group, itinerary choices, and vacation wishes with a reputable charter broker, you will be offered several yachts based in Italy at the broker's recommendation. If you have never before chosen a charter yacht, they likely will all look good. It can be difficult to discern which yacht is the best based solely on looking at brochures.

At this point, your best bet is to listen carefully to the recommendations of your broker, who will have selected the yachts because she believes they fit with what you have expressed as your ideal vacation. If you are a fan of Italian wine, for instance, she may suggest a yacht that keeps a high-quality stash of Barolos and Chiantis onboard. Or, if you are interested in doing some snorkeling around Italy's islands, your broker may recommend a yacht whose crew are well trained in water sports.

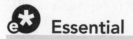 **Essential**

When comparing the costs of a small private yacht and a cruise ship, be sure to add at least $200 per person, per day, to the cruise ship rates (for things like excursions, alcohol, and gambling) and about 25 percent to each yacht's weekly rate (for things like marina fees, crew gratuity, and food). Only then will you get a true cost comparison for total expenses.

Just make sure that you ask your broker why, specifically, she believes each yacht will be good for you and your group. Also feel free to ask for letters of reference from the yacht's previous clients, as well as for information about each yacht's management company.

Day Cruises

Of course, you can sample the feeling of exploring Italy by boat with a ticket aboard one of the countless day cruises that are offered throughout the country. If you're staying in Venice, for instance, there are afternoon tours of the Grand Canal that start at less than $100 per person. You can hop into a traditional day boat in Portofino—often with no reservation required—and enjoy a sunset cruise on Italy's western coast. Sailboats based on Sardinia will take you out for a few hours or even overnight, letting you help with the steering and sails along the way. Countless day boats are available for tours along the Amalfi Coast, as well.

Often, your best bet for a great day cruise is simply happening upon one. Most of the ports that regularly welcome tourists have a steady little industry of local boat owners who are more than happy to take you around for the fee advertised on their chalkboard or handout flyer. This is ideal for those "if-the-mood-strikes" moments, say after a romantic waterfront stroll when you still have an hour or two to wait before your dinner reservation in a nearby *ristorante*.

⊖❗ Alert

Beware of "great day cruises" that cab drivers or *trattoria* waiters suggest to you, unsolicited. Yes, if you ask, these local folks can often recommend a good boat trip that's a few hours long, but if they bring up the topic before you do, then they're probably getting a kickback from a local boat owner.

Venice Canal Tours

The obvious day cruise that most people want to enjoy in Italy is a ride along the Grand Canal in Venice. Expect to pay at least €40 per person for a pre-arranged tour on a decently maintained boat that's semi-private—say, limited to no more than eight people at a time (and not necessarily a gondola). The price of course goes up substantially if you want a boat all to yourself, even if you're only onboard for an hour or so, which is the general length of Grand Canal tours.

Gondola operators on the Grand Canal in Venice know they have a captive audience in tourists, just like the drivers of horse-drawn carriages around New York City's Central Park. A private gondola ride can cost at least twice as much as a semi-private boat tour—and the price goes up at sunset, the most romantic time of the day, often to more than €100 per hour.

Also keep in mind that not all gondola tour guides speak English. That may be all right with you if you simply want to look around and enjoy the ambience, but be sure to ask in advance if you want an actual tour, with descriptions of what you're seeing, in a language that you can understand. Many English-speaking tourists visit Venice each year, so a good number of fluent gondola operators are available. Booking in advance through your hotel or travel agent is the best way to ensure that you'll get one of the better English-speaking guides.

Question

How many gondolas are there in Venice?
Estimates put the number at several hundred, down from a peak of several thousand during the 1700s, when they were a key form of public transportation. A few people still have private gondolas for transit purposes, just like motorbikes or cars in other Italian cities.

Snorkeling and Scuba Diving

Some of the best boat "tours" are actually half- and full-day trips aboard scuba diving or snorkeling boats. Many operators will let observers, including spouses, go along at a deep discount to take in the sights above the waterline while you interact with the fishes below. Financially speaking, these types of day cruises can be a good alternative to "regular" tours, getting you a bit farther away from the hubbub of the primary tourist-boat routes.

There is good snorkeling and scuba diving around the islands of Sardinia and Sicily, of course, but true aficionados tend to head for the Cilento peninsula, which is southwest of Naples. There, you'll see towering cliffs in addition to blue grottoes, making for excellent memories whether you're going underwater or staying dry on the boat.

Ferries

Ferries, locally known as *traghetti* (a single ferry is a *traghetto*), are also an inexpensive way to see a good bit of Italy by boat. You don't get as many bells and whistles as you might with a more tourist-friendly operation, but you also get to pay local commuter prices instead of jacked-up July and August rates.

You can book round-trip ferry tickets and enjoy the ride even if you don't ever get off the boat. The nation's network of ferries offers options for long or short trips. Here are a few good ones to consider.

 Fact

The fifteen-minute ferry ride from Santa Margherita to Portofino is short, but not even close to being the world's shortest ferry ride. Many of the ferries in the New England region of the United States are far shorter, including the scant two-minute ride from Edgartown, Massachusetts, to Chappaquiddick Island.

The main websites to check for ferry routes, pricing, and additional information are Caronte & Tourist (*www.carontetourist.it*), Grandi Navi Veloci (*www.gnv.it*), Medmar (*www.medmargroup.it*), NGI (*www.ngi-spa.it*), SNAV (*www.snav.it*), and Tirrenia (*www.tirrenia.it*).

Santa Margherita to Portofino

This is a short ride, maybe fifteen minutes, but it offers a stunning view of the coastline in one of Italy's prettiest areas. Plus, you can enjoy coming into Portofino without the headache of bumper-to-bumper traffic, which snarls the local roadways during the heights of the summer tourist season.

The ferries from Santa Margherita also run along the Cinque Terre, giving you the option of walking part of the way back along the trail that links the five towns (*cinque* means five). Advance tickets are not required, and the ferry schedule is typically posted at the ferry dock as well as in the local hotels. There are multiple departures daily, and prices depend on which route you select.

Naples to Capri

The ferry ride from Naples to Capri takes about forty-five minutes, and you can also book additional ferry transit from Capri south to Stromboli and the other Aeolian Islands. Those trips take much longer and go farther away from the coast, while the Naples-to-Capri route stays relatively close to shore.

You can also go from Naples to Sicily, but that's more of an all-day transit affair than a fun little ferry ride.

Civitavecchia to Olbia

This ferry ride, from Rome's main port to the island of Sardinia, is eight hours long, but it does offer an option for fleeing the hustle and bustle of the big city for a day on the water. You can spend a night or a long weekend on Sardinia, of course, before your return trip, with special one-way fares available during off seasons for as low as €10 per person. This route includes larger ferries that also allow vehicles, so if you are traveling with a rental car, you can bring it along for the ride.

CHAPTER 18

Beyond Italy and into Europe

You could spend a lifetime traveling in Italy and still not enjoy all of the history and culture it offers. But Italy is just one nation among many in the European Union, all of which is interconnected by a strong transportation network that makes tourism easy. When you think about it, Italy is about the same size in square miles as the state of Arizona. It would be odd for an Italian traveler to go all the way to the United States and visit only Arizona. By the same token, you might want to incorporate other parts of the European Union into your Italy-based vacation.

Incorporating Italy into a European Vacation

Europe's extensive train network is what makes the idea of a broader European vacation so tantalizing. Eurail (*www.eurail.com*) offers passes at multiple price points that will let you travel within a single country, a few regions, a few countries, or all European countries. You buy a single ticket, one that coordinates with your chosen itinerary, and off you go from Bologna to Belgium, Rome to Romania, or Florence to France.

Even better, Eurail pass holders can receive some extra benefits in Italy, including discounted or free seats on some ferries. That's true in Greece, too, so if you plan to travel from, say, Venice to Corfu, you can sometimes go for free if you use the same Eurail pass that can also get you around Italy and into the rest of the European mainland.

It's also worth noting that Eurail passes are more like subway tokens than airline tickets: You can usually decide which train to take while you are traveling, as opposed to having to adhere to a set schedule for takeoffs and landings. This makes your travel options more flexible. The train ticket's description is "good for any three days of rail travel during a fifteen-day time period," as opposed to "good for these specific times and destinations."

Alert

If you are American and traveling as a couple or with a group of no more than five people, then you are eligible for the Eurail "saver" pass, which discounts the adult fare by 15 percent. This can be a substantial savings. With the highest-level ticket, good for train travel on any fifteen days during a two month period, you would save more than €100 per person.

Rental Cars

It is possible to rent a car and drive around Europe, but the cost—especially when you add the price of fuel—tends to be dramatically higher than the cost of buying a rail pass. There are also the worrisome details such as reading street signs posted in a foreign language and driving at speeds well higher than eighty miles per hour on highways such as Germany's Autobahn. And the locals will be in fresh-from-the-factory BMWs, while you might be in a Yugo with a hard-ridden clutch.

The one time when car rental makes sense in Europe is if you plan to travel beyond the major cities, which is where the primary train stations are located. Many of Europe's most charming villages are located in places that are only reachable by car, and if you want to visit those spots, then you will have no choice but to fork over the cash for a rental car.

Should that be the case, then you can reserve a rental car at major airports in Italy or in primary travel hubs in other European countries. Any general travel website can help you do this, including *www.expedia.com* and *www.travelocity.com*.

Airline Flights

Occasional "airfare wars" make short flights between major European cities another option. Depending on when you book, and which routes the European carriers are contesting during your dates of travel, you can sometimes find fares lower than $100 for air travel between European cities. If there is no serious competition happening at any given time, though, you can also expect to find fares well into the $500 or $700 range for round-trip flights from, say, Rome to Paris.

Essential

If you plan to travel by rail during a peak travel time, then you should make a seat reservation just as you would with an airline. Eurail passes do entitle you to unlimited train travel for a certain number of days, but they do not guarantee that the seats you need will actually be available.

Beyond the financial seesaw of airline prices, the thing that makes air tickets less desirable than train passes when traveling in Europe is the fact that airplane schedules are inflexible. If you purchase a seat on a flight that leaves Florence at four o'clock on a Tuesday, then that is the flight you will have to take, no matter what else is happening during your trip. The rail system, by contrast, has more than 1,000 departures each day in Italy alone. Reservations are required for some seats, but in general, air travel around Europe tends to be far less flexible than train travel.

Which Way to Go?

What's best about extending your travel plans beyond Italy is that the country is well positioned for easy travel to multiple other European nations. It's a short travel day from Italy's borders to France, Switzerland, Austria, Germany, Slovenia, and Croatia. The cultures and tourism options in these nations vary widely, so you can tailor your plans to your individual tastes and desires. The rest of this chapter looks at the main sights you might want to put on your itinerary in the European countries that are closest to Italy.

France and Corsica

To look at a map of the Mediterranean Sea, you might think the island of Corsica, just north of Sardinia, was part of Italy instead of France. In fact, the people of Corsica spoke Italian until the late 1800s, but the island today is proudly French. It's a great place for a quick stopover where you can experience that nation's culture within easy travel distance of Sardinia or the Italian mainland. Paris is also within easy striking distance of Italy, and you can compare how world-renowned French art and culture stacks up against your favorite memories from Italy.

Corsica

The island of Corsica is best known as the birthplace of Napoleon Bonaparte. It's 114 miles long with 620 miles of coastline and more than 200 beaches—which of course means jam-packed summertime resorts and all the sunbathing that your skin can stand.

Beyond its beautiful scenery, Corsica is known for its food—a blend of Italian and French cuisines that can't be found anywhere else in the world. Corsica has its own wineries, milk that comes almost exclusively from sheep and goats, and meat that is typically raised in free-range style in the enclaves of the island's mountains. Pork is the primary meat, and local delicacies include *prizutto* (like Parma ham in Italy) and *figatelli* (smoked pig-liver sausage).

 Fact

> The veal that you see in Corsican markets may look paler than what you're used to finding at home. There's nothing wrong with it; in fact, the color comes from the fact that "unnatural" foods or drugs are rarely used to "aid" the growth of Corsican animals, unlike on most industrial-size farms in the United States.

Websites such as *www.corsica-ferries.co.uk* can help you arrange ferry transportation to the island from mainland Italy or from Corsica's southern neighbor, Sardinia, including the ports of Livorno, Civitavecchia, Golfo Aranci, and Santa Teresa. Fares during the off season tend to run around €40 per adult, with increases during the busy summer months. Sleeping cabins are available if you want to make the crossing from the mainland overnight, though even the longer routes, such as the one from Livorno, last only four hours one way.

Paris

Entire libraries have been written about Paris, one of the most popular tourist destinations in the entire world. To walk along the river Seine on a sunny day is an experience that cannot be matched, and much of the art in the city's museums is just as historic and impressive as what you will find in Rome and Florence. Whereas a trip to Florence will help you to appreciate Michelangelo, da Vinci, and Donatello, an afternoon in Paris can introduce you to Monet, Cezanne, and Degas.

Luckily, Paris is an eminently walkable city, which means that even if you have only a single day to look around before or after your trip to Italy, you can make more than a few memories. It is entirely possible to see the Eiffel Tower and the Champs-Élysées during the morning (before the afternoon tourist crush), enjoy a leisurely lunch of crepes and local cheeses alongside a bottle of French Bordeaux or Burgundy wine, and then tour part of the Louvre—which, interestingly given your overall Italian tourism theme, is home to da Vinci's famous *Mona Lisa*.

 Essential

The Louvre isn't the only place to hold master works by French Impressionists. In 1986, a grand Paris train station was converted into the Musee d'Orsay, whose holdings focus on French works created between 1848 and 1915—the height of French Impressionism. This is the better museum if you want to see works by Monet, Cezanne, and Degas.

By high-speed train, the trip from Milan to Paris can take as little as seven hours and costs less than the equivalent of $75 for an economy-level fare. Overnight routes are available, with sleeping cars, at higher prices. Websites such as *www.raileurope.com* offer additional information about schedules and routes.

Switzerland

If you prefer to follow the Alps north from Italy, then you will find yourself in Switzerland, home to world-famous cities including Geneva and Zürich. The national rail network connects all of these to the broader European system—and offers some special "scenic routes" that can make train travel here all the more fantastic.

Eurail considers five train routes in Switzerland to be scenic, promoting them as offering views of "awesome scenery, shimmering lakes, plunging gorges, and snow-capped mountains."

The five scenic Switzerland routes are:

- Glacier Express, running from Davos to St. Moritz
- Golden Pass, running from Luzern to Montreux
- Wilhelm Tell Express, running from Luzern to Locarno (named for a legendary crossbow hero who shot an apple from his son's head, to prevent execution of them both)
- Bernina Express, running from Chur to Lugano
- Centovalli Railway, running from Locarno in Switzerland to Domodossola in Italy

The Bernina Express route has a stop in Tirano, in northeastern Italy, and the entire trip is narrated so that you will know what you are seeing out the train windows. In the summertime, you can do half the train route from Chur to Tirano, and then switch to a bus from Tirano to Lugano, if you would prefer that mode of transportation.

Alert

The Museum of Design Zürich is closed on Mondays, and keeps shorter hours on weekends than on weekdays. From Tuesday through Thursday, hours are 10 A.M. until 8 P.M., while Friday through Sunday, the museum closes at 5 P.M. Tours are given only some days of the week, so contact the museum in advance.

Zürich

Zürich is the main commercial and cultural center of Switzerland, although Berne is the nation's political capital. For tourism purposes, most travelers choose Zürich, especially those who are interested in architecture and art. Some of the churches in this city date back to the 800s, and one—St. Peter—boasts the largest church clock face in the world, at a diameter of twenty-eight feet, five inches (that's six feet bigger than the clock face on London's Big Ben, and two feet bigger than the one on Philadelphia's City Hall).

Art fans head straight to the Museum of Design Zürich, which offers four permanent collections that are difficult to find elsewhere: posters, graphics, design, and applied art. This is not a museum where you stare at ancient paintings. Instead, it is a place where you can see everything from Cuban political posters to puppets. Special exhibitions may concentrate on a particular advertiser, robots, or furniture—all an interesting change of pace from the Renaissance art that dominates the museums in Italy. The museum's website is *www .museum-gestaltung.ch*.

Geneva

Geneva follows Zürich as Switzerland's second most populated city, but is better known because it was enshrined in history as the location where the Geneva Conventions were signed to set the standards for international humanitarian law. The thing to do in Geneva is go watch shopping. Swiss watches are renowned the world over for their high-quality craftsmanship and beautiful design, and Geneva is the home of premier watch-making companies such as Baume et Mercier, Chopard, Patek Philippe, and Rolex—the last of which is the single largest luxury watch brand in the world, creating about 2,000 watches every day.

ⓔ❓ Question

Are Rolex watches less expensive in Geneva?
Sorry, no. Real Rolex watches tend to start at the equivalent of $1,500 and proceed up. The most expensive Rolex purchased is said to have cost the equivalent of nearly $160,000, and the transaction took place in London.

Unfortunately, it is difficult to arrange tours of the premier watch-makers' headquarters and factories in Geneva, but local stores offer good selections of models that you cannot find elsewhere in the world. Your local hotel concierge can direct you to the best shops in your particular area of travel.

Austria

Austria is east of Switzerland, to Italy's north. It is the country where Adolf Hitler was born, and he annexed Austria to Germany during World War II. Soviet soldiers took the city of Vienna in 1945, and Austria was divided into British, French, Soviet, and American zones. It did not emerge as a sovereign nation until 1955. The country's background made it less enviable as a Western-friendly travel destination than, say, England or France for many years, but today Austria is a full-fledged member of the European Union with the concept of neutrality written right into its constitution.

As a tourist location, the city of Vienna beckons, especially to anyone interested in classical music or opera. Austria also offers opportunities to explore the Danube River.

Vienna

Vienna is the capital of Austria, both politically and culturally—and the culture of Vienna is decidedly musical in nature. Austria's roster of native-born composers includes Wolfgang Amadeus Mozart, Joseph Haydn, Franz Schubert, and Johann Strauss, who are world-renowned for works that, in many cases, were first performed in Vienna.

Wiener Staatsoper, the Vienna State Opera, was built in the late 1800s as the city's first opera house. Mozart's *Don Giovanni* was the first performance, and many other performances were held to public acclaim until 1945, when American World War II bombardments destroyed the auditorium, stage, props for more than 100 productions, and more than 150,000 costumes. The opera was rebuilt, and today serves as the breeding ground for artists who become members of the Vienna Philharmonic. Some fifty to sixty operas are performed at the Vienna State Opera each year, many of them intended to lure tourists interested in seeing a Mozart or Strauss work performed in the city.

 Fact

As environmentally friendly countries go, Austria is high up on the list. More than half the country's electricity is generated by hydropower, such as the harnessing of water in dams. Wind and solar resources are also heavily used in Austria, meaning that less than 20 percent of the country's energy comes from oil or gas.

Interestingly, the Vienna State Opera also puts on performances specifically tailored to children, including regular performances of Mozart's *The Magic Flute*, with seats available for free to nine- and ten-year-old children. You can learn more about these, as well as all of the upcoming performances at Wiener Staatsoper, online in English at *www.staatsoper.at*.

Danube River Cruises

The Danube River runs from southern Germany eastward across Europe and into the Black Sea, crossing through Austria's northeastern section, which includes Vienna. Since trains can get you from Italy to Vienna, the city is a natural launching point for a Danube River cruise (especially if you can catch a performance of Strauss's *Blue Danube* waltz before you depart).

Countless options are available for Danube River cruises that last from an afternoon to nearly a month, depending on whether you want a sunset tour or a full-length exploration. One typical itinerary is offered by *www.rivercruisetours.com*, which begins an eight-day journey called "Danube Explorer" in Vienna. You cruise westward from there to a final destination of

Nuremberg, in the German state of Bavaria, where the historic Nuremberg Trials were held following the Holocaust. Along the way, stops include multiple towns as well as an optional day trip to Mozart's birthplace. Any travel agent can help you determine the best Danube River cruise given the time you have available.

Germany

Germany is north of Austria and Sweden, but it's still within a day's travel from many parts of Italy. The trip from Milan to Munich, for instance, takes a little more than seven hours by high-speed train.

❗ Alert

You can save a good deal of money on tickets to performances at Wiener Staatsoper by getting in line for the standing-room-only tickets that are released to the public immediately before each performance. There is no guarantee that you will be a lucky recipient, but if you are, you can watch the opera from "the cheap seats" with local folks.

The German rail network is extensive. More than 33,000 trains run in Germany every day, a staggering number that produces travel options galore. The main tourist city closest to Italy is Frankfurt, in central Germany, while the capital, Berlin, is farther away, in Germany's northeastern corner. Since Frankfurt and Berlin are large-scale cities, you can often find high-speed trains there from international hubs.

Frankfurt

Frankfurt, at least in name, is best known to most Americans as the birthplace of the frankfurter, or hot dog. Though many places vie to say they are the home of the hot dog, it is Frankfurt that claims to have invented the modern-day ballpark delicacy in the late 1400s, when sausages were served inside rolls during imperial coronations.

Plenty of street vendors will be happy to sell you a frankfurter in Frankfurt, which is a good thing, since eating on the run may be all you have time for given the plethora of architectural and historic sites that the city boasts. There's the 311-foot-tall Gothic cathedral of St. Bartholomeus, the gingerbread-looking Roemer city hall, and the stunning Old Opera House, which was reconstructed following heavy damage during World War II. Tours of those three sites alone can take up the better part of an entire day.

Some fifteen museums line the River Main in Frankfurt, creating an area known as Museumsufer, or "museum embankment." It is lovely to stroll not just within them, but also between them, enjoying views of the river as well. Perhaps the most important of the museums, if you have time to visit only one, is the Städel, named for the early nineteenth-century Frankfurt banker who started it. Today, it houses a good number of European paintings, including some by the Italian artist Sandro Botticelli.

Fact

Frankfurt is the only German city with a significant number of skyscrapers. There are about a dozen. Every few years, they all open their doors for public tours simultaneously in what is known as the Wolkenkratzer (skyscraper) Festival. Events include base jumpers, sky divers, fireworks, and laser shows high above most of the other city sights.

Berlin

Berlin is Germany's capital and largest city, with an accumulation of cultural institutions to match. There are more than 150 museums inside the city limits, each one housing a unique collection ranging from classic paintings to dinosaur skeletons. The city is also home to more than fifty performing arts theaters, two zoos, and a sports stadium used for the Olympics in 1936.

The Berlin Wall

The Socialist political party began construction of the Berlin Wall in 1961 as a physical barrier to prevent people from traveling between East and West Germany. It split many families in two and separated workers from their jobs. An unknown number of people died trying to cross the border into West Germany. (Typically, people from East Germany were prevented from traveling to West Germany—not the other way around.)

🔴 Alert

Many street hawkers and souvenir shops in Berlin sell pieces of concrete that they say were once part of the Berlin Wall. Don't fall for it. While there are some pieces of the wall that come with certificates of authentication, most of the rocky chunks you'll find in the local stores are nothing more than worthless rubble.

The fall of the wall in 1989 was the beginning of reunification that led to the present-day borders of Germany. Celebrations were intense, and former *Knight Rider* television star David Hasselhoff became the voice of the new Germany when he stood atop the opened wall and sang "Looking for Freedom" before thousands of screaming fans.

Today, little of the Berlin Wall remains. Souvenir-seekers armed with chisels have chipped away at the wall, pieces of which are now stashed in private collections the world over. A few sections still stand, including one near a former Gestapo headquarters, but the remaining sections tend to be damaged or covered in graffiti, thus making it difficult to appreciate how the wall actually looked.

The Checkpoint Charlie Museum, named for the American checkpoint between East and West Germany, gives you a good idea of the political tensions of the Cold War and the human drama that accompanied the partition of Berlin. You can also enjoy local walking and bicycle tours with guides who discuss the wall's history. Any local hotel concierge can put you in touch with an English-speaking guide of good quality.

Independent Films

One of the more interesting things to do in Berlin is take in a movie. More than 1,000 film and television production companies are based here, and you can often find movies playing on one of the city's nearly 300 screens that you would never be able to find in other parts of the world. Most are produced in German, of course, but occasionally you will find advertisements for showings with English subtitles.

If you are visiting Berlin during the month of February, consider buying a ticket to the Berlin Film Festival, known as Berlinale, where directors from around the globe compete for Golden Bear and Silver Bear awards. Some of the American-made films that you might recognize among the past Berlinale winners include *12 Angry Men*, *Rain Man*, *The People vs. Larry Flynt*, and *The Thin Red Line*. Berlinale's official website, for dates and other details, is *www.berlinale.de*.

Slovenia and Croatia

Slovenia and Croatia are both part of the former Yugoslavia, a country that existed to Italy's east throughout much of the twentieth century. Slovenia was the first of the former Yugoslavian states to declare independence and join the North Atlantic Treaty Organization (NATO) in 2004. Croatia took a bit longer to stabilize to Western standards, and NATO offered the country membership in 2009.

These areas made headlines worldwide during much of the mid-1990s, when the Bosnian War erupted in the former Yugoslavia territories. News reports used words such as "massacre" and "genocide" with alarming regularity, and the resulting impression left in most travelers' minds was that Slovenia and Croatia were areas best left alone. Today, each country is working hard to rebuild itself within the European and international communities, and that includes offering some interesting tourist options.

Škocjan Caves

Slovenia's Škocjan Caves are a UNESCO World Heritage Site, added to the list in 1986 as an "exceptional system of limestone caves." They include many of the world's largest known underground chambers, including underground waterfalls.

The caves are protected as part of a national park that includes an educational walking trail, workshops, and exhibitions. Guided tours of the caves are available year-round, though there are far more tour times available in June, July, August, and September than during any other time of the year. During the coldest winter months, depending on demand, the three scheduled daily tours are sometimes reduced to two.

A museum is located within about ten minutes' walking distance of the park information center, though the museum is open only from June through September. You can learn more and see schedules and rates for your travel dates at the park's official website, *www.park-skocjanske-jame.si.*

Dubrovnik

If you have time to visit only one city in Croatia, consider Dubrovnik, "the Pearl of the Adriatic." Its old city is a UNESCO World Heritage Site, first added to the list in 1979 and then given an extension in 1994, after extensive work to repair the damage done during the Bosnian War. It is renowned for its Gothic, Renaissance, and Baroque churches, as well as its palaces and fountains—much of which were of course influenced by the same architectural movements that you will have discovered in Italy.

Because rebuilding efforts are ongoing, your best bet is to ask a travel agent or local hotel concierge which monuments or churches are ideal for visits during your chosen travel dates. No matter when you travel, rest assured that you will find many of the same sites that have enchanted visitors for centuries.

CHAPTER 19

Key Italian Words and Phrases

A little bit of effort goes a long way when it comes to communicating in Italy. It's amazing how a well placed *per favore* or *grazie* ("please" or "thank you") can indicate to an Italian-speaking local that you are doing your best. This chapter offers a primer on the basics that you may find useful, even if you have no intention of learning the Italian language at a conversational level. Speak what little you can with a smile, and odds are you'll get all the help you need in return.

For When You Need Help

WORDS FOR POLICE, FIRE, AND MEDICAL EMERGENCIES

ambulance	*ambulanza*
American embassy	*ambasciata Americana*
aspirin	*aspirina*
asthmatic	*asmatico*
back	*dorso*
blood	*sangue*
broken arm	*braccio rotto*
broken leg	*gamba rotta*
dentist	*dentista*
diabetic	*diabetico*
doctor	*dottore*
ear	*orecchio*
embassy	*ambasciata*
emergency	*urgenza*
eye	*occhio*
fever	*febbre*
fire	*fuoco*
freezing	*congelamento*
head	*testa*
headache	*mal di testa*
heart	*cuore*
help	*aiuto*
high blood pressure	*ipertensione*
high cholesterol	*alto colesterolo*
hospital	*ospedale*
hot	*caldo*
lost	*perso*
low blood pressure	*pressione bassa*
lungs	*polmoni*

pain	*dolore*
police	*polizia*
police station	*questura*
stolen	*rubato*
stomach	*stomaco*
sweat	*sudore*
thief	*ladro*

HELPFUL PHRASES

Call the police!	*Chiami la polizia*
I'm allergic to penicillin.	*Sono allergic alla penicillin.*
I'm allergic to . . .	*Sono allergic . . .*
I'm looking for a . . .	*Cerco . . .*
I'm looking for a doctor.	*Cerco un dottore.*
I'm looking for the police.	*Cerco la polizia.*
It hurts here.	*Mi fa male qui.*

SYMPTOMATIC WORDS AND PHRASES

to be cold	*avere freddo*
to be hot	*avere caldo*
to be constipated	*avere la stitichezza*
to be pregnant	*essere incinta*
to be sick	*essere malato*
to be tired	*essere assonnato*
to bleed	*sanguinare*
to cough	*tossire*
to faint	*svenire*
to fall	*cadere*
to sneeze	*starnutire*
to vomit	*vomitare*

For Getting Around

DIRECTIONS, HOTELS, BATHROOMS, AND OTHER KEY WORDS

address	*indirizzo*
bathrooms	*stanza da bagno (or gabinetti, or bagni)*
double room (sleeps two people)	*camera matrimonial*
down	*giù*
elevator	*ascensore*
escalator	*scala mobile*
hotel	*hotel*
inside	*interno*
left	*sinistra*
men's bathroom	*uomini*
outside	*esterno*
right	*destra*
sidewalk	*marciapiede*
single room (sleeps one person)	*camera singola*
stairs	*scale*
street	*strada*
street corner	*angolo di strada*
telephone	*telefono*
turn	*giro*
up	*su*
walk	*passeggiata*
women's bathroom	*donne*

HELPFUL PHRASES

Are there any rooms available?	*Avete camera libere?*
I am lost.	*Mi sono perso.*
I'm looking for a . . .	*Cerco . . .*
I'm looking for an elevator.	*Cercu un ascensore.*
Where is the bathroom?	*Dov'è il bagno?*
Would you please write down the address?	*Può scrivere l'indirizzo, per favore?*

STREET SMARTS

accident	*un incidente*
lane	*una corsia*
highway	*un'autostrada*
gas station	*un distributore di benzina*
bypass road	*un tangenziale*
traffic lights	*il semaforo*
pedestrian	*il pedonale*
pedestrian croswalk	*le strisce pedonali*
gas	*la benzina*
diesel	*il diesel*
driver	*l'autista*
lights	*i fari*
speed limit	*il limite di velocità*
one way	*senso unico*
stop	*stop*
dead end	*strada senza uscita*
all routes/directions	*tutte le direzioni*
no stopping	*vietata la sosta*
no parking	*vietato parcheggiare*
rush hour	*l'ora di punta*

CAR TALK

car	*una macchina/un' automobile/un'auto*
car hood	*il cofano*
radio	*la radio*
rearview mirror	*lo specchietto*
seatbelt	*la cintura di sicurezza*
trunk	*il bagagliaio*
steering wheel	*il volante*
tire	*la gomma/il pneumatico*
windshield	*la parabrezza*
windshield wipers	*i tergicristalli*

For Finding Your Way Around

SOME USEFUL DESTINATIONS

museum	*museo*
park	*parco*
gardens	*giardini*
restaurant	*ristorante*
bank	*banca*
church	*chiesa*
cathedral	*cattedrale*
fountain	*fontana*
monument	*monumento*
hotel	*hotel/albergo*
theater	*teatro*
open-air market	*mercato*
supermarket	*supermercato*
bus stop	*la fermata dell'autobus*
coffee shop	*bar*

For Transportation

WORDS YOU MIGHT SEE ON SIGNS

airport	*aeroporto*
arrival	*arrivo*
boarding gate	*cancello d'imbarco*
boat	*barca*
bus	*autobus*
cancelled	*annullato*
closed	*chiuso*
connections	*collegamenti*
danger	*pericolo*
delay	*ritardo*
departure	*partenza*
destination	*destinazione*
exit	*uscita*
fares	*tariffe*
ferry	*traghetto*
flight	*volo*
gate	*cancello*
highway	*autostrada*
no parking	*divieto di sosta*
no vacancy	*completo*
on time	*in orario*
open	*aperto*
rental car	*noleggio auto*
rooms available	*camera libere*
taxicab	*taxi*
ticket	*biglietto*
timetables	*orari*
toll	*pedaggio*
train	*treno*
train platform	*addestrare la piattaforma (or binario)*

HELPFUL PHRASES

first-class ticket	biglietto di prima classe
I want to go to . . .	Voglio andare a . . .
I'd like to rent a car.	Vorrei noleggiare una macchina.
Is this the road that goes to . . .	Questa strada porta a . . .
one-way ticket	biglietto di solo andata
return ticket	biglietto di andata e ritorno
second-class ticket	biglietto di seconda classe
where is . . .	dov'è

For Air Travel

PEOPLE, PLACES, AND THINGS

airplane	un aereo
airport	un aeroporto
baggage	i bagagli
boarding pass	la carta d'imbarco
carry-on luggage	i bagagli a mano
checked luggage	i bagagli da stiva
cart	un carello
check-in desk	il banco di check-in
departures	partenze
early	in anticipo
late	in ritardo
baggage check	la consegna bagagli
passenger	il passeggero
passport	il passaporto
pilot	il pilota
security check	il controllo di sicurezza
shuttle	lo shuttle
steward/stewardess	l'assistente di bordo
visa	il visto

TICKET INFORMATION

airline	la compagnia aerea
first class	la prima classe
flight	il volo
gate	l'uscita
one-way ticket	un biglietto solo andata
round-trip ticket	un biglietto andata e ritorno
terminal	il terminal

 Fact

You will notice that English is often used for terms related to international travel. *La hostess* can be used to mean stewardess, *il duty free* is a duty free shop, *economy* and *coach* are widely used to refer to travel class options, many Italians will check in at *il check-in*, and *un volo con stopover* is a flight with a stopover.

TRAVEL VERBS

to board	imbarcare
to buy a ticket	fare il biglietto
to check bags	consegnare i bagagli
to make a reservation	fare una prenotazione
to sit down	sedersi or accomodarsi
to take off	decollare
to land	atterrare

ARRIVALS AND BAGGAGE

arrivals	*arrivi*
baggage claim	*il ritiro bagagli*
lost luggage	*i bagagli smarriti*
My luggage is lost.	*I miei bagagli sono smarriti.*

IMMIGRATION AND CUSTOMS

immigration	*l'immigrazione*
last name	*il cognome*
first name	*il nome*
customs	*la dogana*
nothing to declare	*niente da dichiarare*
customs declaration form	*il modula dogana*

USEFUL EXPRESSIONS

Here's my passport.	*Ecco il mio passaporto.*
I have a visa.	*Ho un visto.*
I don't have a visa.	*Non ho un visto.*
I would like to declare . . .	*Vorrei dichiarare*

 Fact

Signage in the international airports throughout Italy is almost always written in Italian as well as English. You will have no trouble getting to your ticket counter, security checkpoint, departure gate, and anywhere else you need to go. In addition, most people who work at airport information desks speak English in addition to Italian.

For Ordering Meals

BASIC RESTAURANT VOCABULARY

to be hungry	*aver fame*
to be thirsty	*avere sete*
to order	*ordinare*
to drink	*bere*
to eat	*mangiare*
check/bill	*il conto*
cover charge	*il coperto*
service charge	*il servizio*
menu	*il menu*
tip	*la mancia*
What would you like? I would like . . .	*Che cosa mangia? Io vorrei . . .*
I am a vegetarian.	*Sono vegetariano.*
I am on a diet.	*Sono a dieta.*

 **Essential**

Some restaurants will add a cover charge—il coperto—and a service charge—il servizio—to your bill. This, by law, must be clearly marked on the menu. As a general rule, Italian waiters will not expect a tip, though adding a few euros to your payment will be appreciated.

WORDS FOR BASIC FOODS

apertif	*apertivo*
appetizer	*antipasto*
beef	*manzo*
bread	*pane*
butter	*burro*
cheese and fruit	*formaggio e frutta*
chicken	*pollo*
clams	*molluschi*
dessert	*dolce*
first course	*primo*
fish	*pesce*
garlic	*aglio*
lamb	*agnello*
lobster	*aragosta*
mushroom	*fungo*
mussels	*cozze*
olive oil	*olio d'olivia*
onion	*cipolla*
pepper	*pepe*
pork	*maiale*
post-dinner drink	*digestivo*
salad	*insalata*
salt	*sale*
second course	*secondo*
shrimp	*gambero*
side dish	*contorno*
soup	*minestra*
steak	*bistecca*
sugar	*zucchero*
tomato	*pomodoro*
veal	*vitello*
vegetable	*verdura*

UTENSILS, SERVICE, AND OTHER BASICS

chair	sedia
check	assegno
fork	forchetta
gratuity	gratifica
knife	coltello
napkin	tovagliolo
per person	per la persona
plate	piatto
spoon	cucchiaio
table	tavola
tax	tassa
waiter	cameriere
waitress	cameriera

DRINKS

beer	birra
coffee	caffé
decaffeinated coffee	caffé decaffeinato
decaffeinated tea	tè decaffeinato
hot chocolate	cioccolata calda
iced tea	ha ghiacciato il tè
lemonade	limonata
red wine	vino rosso
tea	tè
water	acqua
white wine	vino bianco
wine	vino

 Alert

Tax and gratuity are often added to your restaurant check in Italy and presented to you as part of the total bill. You are not expected to offer an extra gratuity in addition to the one on the check. If no gratuity is included, Italians tend to tip less than Americans. Whereas you might leave a 15 percent tip at home, a 5 percent gratuity in Italy will do.

HELPFUL PHRASES

children's menu	un menù per bambini
I'm allergic to nuts.	Sono allergic ai noci.
less, please	meno, per favore
more, please	più, per favore

Fact

Outside of the primary tourist areas in Italy's bigger cities, restaurant owners often will not often bring the check until you request it, for fear of being rude or rushing you through your meal. Don't feel bad about requesting the bill. Otherwise, you may sit around all night waiting for it to come.

For Being Polite

excuse me	*mi scusi (also used for "I'm sorry")*
goodbye	*arrievederci*
hello (daytime)	*buon giorno*
hello (nighttime)	*buona sera*
just a moment	*un momento*
no	*no*
please	*per favore*
thank you	*grazie*
yes	*si*
you're welcome	*prego*

CONVERSATION STARTERS

How are you?	*Come stai?*
Fine, thanks.	*Bene, grazie.*
Excellent!	*Ottimo!*
My name is . . .	*Mi chiamo . . .*
What's your name? (formal)	*Come si chiama Lei?*
What's your name? (informal)	Come ti chiami?
His name is . . .	*Lui si chiama . . .*
Her name is . . .	*Lei si chiama . . .*
I am . . .	*Sono . . .*

Where are you from?	*Di dove sei?*
I am from . . .	*Sono di . . .*
I come from	*Vengo da. . .*
. . . the United States	*gli Stati Uniti*
. . . England	*l'Inghilterra*
. . . Australia	*l'Australia*
. . . Canada	*la Canada*
. . . France	*la Francia*
. . . Spain	*la Spagna*
. . . China	*la Cina*
. . . Japan	*il Giappone*
May I introduce you to . . . ?	*Posso presentarti . . . ?*
Nice to meet you.	*Piacere di conoscerti.*
See you . . .	*Ci vediamo . . .*
. . . tomorrow.	*. . . domani.*
. . . this afternoon.	*. . . questo pomeriggio.*
. . . this evening.	*. . . stasera.*
. . . next week.	*. . . la settimana prossima.*
. . . in an hour.	*. . . tra un'ora.*
. . . later.	*. . . piu'tardi.*
Do you speak . . . (informal)	Parli . . .
Do you speak . . . (formal)	Parla . . .
. . . English?	. . . inglese?
. . . German?	. . . tedesco?
. . . French?	. . . francese?
. . . Spanish?	. . . spagnolo?
Where is . . . ?/Where are . . . ?	Dov'è. . . ?/Dove sono. . . ?
Can you tell me . . . ? (informal)	Puoi dirmi . . . ?
Can you tell me . . . ? (formal)	Può dirmi . . . ?
Can you show me . . . ? (informal)	Puoi mostrarmi . . . ?
Can you show me . . . ? (formal)	Può mostrarmi . . . ?

Other Helpful Phrases and Words

HELPFUL PHRASES

Do you speak English?	*Parla inglese?*
Do you take credit cards?	*Accettate carte di credito?*
How do you say . . . in Italian?	*Como si dice . . . in Italiano?*
How much is . . .	*Quanto costa . . .*
Please show me	*Può mostrarmelo, per favore*
Please show me on the map.	*Può mostrarmelo sulla pianta, per favore.*
Please write it down.	*Può scriverlo, per favore.*
What time is it?	*Che ore sono?*
How are you?	*Come stai?*
Fine, thanks.	*Bene, grazie.*
Excellent!	*Ottimo!*
My name is . . .	*Mi chiamo . . .*

 Alert

Ciao (pronounced "chow") is an informal greeting that means hello, but it is considered impolite to address strangers this way. Stick with the more formal *buon giorno*, or, if it's evening, say *buona sera*. If someone says *ciao* to you first, as you are leaving, then it is polite to say *ciao* in response.

HELPFUL WORDS

ATM	*bancomat*
bandage	*fasciatura*
bank	*banco*
hairbrush	*spazzola*
key	*chiave*
luggage	*bagaglio*
market	*il mercato*
passport	*passaporto*
post office	*la posta*
razor	*rasoio*
shampoo	*shampoo*
soap	*sapone*
sunscreen	*crema solare*
tampons	*tamponi*
tissue	*tessuto*
today	*oggi*
tomorrow	*domani*

MONTHS OF THE YEAR

January	*Gennaio*
February	*Febbraio*
March	*Marza*
April	*Aprile*
May	*Maggio*
June	*Giugno*
July	*Luglio*
August	*Agosta*
September	*Settembre*
October	*Ottobre*
November	*Novembre*
December	*Dicembre*

NUMBERS

zero	*zero*
one	*uno*
two	*due*
three	*tre*
four	*quattro*
five	*cinque*
six	*sei*
seven	*sette*
eight	*otto*
nine	*nove*
ten	*dieci*
twenty	*venti*
thirty	*trenta*
forty	*quaranta*
fifty	*cinquanta*
sixty	*sessanta*
seventy	*settanta*
eighty	*ottanta*
ninety	*novanta*
one hundred	*cento*

DAYS OF THE WEEK

Sunday	*Domenica*
Monday	*Lunedi*
Tuesday	*Martedi*
Wednesday	*Mercoledi*
Thursday	*Giovedi*
Friday	*Venerdi*
Saturday	*Sabato*

For Your Accommodations

APPLIANCES AND ELECTRONICS

air conditioning	*l'aria condizionata*
alarm clock	*la sveglia*
central heating	*il riscaldamento centrale*
computer	*il computer*
DVD player	*il lettore DVD*
electric socket	*la presa (di corrente)*
electrical switch	*l'interruttore*
iron	*il ferro da stiro*
printer	*la stampante*
radio	*la radio*
telephone	*il telefono*
television set	*il televisore*
VCR	*il videoregistratore*

IN YOUR ROOM

armchair	*la poltrona*
balcony	*il balcone*
bed	*il letto*
blanket	*la coperta*
carpet	*la moquette*
ceiling	*il soffitto*
chair	*la sedia*
chest of drawers	*il cassettone*
clean	*pulito*
closet, wardrobe	*l'armadio*
cloth, rag	*lo straccio*
couch, sofa	*il divano*
curtain	*la tenda*
desk	*la scrivania*
dirty	*sporco*

IN YOUR ROOM *continued*

door	*la porta*
drawer	*il cassetto*
dry	*secco*
dust	*la polvere*
fireplace	*il caminetto*
floor	*il pavimento*
floor, story	*il piano*
furniture	*i mobili*
garbage	*la spazzatura*
key	*la chiave*
lock	*la serratura*
pillow	*il cuscino*
radiator	*il termosifone*
roof	*il tetto*
room	*la stanza*
rug, mat	*il tappeto*
sheets	*le lenzuola*
staircase, stairs	*la scala*
stool	*lo sgabello*
table	*il tavolo*
telephone	*il telefono*
vase	*il vaso*
wall	*la parete*
wallpaper	*la carta da pareti*
window	*la finestra*

BATHROOM

bath; bathroom	il bagno
bathtub	la vasca da bagno
brush	la spazzola
hairdryer	il phon
mirror	lo specchio
shampoo	lo shampoo
shower	la doccia
shower curtain	la tenda da doccia
sink	il lavandino
soap	il sapone
toilet	la toilette
toilet paper	la carta igienica
toothbrush	la spazzola per i denti
toothpaste	il dentifricio
towel	l'asciugamano

For Doing Your Laundry

LAUNDRY VOCABULARY

to wash	lavare
to dry clean	lavare a secco
to dry	asciugare
bleach	la candeggina
dryer	l'asiugatrice
fabric softener	l'ammorbidente
to do the laundry	fare il bucato
soap	il sapone
stain	la macchia
starch(ed)	inamidato
washing machine	la lavatrice

For Chatting about the Weather

WEATHER WORDS AND EXPRESSIONS

How's the weather?	Che tempo fa?
It's sunny.	C'è il sole.
It's nice.	Fa bel tempo.
It's cold.	Fa freddo.
It's hot.	Fa caldo.
It's snowing.	Nevica.
It's raining.	Piove.
It's windy.	Tira vento.
It's foggy.	C'è la nebbia
storm	il temporale
lightning	il lampo
changeable	variabile
air	l'aria
rain	la pioggia

 Alert

Italy's weather tends to be more moderate than the frigid winters and hot and humid summers in some parts of the United States. Many people consider the spring (April and May) and autumn (September and October) to be the best times to visit Italy. The weather is mild and there are fewer tourists at these times.

For Doing Business in Italy

BUSINESS VOCABULARY

boss, manager	*il dirigente*
business card	*la carta da visita*
CEO	*l'amministratore delegato*
company	*l'azienda*
contract	*il contratto*
corporate planning	*la programmazione aziendale*
interview	*l'intervista*
job	*il lavoro*
meeting	*la riunione*
resume	*il CV/il curriculum*
salary	*il salario*
to work	*lavorare*

 Fact

Italy is a major producer of furniture and housewares. Try to find a furniture store or housewares store—you may just find something to bring home with you.

343

What Your Teacher Never Taught You

By no means exhaustive, nor rife with vulgarities, the following list contains some fun and colorful expressions to be used in a variety of situations.

accidenti	a mild expletive, like darn or heck
alito puzzolente	bad breath
amore a prima vista	love at first sight
arrapare	to become sexually excited
bel niente	nothing, nada, zip
bischero	a stupid person (Tuscany)
casino	can mean "a lot" or "a mess" (*Mi è piaciuto un casino.* I liked it a lot. *Che casino!* What a mess!)
chiudere il becco	to shut up, to shut one's trap
fannullone	a lazy bum
fregare	to cheat or swindle somebody
fuori di testa	to be out of one's mind
leccaculo or leccapiedi	brownnoser
mollare qualcuno	to dump someone
morire dalla noia	to die of boredom.
parolaccia	dirty word
pigrone/a	a lazy bum
portare male gli anni	to age badly
roba da matti	crazy stuff
preso in giro	to be made fun of, made a fool of
scemo/a	a stupid person, a jerk
schifo	disgust, grossness (widely used in expressions like *Che schifo!* "Ew! Gross!")
scocciare	to irritate or annoy
valere la pena	to be worthwhile

CHAPTER 20

Sample Itineraries

Italy is an amalgam of regions that each contribute something unique to the experience of Italy as a whole. From the pizza makers in Naples and the wine growers in Tuscany to the museum curators in Florence and the ferry drivers in Sicily, Italy offers countless choices for the itinerary of your dreams. This chapter offers some suggestions for trips of varying lengths—but keep in mind that as with any destination, Italy can be anything you choose to make of it.

If You Have a Day in Italy

One day in Italy isn't much time at all, but it's certainly better than no days in Italy! If you have just twenty-four hours to explore, then your best bet is to head for a major city. That way, you can check out a few key museums and historic sites, and you can sample the region's cuisine in one of the countless restaurants that each major city offers.

Three good choices for single-day tours are Rome, Florence, and Venice. Each of these cities is beautiful in its own right, will give you at least one "major" sightseeing memory, and offers the "flavor" of its general region within the country.

Rome

The big question to ask yourself during a single day in Rome is: Would you rather beat the crowds at the Colosseum or the Sistine Chapel?

 Alert

The line to get into the Sistine Chapel is typically at least an hour long, even during the off-season winter months. If this is one of your must-see sights during a day in Rome, then arrive first thing in the morning to ensure that you will get inside. Often, visitors who arrive after lunchtime are turned away because no more tours are being accepted.

These are two of the biggest sightseeing draws in Rome and Vatican City. You will likely want to visit them both during a single day in Rome, and you should go first to the one where you think you will want to spend the most time. If you plan to take the full-on tour of the Colosseum, learning about its history and architecture for an hour or two, then consider being on line first thing in the morning. That's especially true during the summer months, when the open-air structure can feel stiflingly hot with all the tourists lingering under the midday sun.

Even a full-length tour of the Colosseum will still leave you plenty of time to grab a cab (or walk, if you're in good shape) over to Vatican City, where you can get on line to view the Sistine Chapel. Be sure not to dilly-dally, though, as the chapel typically closes early in the afternoon, and you will want to be in line to get inside by about noontime. Save St. Peter's Basilica for after the Sistine Chapel. It's just a few steps away, and it stays open later.

ⓔ✱ Essential

If you have time for only one real meal in Florence, look for a *ristorante* with a good local wine list. You can often find Brunello di Montalcino vintages here at far lower prices than the popular wines command in the United States, and you will absolutely see labels from producers who are better known locally than they are internationally.

A morning of touring the Colosseum and the Sistine Chapel should help you work up a pretty good appetite. After you finish your look around Vatican City, meander over to the Spanish Steps, which are about a half-hour walk away. You'll get a great feel for the architecture of the city, and you'll bump into countless *trattoria* signs offering pretty much every kind of Italian cuisine you might want.

Florence

It would be downright criminal to spend a day in Florence, the cradle of the Renaissance, without taking some time to appreciate all the magnificent artwork in the city. Allow at least a few hours in your schedule for a visit to the Uffizi Gallery, where you can view pieces by the Italian masters Botticelli, da Vinci, Michelangelo, and Raphael. Arriving first thing in the morning is key; it allows you to get the first tickets of the day. Otherwise, you may have to wait in the entrance line for as long as five hours—obviously not an ideal way to spend so many of your precious twenty-four hours in Italy.

From the museum, make your way over to Florence Cathedral. Even if you have no interest in religious history, the architecture of this building is extraordinary. This is a 500-foot-long cathedral, one unlike anything else you are likely to see in a lifetime. You can also get a good look at the dozens of stained-glass windows for which the cathedral is renowned.

Alert

Check the weather forecast before walking over to St. Mark's Square. It's the lowest point in Venice and floods regularly during heavy rains. Waters rose as high as five feet during December 2008 rainstorms. As a general rule, there is at least minor flooding in Venice some 200 days each year.

End your day in Florence with a walk over the Ponte Vecchio, one of the oldest bridges in Europe. This shop-lined tourist hotspot is a good place to pick up souvenirs for anyone back home, and the neighborhood also offers plenty of places to enjoy some local Tuscan cuisine.

Venice

The two must-see stops during a single day in Venice are the Grand Canal and St. Mark's Square. You can tour the Grand Canal for far fewer euro if you choose a ferry-style boat instead of a gondola. The ferry boats often offer guided tours in English for longer amounts of time than the gondolas, and at lower prices. You'll get more for your money that way and will still have plenty of time to see more of Venice afterward.

Head from the canal over to St. Mark's Square, which is famous in its own right but is also the gateway for you to see St. Mark's Basilica, Palazzo Ducale, and Campanile. That's a full afternoon's worth of sightseeing, after which you can step into a nearby *trattoria* or *ristorante* to try the regional specialty: risotto. Consider a seafood- or fish-based risotto, which will also give you a good excuse to enjoy a bottle of local Pinot Grigio white wine.

If You Have a
Long Weekend in Italy

Three days in Italy opens your options dramatically, especially if you invest in an all-you-can-ride train pass from Eurail (*www.eurail.com*). The lowest-level Italy pass costs about the equivalent of $200, and it lets you ride as many trains within the country as you want for three days. (Four-day passes are available, too, for about $225.)

Essential

You don't need a reservation for train seats in Italy, but commuter-time trains tend to fill up fast. If you're planning to be aboard during rush hour, you might consider making a reservation in advance. With only a few days in Italy, you don't want to waste time standing around in a train station, waiting instead of sightseeing.

Day 1

If you start your long weekend in Rome, you can follow the one-day itinerary described earlier in this chapter.

Day 2

On your second morning, get up early and take the three-hour train ride to Pisa, where you can see the Leaning Tower and have lunch in a local *trattoria*. It's just an hour's train ride from Pisa to Florence, where you can spend the afternoon admiring the master-works at the Uffizi Gallery. Enjoy another fantastic Tuscan meal for dinner, and you'll be ready to sleep like a baby.

Day 3

Wake up in Florence, where you can sightsee again during the morning before getting back to the train station and heading to Venice, which is a two-hour ride if you catch a high-speed line. You can be on the Grand Canal in time for an afternoon cruise, and then enjoy a leisurely, last-night-in-Italy dinner overlooking St. Mark's Square.

Day 4

Overnight in Venice before flying home the next morning. The airport is connected to the train line, so you can use your Eurail pass once again before it expires, thus saving beaucoup bucks for a taxi.

If You Have a Week in Italy

If your schedule allows you a full week in Italy, then you will have the option of getting to some of the more "distant" spots within the country. That doesn't necessarily mean little villages out in the middle of nowhere, but it does mean moving beyond the major cities and into other locations that require longer travel times.

Two good examples of such places are the islands of Sicily and Sardinia. They're about as far away as you can get from Venice, but with a full week's time to travel, they are easily within reach—even if you include a stop in Naples on your way there.

Days 1–3

Consider spending your first three days in Italy doing the "long weekend" itinerary—only in reverse. Begin your stay in Venice, then travel west to Florence and west again to Pisa, then south to Rome along Italy's western coast.

Day 4

On your fourth day, you will awake in Rome and be well positioned to catch an early-morning southbound train to Naples, which is a two-hour ride away. Your fourth day in Italy can thus be spent exploring the ruins of Pompeii, or, if the weather is bad, the artifacts inside the city's Museo Archeologico Nazionale. (Either way, you'll get to fill your head with lots of Mount Vesuvius memories.) Of course, you need to stop at a *pizzeria* for an authentic pizza dinner that night. Order the classic version with tomatoes so that you'll feel like a local. Overnight in Naples.

Fact

The tomatoes in Naples might taste different than the ones you get at home. The local type are called San Marzano tomatoes, and they have no seeds. These are usually the kinds of tomatoes used to make the classic Italian "peeled tomatoes" that are canned, shipped worldwide, and used in countless people's homemade marinara sauce recipes.

Day 5

Begin day five at the ferry dock. You can catch a ride to either Sardinia or Sicily from there, though do expect to spend the entire day on the water. You can enjoy the fresh sea air after your previous four days of running around from city to city on the mainland. You should get to either Sardinia or Sicily in time for a hearty dinner of freshly caught Mediterranean seafood.

Days 6–7

Relax on the beaches, do some snorkeling, and soak up some last bits of Italian culture before you head back home. If your final destination is in Sicily, be sure to order a dish with Marsala sauce—and grab a few bottles of the locally bottled stuff to use in your own recipes after you leave Italy from the island's airport.

If You Have
Two Weeks in Italy

With fourteen days in Italy, you can visit all the major cities as well as some off-the-beaten-path towns and villages that most tourists never even realize exist.

Days 1–3

Start your itinerary in Venice, just as you would for the one-week itinerary, but instead of moving from there straight to Florence at the end of your second day, go instead to Milan or Bologna. If you want to shop, Milan is the place to be. If you want to see great architecture and enjoy hearty meat sauces atop pasta, then Bologna it is. Both cities are easily accessible by train, and routes are covered by a standard Eurail pass.

Days 4–5

Take a morning train to Florence. Schedule two nights' hotel here, giving you three days of touring. That way, you can enjoy the best of the city sights and take a day trip to a local village. The Tuscany countryside is gorgeous, the food doesn't get any fresher, and the wine doesn't get any better. You might even pay a visit to Montalcino, where they bottle the world-famous Brunello reds.

Days 6–7

Spend days six and seven exploring Rome and Vatican City. The train from Florence is easy, and having two days instead of one means that you won't have to fight the afternoon crowds at the Colosseum or the Sistine Chapel. Plan to spend each of your two mornings at one or the other, with the rest of your day devoted to seeing Rome's museums, archaeological ruins, shops, and *trattorias*.

℮❓ Question

What is the "fashion row" of Rome?
The capital city is not known for fashion on the same scale as Milan, but there is an area within view of the Spanish Steps where you can wander in and out of shops and boutiques selling Italian haute couture. Just follow the well-dressed crowds carrying shopping bags, and be prepared to pay top euro for the latest fashions.

Days 8–9

Take the train to Naples, where you will be able to indulge in a two-day stay that lets you enjoy the sights at Pompeii and Mount Vesuvius at a leisurely pace—visit one each day—followed by some tours of the architectural sights and museums within the Naples city limits during your afternoons. Two days in Naples also will give you a chance to sample multiple pizzerias in the food's birthplace, so that you can get a true taste (in every sense) of just how staunchly Neapolitans defend their thin-crust style and traditional toppings.

Days 10–11

Take the train south from Naples on the spectacularly scenic, five-hour ride to Reggio di Calabria. This is the long way to the "toe of the boot," but it's worth the time if you can get a window seat. Have your camera ready for gorgeous coastal views. In this instance, the ride *is* the destination.

Once you arrive at Reggio di Calabria, you will be just across from Sicily, which is so close that you will be able to see it on clear days. Some train cars get put right onto ferries and moved over to train tracks in Sicily, while other trains force you to get off and take the ferry crossing on foot. Either way is a breeze, and you can overnight in Sicily and then spend the next day touring the island, eating veal Marsala, or simply soaking up some sunshine on the beach.

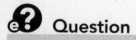 **Question**

Is Reggio di Calabria worth an overnight stop?
Not really. The local shop owners might argue that answer, but the reality is that most visitors much prefer moving immediately from the Reggio di Calabria station on to Sicily, where the beaches, sightseeing, and restaurants are all far more tourist-friendly.

Days 12–14

Sicily might be where you want to end your two-week Italy itinerary, given how much traveling you will have already done from location to location. And there's definitely plenty to do on the island if you want to spend your last few days there.

However, if you have one more travel day in your weary bones, then consider spending day twelve or thirteen on the ferry from Sicily to Sardinia. Better yet, book an overnight trip, as the ferry ride can be long—as long as fifteen hours from Palermo, in northwestern Sicily, to Cagliari, in southeastern Sardinia. Since an overnight trip gets you into Sardinia the morning of your thirteenth day, the overnight ferry ride gives you two days to play on some of Italy's finest beaches before flying home. If you can afford it, a hotel on the ritzy Costa Smeralda, along Sardinia's northeastern shore, will offer you beachfront memories to last a lifetime.

If You Have a
Month in Italy and Europe

A month-long itinerary will give you even more time to relax in Italy's major cities, deviate from the train lines to explore even more local villages, and cross Italy's borders to enjoy some of the additional fun that is so close by in Europe.

However, unlike the other itinerary suggestions in this chapter, it's best to start a month-long itinerary in Italy's islands, from which you can work your way north and eventually up into Austria, Switzerland, or the other countries of your choice.

Essential

You may be the type of traveler who prefers your most leisurely days at the end of a long trip, instead of at the beginning. If that's the case, you can reverse this suggested month-long itinerary and end your trip in the Italian islands instead of starting there. For most people, though, the opposite is better, allowing you to adjust to Italian time slowly.

Week One

Fly into Rome or Naples on your first day and catch a ferry ride over to Sardinia. Indulge in a two-night, three-day stay, relaxing on the beaches and dining in waterfront seafood restaurants. On your fourth afternoon, step onboard a ferry for the overnight crossing to Sicily, where you can spend days five and six. Work your way around the island from west to east, ending in Messina, where you can spend your sixth evening in a hotel near the local ferry dock.

Wake early and catch the ferry across to mainland Italy, where you can board the northbound train in Reggio di Calabria. Arrive in Naples at the end of your seventh day, and prepare to begin your exploration of mainland Italy.

Week Two

Depending on your personal interests, you can divide the seven days of your second week between Naples, Rome, and Florence. If cities are not your thing, reserve one day for each metropolis and spend the rest of your time touring the countryside in Campania and Tuscany. If you plan to explore Tuscany, rent a car so you can get off the beaten path and into as many charming villages as you can find. Rent the car at the Naples airport and drop it off in Florence.

e! Alert

The Vatican Museums alone comprise some twenty different museums, including everything from the Sistine Chapel to the Egyptian Museum and the Gallery of Tapestries. Some art students spend entire weeks visiting just one. If you tend to linger, then count on at least a full day in Vatican City during week two of your month-long itinerary.

Conversely, if you love to sightsee in the cities, you might consider sticking with the train lines and adding even more days in Naples, Rome, and Florence. They are arguably the most interesting of Italy's cities—primarily in terms of sights and museums—and you could let your time in them cross over into week three, if you so desire.

Week Three

Where you go during week three of your itinerary will depend on where you want to go later, during week four.

Beginning from Florence, you will need to decide whether you want to go to Italy's northeast—perhaps positioning yourself to move later into Austria, Slovenia, or Croatia—or to Italy's northwest, which would put you closer to the borders of France and Switzerland. It is possible to crisscross the north of Italy in one week before moving on to the rest of Europe, but the pace would be harried.

If you choose to head northeast via the train system from Florence, then you can take the whole of week three to explore Bologna and Venice. Or, spend a few days in those two cities with a few "countryside" days out in the villages and vineyards. As with Tuscany, you have options in this part of Italy. The pace can be as slow as you want it to be, and as far away from the rest of the tourists as you desire. As long as you end week three in Venice, you will be well-positioned to move into eastern Europe via train or ferry.

ⓔ✔ Fact

Venezia Lines (*www.venezialines.com*) operates ferries from the port of Venice into five different ports in Croatia: Mali Losinj, Porec, Pula, Rabac, and Rovinj. These destinations are all along the island-filled northwest coast of Croatia. It would take months in the archipelago to see each island only once.

Alternatively, you can head northwest from Florence, beginning with a day in Pisa to see the Leaning Tower and then moving on to Genoa. The aquarium at the port of Genoa is worth a few hours of your time, and it's within easy walking distance of the main part of the city for shopping and sightseeing. After a day or two in Genoa, you can venture by rental car into the countryside to the villages and vineyards where the locals bottle world-famous Barolo and Barbaresco vintages. From there, make your way to the city of Milan, which is Italy's northernmost major train hub with connections into the rest of Europe. You can drop off your rental car and return to mass transit for your trek into greater Europe.

Week Four

Spend your fourth week moving beyond Italy's borders, into greater Europe. After three weeks of exploring from Sicily in the south all the way to the country's northern cities, you will have a good appreciation for the whole of Italian culture—and you will be better able to see how the spread of the Roman Empire so long ago continues to influence the European lifestyle today. That's especially true if you move east toward Croatia and beyond to Greece, where many amphitheaters, temples, and other ruins from Roman times serve as remarkable tourist sites today.

Chapter 18 offers detailed suggestions for easy destinations via train in the countries that surround Italy's northern border. Whether you want to finish your month-long vacation in Paris or Munich, you can easily do so by departing from Venice or Milan with your Eurail pass firmly in hand.

If You Have Two
Months in Italy and Europe

Western Europe is about one-third the size of the continental United States. Imagine Portugal, all the way at Europe's western edge, being where the state of Texas is on a United States map. The toe of Italy's "boot" would be where the southern tip of Florida is. Vienna would be atop Raleigh, North Carolina; Hamburg would be around Pittsburgh, Pennsylvania; and Paris would be in southern Illinois.

If someone told you that you could start in Texas and spend two months making your way in a giant circle from Texas to Florida, north to Pennsylvania, and over to Illinois, you would understand that the distances make sense. The same is true for seeing Italy and much else in Europe. It sounds like a big journey, but over the course of two months' time, you can squeeze in a lot of sights.

Even better, the luxury of having two whole months to explore Italy and Europe means you can take all the extra time you want to move beyond Italy's major cities and into its villages before crossing the border and exploring not just adjacent European nations, but others beyond them. If you make it to Paris with a week still left in your schedule, then you can easily take the train to world-famous cities such as Barcelona and Madrid in Spain, Lisbon in Portugal, and Brussels in Belgium. It's less than a day's train travel between each of these cities, putting many of them within reach depending on how much time you leave in your schedule after departing from Italy.

Alert

Great Britain's trains do not operate as part of the Eurail pass network. There is a high-speed train that you can take from France to England through the underwater Chunnel, but you will have to buy a separate ticket. Eurostar (*www.eurostar.com*) operates the passenger trains, with tickets also available through Rail Europe (*www.raileurope.com*).

Or, if you go in the direction of Croatia and Greece, you can extend your journey eastward beyond Athens into the Greek Isles. High-speed ferries connect many of the Greek islands to one another, giving you even more opportunities to see the ruins of Roman civilization. You might even make the short crossing from, say, the island of Rhodes over to the southern coast of Turkey, where even more archaeological treasures from the beginning of civilization are within easy touring distance of the major port cities such as Marmaris and Bodrum.

You might even make time to go north into Turkey and tour the ancient city of Ephesus before catching a flight home from Istanbul—which many centuries ago was known as Constantinople, the capital of the Roman Empire. A full-circle journey, indeed.

APPENDIX A

Helpful Websites

Travel agents can be extremely helpful when planning an overseas trip to a nation where you don't speak the local language. If you don't have a travel agent, you can find one at *www.asta.org*, the official website of the American Society of Travel Agents (the world's largest professional group in that sector). If that's not your cup of tea, you can do all of your trip-planning yourself using a plethora of helpful resources available online. This appendix gives you good places to start looking for everything you might need.

For Transportation in Italy

www.expedia.com
www.priceline.com

Any aggregating travel website, such as Expedia or Priceline, can show you prices and help you book airfare, hotels, rental cars, and—in some cases—cruise ships in Italy. Some sites even offer package deals. Beyond those basics—and in particular for traveling by rail—you will need to use dedicated resources that focus primarily on what's available in Italy.

AEROPORTO DI FIRENZE

www.aeroporto.firenze.it

This is the official website of the airport that services Florence. The site has an English version with timetables, transportation information, and everything else you might need before a flight.

AEROPORTO DI ROMA

www.adr.it

This is the official website of the airport that services Rome. It offers an English version with directions to and from the terminals, timetables for incoming and outgoing flights, and real-time information about delays, cancellations, and the like.

AEROPORTO DI VENICE

www.veniceairport.it

This is the official website of Marco Polo Airport, which serves Venice. It includes an English version with all the information you might need about flight times, departure gates, delays, and the like. A special section talks about passengers arriving in Venice to board cruise ships, including procedures for skipping check-in lines at the airport after disembarking a ship for your return flight home.

CAREMAR

www.caremar.it

Caremar is a ferry company that operates out of the Campania region, including mainland ports in Anzio, Formia, Pozzuoli, Naples, and Sorrento. Ferries from the mainland ports run to nearby islands including Ischia, Ponza, and Capri. Not all destinations are available from each of the mainland ports, so check the website for more information.

EURAIL

www.eurail.com

This is the place to buy multiday train passes for use in Italy and the rest of the European rail network. Timetables, maps, airport-train links, travel guides, popular routes, and even partner ferry schedules are available here. You can also switch the currency settings to show prices in United States dollars instead of euros, for easier budget planning.

ITALIAN GOVERNMENT TOURIST BOARD—AIRPORTS

www.italiantourism.com/air.html

This section of the Italian Government Tourist Board's website offers a list with live links to the websites of every airport in Italy. There are also instructions for how to make connections to trains, buses, taxis, water taxis, and rental cars from individual airports to the nearest major cities.

ITALIAN GOVERNMENT TOURIST BOARD—DISTANCES

www.italiantourism.com/distanze.html

This section of the Italian Government Tourist Board's website is incredibly useful for figuring out how long it will take you to get from one point in Italy to another. There are tables for road distances as well as ferry distances, plus journey times expressed in terms of air, train, and road travel between major cities. For instance, with one glance, you can see that when going from Rome to Naples, your options are a forty-five minute plane ride, a two-hour train ride, or a two-and-a-half-hour drive.

ITALIAN GOVERNMENT TOURIST BOARD—FERRIES

www.italiantourism.com/ferries.html

This section of the Italian Government Tourist Board's website offers an excellent overview of the dozen or so ferry companies that operate routes into and out of Italian ports, including live links to their individual websites and timetables (even for small ferry operators). The overview page also has brief descriptions of Italy's larger lakes, with information about towns where you can go to rent a day boat for an afternoon.

ITALIAN GOVERNMENT TOURIST BOARD—TRAINS

www.italiantourism.com/railway.html

This section of the Italian Government Tourist Board's website provides a complete overview of the types of trains you will find in Italy, from high-speed to local (written on timetables as *regionale*). There are also good explanations about making seat reservations, buying tickets in first or second class, and traveling on trains with a person in a wheelchair.

ITALIARAIL

www.italiarail.com

ItaliaRail is a North America-owned website dedicated exclusively to travel by train in Italy. You can buy Eurail passes here (for Italy and for multiple countries in Europe) and find tourist information about some cities, special deals and discounts, and helpful maps of train routes from multiple operators.

RAIL EUROPE

www.raileurope.com

Rail Europe is a North America–owned company that has helped people purchase train tickets throughout Europe for more than seventy-five years. French and Swiss national railroads are primary shareholders in this company, whose website offers schedules, timetables, special deals, and more.

SNAV

www.snav.it

SNAV is a ferry company that offers departures from both sides of the Italian mainland to Sicily, Sardinia, Croatia, and Greece. This company's operations begin in the southern half of Italy, starting with Civitavecchia (Rome) on Italy's western coast and Ancona on Italy's eastern coast. No departures are available farther north, even from port cities such as Genoa and Venice. The website includes special offers for passenger transit as well as details about shipping and freight services.

TIRRENIA NAVIGAZIONE

www.tirrenia.it

Tirrenia Navigazione is a ferry company that offers service to ports on both sides of the Italian mainland, as well as ports on Sicily and Sardinia. A handful of routes are also offered from Genoa to Tunis and from southeastern Italy to Croatia. Discount offers are typically posted on the website's home page.

TOREMAR

www.toremar.it

This is a ferry company that offers service from the Italian mainland cities of Livorno and Piombino to the small islands of Gorgona, Capraia, and Elba. Service is also available from Porto S. Stefano, an island south of Elba, to the nearby island of Giglio. Note that at the time of this writing, information on the website was available only in Italian.

TRENITALIA

www.trenitalia.com

This is a website where you can buy train tickets for use exclusively within Italy's borders. There is also good information here about train stations big and small, if you are wondering what you can expect to find at your ultimate destination.

For Pre-Arranged Tours in Italy

As with transportation, travel agents can be tremendously helpful in securing pre-arranged tours. There are plenty of online operators that will let you book tours of everything from Vatican City to St. Mark's Square in advance of your trip, but a local travel agent may have personal connections that can ensure you an English-speaking guide, a good deal, and proper service. With that said, here are some websites that you can use to pre-book tours on your own.

ITALIA TOURS

www.italiatours.com

Italia Tours offers everything from rental cars and day trips to city tours and multiday itineraries. There are self-drive gastronomy tours, guided tours of Tuscany, tours that include cooking classes, and vacation packages for virtually every part of Italy that you can imagine. Some tours are escorted, and some include chauffeured vehicles.

ITALY SOURCE

www.italysource.com

Italy Source is a U.S.-based company that specializes in tours of Italy and parts of Switzerland and France. The website offers helpful articles about good times to travel, optional itineraries for first-time Italy visitors, price levels for vacations of varying lengths, and more. Tours are organized by region, price, and type (such as honeymoons and anniversaries).

PERILLO TOURS

www.perillotours.com

Perillo Tours is a family-owned business that has offered tours in Italy since 1945. The company caters to travelers from the United States by offering tours with full, American breakfasts, competitive airfare rates from more than 130 cities in the United States, and deluxe hotels that offer the kinds of amenities that are typical on American soil. Some tours include "a touch of Switzerland" in addition to the northern Italian regions.

ROAD TO ITALY

www.roadtoitaly.com

Road to Italy offers private tours, group tours, honeymoon packages, and day trips throughout the country. There are also half- and full-day shore excursions available from Civitavecchia, Livorno, Naples, Venice, Palermo, Messina, and Catania. Day trips from Tuscany focus on food and wine, art and history, or specialty subjects.

TOUR ITALY NOW

www.touritalynow.com

This company offers private, group, and honeymoon tours on a prepackaged or customized basis. The site also has a good number of helpful articles about what to see and do in Italy, including must-see sights, a cruise guide, an article about renting homes versus hotel rooms, and general tips for traveling throughout Italy's various regions.

For English-to-Italian Translations

Can't find a word or phrase that you need? The following websites offer free computer-generated English-to-Italian translations. In some cases, the sites also offer for-a-fee translation by a human being at the other end of your Internet connection.

BABELFISH

www.babelfish.yahoo.com

This is the free translation service of Yahoo! It lets you translate large blocks of text up to 150 words long, or single web pages. An interesting feature is that after you have translated a phrase, you can click "search the web" to find more information based on your translation's results.

FREE TRANSLATION

www.freetranslation.com

The Free Translation website can help you to translate words, phrases, or entire websites from English to Italian. The standard word limit for free translation is 750 words, which should be more than enough for you to figure out how to ask a local Neapolitan, "Where can I get an adapter for my iPod Nano?"

WORD REFERENCE

www.wordreference.com

Word Reference is a website that offers translations of single words along with expansive definitions, which is good in cases when individual words have multiple meanings. The site offers an application that lets you use its services as a download on iTunes.

For Italian Food and Wine Research

It pays to bone up (pun intended!) on different kinds of meats, cheeses, pastas, sauces, and wines before heading to Italy. You will encounter countless ingredients and dishes when you get to Italy. Only if you learn a little bit in advance will you be able to enjoy the best of Italy's food and wine—in keeping with your own tastes.

ITALIAN FOOD FOREVER

www.italianfoodforever.com

This is the website of an English-speaking woman who married into a large, Italian family, who taught her to cook traditional food from "the Old Country." The site's glossary is exceptionally thorough in offering the Italian words for specific menu items that you might see, such as *affettato* (cold cuts served as an appetizer), *bavette* (a type of pasta), and *capsicum* (bell pepper).

LIFE IN ITALY

www.lifeinitaly.com

The Life in Italy website is all about Italy as it exists today, instead of the food and wine traditions of the past. There are individual sections about food, wine, and liquors, including articles about specific ingredients such as anchovies, saffron, and pasta shapes. The wine section includes lists of top producers of popular styles, including Barolo and Chianti.

WINE ENTHUSIAST

www.winemag.com

This is the website of *Wine Enthusiast* magazine. If you type the word "Italy" into the search box, you will find more than 100 articles about the various regions, grapes, and wineries in the country. Some articles give suggestions for Italian food and wine pairings, while others offer up-to-the-minute information about trends and newly released vintages. The "wine ratings" section of the site lets you search by label name and year to determine which Italian bottling the staff considers to be "best buy" and "editor's choice."

WINE SPECTATOR

www.winespectator.com

This is the in-depth website of *Wine Spectator* magazine. It includes articles about wines from all over the world, and Italy gets its fair share of representation. This site is a good place to look for up-to-the-minute news about what is happening in Italy's wineries, notes from recent tastings of newly available vintages, and reviews of virtually every wine that you can find for purchase. Many—but not all—of the sections are free, including the "ABCs of Wine" tutorial pages.

For Travel Information about the Rest of Europe

The following websites are good resources if you plan to extend your stay in Europe beyond Italy's borders.

CROATIA NATIONAL TOURIST BOARD

www.croatia.hr

This official national website includes destination articles, hotel and transportation services, and a section called "Tourism Plus" that lets you search for itineraries based on activities such as golf, camping, hunting, snow skiing, and rafting. There is also an "Events" section with a searchable database of upcoming festivals and other celebrations. You can search by region, island, town, or date.

EUROTRIP
www.eurotrip.com

This is a favorite website among travelers looking to save a few bucks by backpacking, sleeping in hostels, and such. You will find links to articles titled "Cheap Flight Tactics," "Hostels for a Newbie," and "I Don't Quite Understand the Eurorail System" (presumably, you will if you read the entire article). An interesting feature on this site is the ability to search for affordable hostel rooms in all European countries at once.

FRANCEGUIDE
http://us.franceguide.com

This is the English version of the official website of the French Government Tourism Office. In addition to all the hotel, transportation, and general travel information that you would expect to find on a site of this nature, Franceguide also offers contests where you can enter to win free vacations in Paris and beyond.

GERMANY TOURISM
www.germany-tourism.de

Germany Tourism is the official website of the German National Tourist Board. It offers tips for planning itineraries in all parts of the country, weather forecasts for all major German cities, discounts on everything from hotels to day trips, and ideas for groups or special occasions, including honeymooners, gay and lesbian travelers, religious travelers, and families. A special section is devoted to "heritage seekers," including a timeline of immigration to the

United States dating back to the seventeenth century, before there actually was a United States of America.

I LOVE SLOVENIA
www.slovenia.info

This is the official website of the Slovenian Tourist Board. It includes information about the country's regions and main sights, a map, a route planner, and ideas for travel based on food, wine, health, and other activities. You can also download promotional commercials produced for television stations that show different parts of Slovenia that are most eager to welcome tourists.

MY SWITZERLAND
www.myswitzerland.com

This is the official website of the Swiss National Tourist Office. It offers destination articles, hotel reservations, updated information for travelers, and ideas for planning vacations during every season of the year. You can also buy tickets through this website for train transportation in Switzerland.

VACATION IN AUSTRIA
www.austria.info

Vacation in Austria is the official website of the Austrian National Tourist Office. There are downloadable brochures, interactive maps, picture galleries, tips for itineraries based on interests such as architecture and wine, "dream vacation" suggestions, hotel reservations, and more. News and updates are posted on the home page, and there is a link where you can send a question to an expert on the staff.

VISIT EUROPE

www.visiteurope.com

This site is maintained by the European Travel Commission, an association of national travel associations with nearly forty members, including all of the European Union countries. The site offers an interactive map of Europe that lets you zoom in and out of countries and regions, learning about everything from the Danube River to the Alps. There is a currency converter to help you figure out how many American dollars you are spending with each euro, plus practical tourism information, downloadable brochures, and news about upcoming events across Europe.

Buon viaggio!: Travel Essentials

Passports and Visas

Before your first taste of authentic *crostini misti* and a glass of *Chianti*, you'll have some paperwork to do. Check to see that your passport is current, and remember that returning to the United States with an expired passport is illegal.

Visas are generally required for citizens of the United States only if they stay in Italy for longer than three months. If that's the case, you'll need an application form, a detailed itinerary, proof of adequate medical insurance, a valid return airline ticket, and proof of accommodations. Also carry two or more forms of identification on your person, including at least one photo ID. Many banks require several IDs in order to cash traveler's checks.

Fact

Freedom of movement isn't just for those wearing stretch pants. If you're an EU citizen, you can take the specially designated lane at the airport and breeze right through customs. It's all part of the efforts to ease border-patrol regulations and ease travel between participating countries.

Customs

Going through *la dogana* (customs) shouldn't be much of a bother as long as you have all the right identification. In addition, if you've purchased goods and gifts at a duty-free shop, you'll have to pay a duty if the value of those articles exceeds the allowance established by the Italian customs service.

"Duty-free" simply means that you don't have to pay a tax in the country of purchase. Be sure to keep receipts for major purchases while in Italy—non-European Union citizens can claim a refund for the value added tax (VAT or IVA).

Where to Turn When You Need Assistance

Sometimes it happens no matter what you do to prevent it. You thought your wallet was safe in your pocket but you misplaced it. Your passport fell out of your pocket on that rough ride from Naples to Capri. If you lose your passport, immediately notify the local police and the nearest embassy or consulate. There are consulates in most major Italian cities, including Florence, Milan, Naples, Palermo, and Venice. They answer the phone around the clock and also have lists of English-speaking doctors and lawyers.

Essential

The U.S. Embassy is at Via V. Veneto, 119a, 00187 Rome. There are U.S. Consulates in Florence, Milan, and Naples (*www.usembassy.it*). They all issue new passports the same day but are closed on U.S. and Italian holidays.

Exchanging Money

Many tourists may be used to the old and faithful traveler's checks. But there are other, more convenient, and perhaps easier ways of getting your hands on some euro while you vacation in Italy.

ATMs are Called Bancomat

Buying euro from your bank in the United States can be expensive. Most banks will charge up to 10 percent in fees. The same goes for exchanging money at exchange airports, counters, and hotels in Italy. The best exchange rates can be found at ATMs (*bancomat*, pronounced BAHN-koh-maht). Check with your bank before you leave to determine if there are any service charges involved with ATM use abroad. Your bank may allow free ATM use through a specific Italian network (Cirrus and BankMate are two of the most widely available). ATMs in Italy will usually only allow you to withdraw money from your primary account (usually your checking account). If you're used to keeping a low balance in your checking account and a high balance in savings, you may want to call your bank to make sure that your checking and savings accounts are linked.

Banks

If you do not have an ATM card, your best bet is to exchange money at a bank. Be advised, though: Banks in Italy are usually open from 8:35 A.M. to 1:35 P.M., and again from 3:00 P.M. to 4:00 P.M. Paperwork can take some time, and the exchange rate, though it may be better than what you might find at the airport, still leaves a bit to be desired.

Credit Cards

Major credit card accounts usually offer cash advance type services. These transactions benefit from the anti-fraud protection that accompanies your account (save your receipts!). Though the exchange rates can be compatible, check on the types of fees and charges associated with these transactions. If you plan on using a credit card for purchases while you are in Italy, make sure to call your bank or credit card company before you leave to confirm that you will be using your card in Italy. Not doing so may alert your credit card company's anti-fraud department at an inopportune time!

Traveler's Checks

Many travelers still insist on the convenience and safety that traveler's checks offer. With the prominence of ATMs and credit card use, travelers will find that traveler's checks are not as widely accepted as they used to be. You will be able to exchange them in banks and in hotels, but don't count on them being accepted at local shops and restaurants.

The Euro

The euro is used as the national currency in twelve European countries, including Italy. The seven banknote denominations (5, 10, 20, 50, 100, 200, 500) have a common design in all countries, but the eight denominations of coins have a single European design on one side, and unique national designs on the other.

Coin	Design
1 cent	Castel del Monte in Apulia
2 cent	The Mole Antonelliana Tower in Torino
5 cent	The Colosseum in Rome
10 cent	Sandro Botticelli's Birth of Venus
20 cent	Unique Forms of Continuity in Space by Umberto Boccioni
50 cent	Statue of Emperor Marcus Aurelius on horseback
1 euro	Leonardo da Vinci's famous drawing of the human body
2 euro	Drawing of Dante Alighieri by Raphael

Useful Vocabulary and Phrases

The following terms and expressions will help you navigate Italian financial institutions—or at least they will help you as you try to exchange money.

MONEY AND THE BANK

money	*il denaro/i soldi*
the euro	*l'euro*
change	*il cambio*
banknote	*la banconota*
coin	*la moneta*
currency	*la valuta*
dollar	*il dollaro*
British pound sterling	*la sterlina*
check	*l'assegno*
traveler's check	*il travelers check*
to cash (a check)	*incassare un assegno*
bank	*la banca*
counter	*lo sportello*
teller window	*la cassa*
exchange rate	*il tasso di cambio*
to sign	*firmare*

At the Bank

To which counter do I go to change money?
A che sportello devo andare per cambiare del denaro?

Is there a commission?
C'è una commissione da pagare?

What's the exchange rate for the dollar?
Qual'è il tasso di cambio per il dollaro?

Where do I have to sign?
Dove devo firmare?

What is today's date?
Qual'è la data di oggi?

What time does the bank open?
A che ora apre la banca?

What time does the bank close?
A che ora chiude la banca?

Do you accept credit cards?
Accettate la carta di credito?

Can you change money for me?
Potete cambiare delle banconote per me?

Can you change dollars for me?
Potete cambiare dei dollari per me?

Can you change American/Australian/Canadian dollars for me?
Potete cambiare dei dollari Americani/Australiani /Canadesi per me?

Where can I get money changed?
Dove posso cambiare delle banconote?

Where can I get foreign money changed?
Dove posso cambiare della valuta straniera?

Where can I change a traveler's check?
Dove posso cambiare un travelers check?

What is today's exchange rate?
Quantè il cambio di oggi?

Where is an automatic teller machine (ATM)?
Dove posso trovare un Bancomat?

Making a Telephone Call

At some point you'll want to speak on the telephone, whether it's to make hotel reservations, purchase tickets to a show, or arrange for a taxi to pick you up. The *alfabeti telefonici* (phonetic alphabet) is useful when spelling out words over the telephone, for example, or when speaking to officials.

Italians tend to use the names of Italian cities (when there is a corresponding town) rather than proper nouns to spell out words. For example, while you might say "M as in Michael," an Italian is more likely to say *M come Milano* (M as in Milan). The following list will give you examples for all other letters.

Italian Letter	Italian Word	Italian Letter	Italian Word
A	*Ancona*	N	*Napoli*
B	*Bologna*	O	*Otranto*
C	*Como*	P	*Padova*
D	*Domodossola*	Q	*quarto*
E	*Empoli*	R	*Roma*
F	*Firenze*	S	*Savona*
G	*Genova*	T	*Torino*
H	*hotel*	U	*Udine*
I	*Imola*	V	*Venezia*
J	*Jérusalem*	W	*Washington*
K	*kilogramma*	X	*Xeres*
L	*Livorno*	Y	*York*
M	*Milano*	Z	*Zara*

Calling Italy from the United States and Canada

To place a call from the United States or Canada, first dial the United States international code 011, then dial Italy's country code 39, then dial the city code (06 for Rome, 055 for Florence), and finally dial the number, which can be six or seven digits. For example, if the Italian phone number is 055-55-55-55, you must dial the following: 011 39 0 55 55 55 55.

Calling Another Country from Italy

To place a call to another country from Italy, first dial the Europe long distance code 00, then the country code (1 for the United States and Canada), then the area code and number.

COUNTRY CODES OF OTHER COUNTRIES

United States	1
Canada	1
United Kingdom	44
France	33
Germany	49
Spain	34
Switzerland	41

Placing a Call Within Italy

Italian phone numbers are comprised of an area code (this can be from two to fours digits and begins with a zero) and the phone number. Cell phone area codes begin with the number 3, and area codes that begin with the number 8 are toll-free. To make a call from one area code to another, you must dial the full area code and number. To call within the same area code, you must dial the area code as well.

 Alert

Remember, Italy is six hours ahead of the United States eastern standard time (EST). For example, at midnight in Boston, it is 6:00 a.m. in Rome.

Public Phones

Public phones are easy to find. They're literally everywhere, and most bars and coffee shops will have one on the premises. The phone booths are egg-shaped and are usually painted a bright orange color for easy recognition. You can pay for a public phone with coins (*monette*), with a phone card (*scheda telefonica*), or with a credit card (*carta di credito*). Some older phones will only take coins, and some newer phones will only take a phone or credit card.

You can purchase phone cards from machines at the airport, train stations, and most tobacco stores and bars. They are available in various denominations. To use the phone card, you must first break off the perforated corner in the upper part of the card, which will allow the card to fit into the slot on the phone. Once you've inserted the card, it is activated.

You may come across public Internet Corners. They can be used with the phone cards. These stations may not work very well, so do not depend on them for Internet access.

Emergency Numbers

In the rare instance that you need to get in touch with emergency services, here is how to reach them:

- **112** Emergencies. Much like 911 in the United States, this is a European Union-wide emergency number with multilingual operators that can route your emergency to the appropriate agency.
- **113** Emergencies (local police)—*Polizia di stato*, national civilian police
- **115** Fire department
- **117** *Guardia di finanza* (financial police). If a business has cheated you, this is the number to call.
- **118** Ambulance.

Cell Phones

We've become accustomed to the convenience of personal cell phones. Whether you plan on bringing your cell phone with you or buying (or renting) one while you're there, this section will give you some valuable pointers.

GSM (Global System for Mobile Communications) is a type of cell phone and network that is used in most countries in the world, including Europe. You will need a GSM phone in Italy. GSM phones are sometimes called world phones because they can be used around the world.

Check with your cell phone service provider to determine if yours is a GSM phone. If it is not, world phones can be purchased easily and inexpensively from numerous online vendors. If you have a GSM phone, check with your service provider to determine the costs involved with using your phone while you are abroad. Some companies offer reasonable rates for use abroad, while others are quite expensive.

If your U.S. cellular service provider does not offer international service, it is possible—and often economical—to rent a world phone complete with a SIM card from a reputable online source such as RangeRoamer (*www.rangeroamer.com*) or Call in Europe (*www.callineurope.com*). Waiting until you arrive in Italy and renting a phone at the airport or from a cell phone store is possible but time-consuming.

SIM Cards

A SIM (Subscriber Information Module) card is a small chip inserted into your phone that contains your cell phone number and your account information. The SIM Card can easily be switched from one phone to another. Provided you're in possession of a world phone, it may be possible for you to purchase a SIM card in Italy and simply use it while you travel. This is a good option all over Europe because cell phone plans in Europe do not require lengthy contract commitments. SIM cards come with a certain number of pre-paid minutes; once you've used your minutes, you can either discard the SIM card or purchase more minutes. Also, there is no per-minute charge for incoming calls.

TELEPHONE VOCABULARY

cell phone	*telefonino/cellulare*
	teh-leh-foh-NEE-noh/chehl-loo-LAH-reh
reverse charges/ collect call	*a carico del destinatario*
	ah KAH-ree-koh dehl des-tee-nah-TAH-ree-oh
busy	*occupato*
	ohk-koo-PAH-toh
Please hold	*stia in linea*
	STEE-ah een LEE-nay-ah
to hang up	*riagganciare*
	ree-ah-gahn-CHAH-ray
to call back	*richiamare*
	ree-kyah-MAH-ray
to ring	*squillare*
	skwee-LAH-ray
telephone	*il telefono*
	eel teh-LEH-foh-noh
telephone booth	*la cabina telefonica*
	lah kah-BEE-nah teh-leh-FOH-nee-kah
telephone call	*la telefonata*
	lah teh-leh-foh-NAH-tah
telephone directory	*la guida telefonica*
	lah GWEE-dah teh-leh-FOH-nee-kah
telephone number	*il numero di telefonico*
	eel NOO-meh-roh teh-leh-FOH-nee-koh
dialing tone	*il segnale acustico*
	eel sehn-YAH-lay ah-KOO-stee-koh

Italian Art and Culture

Learn more about the art and culture of Italy and you'll learn more about the country itself. It's practically impossible to think of Italy and not recall the Renaissance or the opera. Today, Italians have a broad range of interests, including playing sports, watching movies, and reading books and magazines. Italy's many cultural riches can entertain you and enrich your travel experience.

Art and Soul

Whether you travel to Italy, page through a coffee-table book featuring Italian artists, or listen to opera on the radio, Italian art is unavoidable. Amazing Italian art predates the Roman Empire and stretches into the present day.

Essential

When referring to a particular artistic period in a century between 1100 and 1900, Italians drop the mille (thousand). For example, the 1300s are called il Trecento, the 1400s are called il Quattrocento, and so on.

Famous Artists

Michelangelo, Raffaello, Leonardo, and Donatello have at least one thing in common: Most people nowadays know these artists by their first names. Obviously, they had *cognomi* (last names) too:

Michelangelo Buonarroti
Raffaello Sanzio
Donato di Betto Bardi (Donatello)
Leonardo da Vinci

 Fact

Leonardo da Vinci literally means "Leonardo from Vinci." Vinci is a small town in the province of Firenze, in Tuscany, to the northwest of the city of Florence. Leonardo was born on April 15, 1452, in a small farmhouse about two miles from the town of Vinci. His full name was Leonardo di ser Piero da Vinci (Leonardo, son of Piero, from Vinci).

Other well-known names include Giotto di Bondone, Tommaso Giovanni di Simone Guidi (Masaccio) and Alessandro di Mariano Filipepi (Sandro Botticelli).

Marble, Wood, Bronze

If it was solid and durable, chances are a Renaissance artist could grab a chisel and begin to sculpt. Donatello, for example, was an extremely influential Florentine sculptor of the *Quattrocento*. He did freestanding sculptures in marble, bronze, and wood and was also known for pioneering *schiacciato* (shallow relief). This new technique helped him achieve a sense of depth in his paintings using perspective rather than through the use of high relief.

Michelangelo believed it was his duty to liberate the figure that was straining to be released from the marble. His unfinished slave sculptures, several of which can be viewed in Florence's *Galleria dell'Accademia*, are perhaps the best examples of how he chipped away just enough marble to liberate the figures.

Artistic Vocabulary

You're standing in line at the Uffizi in Florence or the *Capodimonte Museum* in Naples and can't wait to see all that amazing artwork. Or you're a student in an art history class studying Michelangelo, Ghirlandaio, and Caravaggio. Put your free time to good use and review some vocabulary words that relate to art and museums.

VOCABULARY: AT THE MUSEUM

apprentice	*l'apprendista*
art	*l'arte*
artist	*l'artista*
canvas	*la tela*
caption	*la didascalia*
corridor	*il corridoio*
frame	*la cornice*
gallery	*la galleria*
marble	*il marmo*
masterpiece	*capolavoro*
paint, to	*dipingere*
paint	*la vernice*
paintbrush	*il pennello*
painter	*il pittore*
relief	*il rilievo*
Renaissance	*il Rinascimento*
sculpt	*scolpire*
sculptor	*scultore*
sculpture	*la scultura*
studio	*la bottega*

The Opera

The theatrical form of opera, which combines acting, singing, and classical music, originated in Italy more than 400 years ago. Most operas were originally sung in Italian, and today there are historic opera houses throughout Italy where the divas still sing.

The common operatic term *bel canto* (beautiful singing) points out why so many people refer to Italian as a language that's "sung" by native speakers. Since Italian speakers place the vowels in a forward position (in front of the mouth) just as singers do when singing, it's easy for Italians to switch from speaking to singing. That's probably why so many Italians seem to be blessed with "natural" singing voices. The formation of vowels is integral not only in singing opera but in speaking Italian as well.

Question

Who is the *prima donna*?
The *prima donna* is the principal female singer in an opera or concert organization. The term literally means "first lady" and has mutated in current usage to mean an extremely sensitive, vain, or undisciplined person.

If you want to get a head start on understanding a performance, be sure to read the *libretto* (literally, "little book") first. The *libretto* is a play-by-play of all the action onstage, and reading it will enhance your time at the theater. Although you might not be able to follow the songs word for word, what's more important is to get a feel for the action, the excitement, and the drama.

Here are just a few operas that are recognized as masterpieces and are sure to give you a thrill:

Aida, **by Giuseppi Verdi,** was first produced in Cairo in 1871. The opera is set in ancient Egypt and is named after the Ethiopian princess who is its heroine.

Il Barbiere di Siviglia **(The Barber of Seville)** is a comic opera composed by Gioacchino Rossini and first produced in Rome in 1816. The barber of the title is Figaro, a character who also appears in Mozart's *Le Nozze di Figaro,* a sequel.

La Bohème is an opera in four acts by Giacomo Puccini, first produced in Turin in 1896.

Rigoletto is an opera by Verdi produced in Venice in 1851. The title is taken from its baritone hero, a tragic court jester. "*La donna è mobile*" (the woman is fickle) is its most famous aria.

La Traviata is another opera written by Verdi. The title is variously interpreted to mean "the fallen woman" or "the woman gone astray." The work, in three acts, was first performed in Venice in 1853. This is the opera Richard Gere takes Julia Roberts to see in the movie *Pretty Woman.*

Operatic Vocabulary

If you ever have the opportunity, hearing a performance at Milan's *La Scala* will leave you speechless. To help you find your way out there, you might need to know a few vocabulary words. See the music vocabulary lists on the following pages.

VOCABULARY: THE OPERA

accompanist	l'accampagnatore
act	l'atto
to act	recitare
backstage	il retroscena
ballet	il balletto
ballet dancer	il ballerino
cadence	la cadenza
check room	il guardaroba
comedy	la commedia
comic opera	l'opera buffa
concert	il concerto
conductor	il direttore d'orchestra
costumes	i costumi
curtain	il sipario
dance	la danza
dancer	il ballerino
drama	il drama
dress rehearsal	la prova generale
duet	il duetto
to improvise	improvvisare
intermission	l'intervallo
lobby	l'ingresso
lyric	il lirico
music	la musica
musical	il musicale
orchestra	l'orchestra
overture	il preludio
part	la parte
performance	la rappresentazione
play	l'opera drammatica
producer	il produttore
production	la messa in scena
program	il programma

scene	*la scena*
scenery	*lo scenario*
show	*lo spettacolo*
singer	*il cantante*
song	*il canzone*
stage	*il palcoscenico*
symphony	*la sinfonia*
tenor	*il tenore*
ticket	*il biglietto*
title	*il titolo*
tragedy	*la tragedia*
voice	*la voce*

VOCABULARY: CONCERTS

to applaud, to clap	*applaudire*
applause	*l'applauso*
cello	*il violoncello*
chorus	*il coro*
clarinet	*il clarinetto*
classical music	*la musica classica*
concert	*il concerto*
drums	*la batteria*
flute	*il flauto*
guitar	*la chitarra*
instrument	*lo strumento*
jazz	*il jazz*
to listen (to)	*ascoltare*
oboe	*l'oboe*
opera	*l'opera*
orchestra	*l'orchestra*
piano	*il pianoforte*
to play by ear	*suonare a orecchio*
to play by sight	*suonare a prima vista*

VOCABULARY: CONCERTS *continued*

to play the guitar	*suonare la chitarra*
to play the piano	*suonare il pianoforte*
rock music	*la musica rock*
saxophone	*il sassofono*
show	*lo spettacolo*
to sing	*cantare*
singer	*il cantante*
song	*la canzone*
stage	*il palcoscenico*
trombone	*il trombone*
trumpet	*la tromba*
violin	*il violino*

Architecture

It is widely believed that the Roman Empire's most significant contribution to the modern world is its architecture. The Romans perfected the use of the arch and made significant advancements in the use of concrete to build aqueducts, stadiums, villas, and palaces. Learning about architecture is another way to increase your Italian vocabulary, whether you'd like to learn about the three primary orders of columns—Corinthian, Doric, or Ionic— or the many different types of architectural styles—including Byzantine, Gothic, Romanesque, Renaissance, Mannerism, and Baroque. Another example? The palladium window derives from an Italian architect, Andrea Palladio, who led a revival of classical architecture in sixteenth-century Italy and designed many major buildings, including the church of San Giorgio Maggiore in Venice, built in 1566.

Churches

How was a priest to teach his mostly illiterate congregation about the Bible? With pictures! That's one reason why so many churches in Italy have paintings, frescoes, and mosaics everywhere. Commissioned artists created pictorial representations of Biblical stories, from the flood to the martyrdom of saints, from heaven to hell, from Christ's birth to His crucifixion and resurrection. Since very few people could read, this was one way for them to visualize the sermons offered from the pulpit. Images of sinners burning in hell probably convinced a number of churchgoers to mind their actions.

Essential

If you're interested in learning more about architecture and have some time on your hands, try the ten-volume treatise *De Architectura*. It was written in the first century B.C. by Vitruvius, a Roman architect and military engineer. The work is considered the bible of classical architectural theory and also served to inspire the Italian Renaissance's architects and educated men.

It's not surprising to see so many impressive-looking churches in a country where the seat of Roman Catholicism is located. Throughout Italy, there are cathedrals and basilicas in styles such as Byzantine, Gothic, Romanesque, and Renaissance. If you're looking for some of the best examples of celestial art and architecture, you can't go wrong visiting these churches:

***Basilica di San Francesco*, Assisi.** Built in memorial of St. Francis, this unique church, with two separate levels, has a number of important frescoes by artists such as Giotto, Cimabue, Simone Martini, and Pietro Lorenzetti.

Cathedral, Baptistry, and Tower Pisa. The famous leaning tower isn't the only architectural masterpiece in Pisa. The green-and-white marble stonework of the adjacent buildings is every bit as stunning.

Baptistry Duomo, Florence. The octagonal duomo by Filippo Brunelleschi can be seen for miles around, and the ceiling of the Baptistery is covered in amazing mosaics.

St. Mark's Basilica, Venice. The curving domes of the church are encrusted with golden mosaics that are the epitome of Byzantine art.

***San Miniato al Monte Basilica*, Florence.** This church overlooking a hillside has many important frescoes.

Basilica of Sant'Ambrogio, Milan. This is an amazing Gothic church in the center of the city. Visitors can even walk on the roof for a closeup look at the spires.

Santa Maria Novella church, Florence. Wealthy businessmen commissioned several of the city's most important Renaissance artists to create frescoes in the chapels that line this church.

Architectural Vocabulary

It helps to know what you're talking about when it comes to architecture in Italy. Following are common words you are likely to encounter.

VOCABULARY: ARCHITECTURE

abbey	l'abbazia
altar	l'altare
arch	l'arco
balcony	la loggia
baptistery	il battistero
bell tower	il campanile
canopy	il baldacchino
chapel	la cappella
church	la chiesa
cloister	il chiostro
crypt	la cripta
crucifix	il crocifisso
Last Supper	il cenacolo
nave	la navata
palace	il palazzo
pilaster	il pilastro
refectory	il refettorio
rose window	il rosone

Roman Ruins

There's something almost otherworldly about historical ruins—maybe it's the thought of connecting with an ancient people, admiring their craftsmanship, or wondering about the lives of those who lived long before us. At the Roman Forum, for example, Roman senators met to conduct the business of governing the empire. Today, you can wander the Via Antica and see many of the buildings and monuments that date back more than 2,000 years.

There are many other incredible ancient ruins in Italy, and you might consider taking a tour from an Italian speaker to learn twice—first the language, and second the history of the location. Take a guidebook along to translate the terms you don't understand and then describe what you've seen in Italian. Here are a few places worth visiting:

Pompeii. One of the most popular ghost towns, it was leveled in A.D. 79 when Mount Vesuvius erupted and covered the entire city in ash. Thousands of years later, it is still Italy's most-visited tourist attraction. Today, it's still possible to see many houses and public buildings that were part of the city.

The Colosseum. This structure was the scene of gladiator fights, naval battles, chariot races, and fights with hungry lions. What remains of this huge amphitheater is remarkable, considering that emperors and popes mined the ruins for centuries to use its marble for other buildings in Rome.

Roman Forum. Imagine Caesar walking the stones of the Roman Forum, scheming to achieve domination of the Western world.

Etruscan ruins. These ruins are older than the Roman Empire, and there are a number of sites you can visit throughout Tuscany.

Sicily. This is the mother lode of Greek archeological finds. Remarkable examples of Greek temples can be found at Syracuse, Agrigento, Selinunte, and Segesta. The theater at Taormina is especially well-preserved.

✅ Fact

There's a price to pay for everything—even church. Some churches in Italy now request an entrance fee to offset the cost of maintenance, claiming that the artwork found on their walls, by such artists as Filippo Brunelleschi, Masaccio, and Giotto, are equal to any found in museums. Town residents are exempt from paying.

Il Cinema Italiano

Watching Italian movies is a great way to prepare for a trip to Italy. During the 1940s neorealism emphasized location shooting and authentic drama. In the 1950s, the lighthearted *la commedia all'italiana*, with stars such as Totò, left audiences howling. In the 1960s, Progressive directors such as Federico Fellini and Michelangelo Antonioni created films of great individual expression.

Here is a list of recommended films related to the Italian language. Pass the popcorn and watch the screen light up with Roberto Benigni, Sophia Loren, Marcello Mastroianni, and many others.

- *Ladri di biciclette (Bicycle Thief)*, **1948**. Many critics consider this Oscar-winning classic to be one of the greatest films ever made. Vittorio De Sica used nonprofessional actors to tell the simple, human tragedy of a working man whose bike, which he needs for his job, is stolen, sending him and his son on a harrowing search through the streets of Rome.
- *Riso amaro (Bitter Rice)*, **1948.** Silvana Mangano became an international sensation with her performance as a shapely city woman working in the rice fields of Italy's Po Valley after World War II. The sexy Mangano is caught in a love triangle with the respectable Raf Vallone and the unscrupulous Vittorio Gassman.
- *Ciao professore!*, **1993.** This tender and often hilarious comedy from Lina Wertmuller centers on a teacher who is mistakenly assigned to a third-grade class in an impoverished town in southern Italy. The teacher soon faces the Mafia, truancy, and pupils with family problems as he tries to steer his students in the right direction.
- *Nuovo Cinema Paradiso* (**Cinema Paradiso**), **1988.** This charming, bittersweet tribute to the power of movies, directed by Giuseppe Tornatore, won 1989's Best Foreign Film Academy Award. A film director looks back on his childhood in Sicily,

where he served as an apprentice to the projectionist at his small town's only movie theater.

- *Morte a Venezia (Death in Venice)*, **1971.** This is Luchino Visconti's brilliant version of Thomas Mann's classic story. Dirk Bogarde stars as a jaded, middle-aged composer on holiday in Venice who spots a handsome young boy on the beach. His doomed obsession with the youth renews his interest in living.
- *Divorzio all'Italiana (Divorce, Italian Style)*, 1961. This marvelous Oscar-winning farce stars Marcello Mastroianni as a man facing midlife crisis who discovers it's easier to kill his annoying wife than divorce her. Eventually he falls for a gorgeous younger woman, played by Stefania Sandrelli.
- *Il Giardino dei Finzi-Contini (The Garden of the Finzi-Continis)*, **1962.** Director Vittorio De Sica's Oscar-winning drama centers on an upper-class Jewish family living in fascist Italy, oblivious at first to the growing tide of anti-Semitism that soon threatens their existence.
- *Il postino (The Postman)*, **1994.** This lovely romance is set in a small Italian town during the 1950s where exiled Chilean poet Pablo Neruda has taken refuge. A shy mailman befriends the poet and uses his words—and, ultimately, the writer himself—to help him woo a woman with whom he has fallen in love. It stars Philippe Noiret and Massimo Troisi, who died a day after filming ended.
- *La strada (The Road)*, 1954. Federico Fellini's Oscar-winning study of members of a traveling circus troupe relates how a brutal strongman uses a simpleminded woman who loves him, forcing her to find solace with a good-hearted clown.
- *Le sette bellezze (Seven Beauties)*, 1976. Giancarlo Giannini stars in Lina Wertmuller's dark seriocomic movie as a small-time hood in World War II Italy trying to support his sisters. His desperate attempts to stay alive take him from jail to a

mental hospital and eventually put him in the hands of an obese concentration camp commandant.

ⓔ✱ Essential

The movie *Ladri di Saponette* (1989), also known as *The Icicle Thief,* is a shameless parody of Vittoria De Sica's neorealist classic *Ladri di Biciclette (The Bicycle Thief)*. It's a black-and-white film that satirizes TV commercials and lampoons advertising. The video has no relation to De Sica's film but is worth mentioning for its own warped vision of the small screen.

The Art of Dubbing

Italy is a nation that shies away from subtitles, and dubbing in Italian movies is acknowledged to be first-rate. In fact, Italy has an internationally renowned dubbing school and tradition. Dubbing and voice-over for film, video, and documentary scripts requires training in a formal setting. For years, the same actors and actresses have dubbed the voices of well-known actors. Ferruccio Amendola, for instance, was an outstanding dubber who gave the Italian voices to actors such as Al Pacino, Dustin Hoffman, and Robert De Niro.

Italian Literature

There are a number of Italian texts, both classic and contemporary, that are must-reads for anyone interested in the history, culture, and language of Italy. Whether it's a trip to hell and back, a year's worth of love poems, or ribald humor during the plague, there's a tale for everyone.

Dante, Petrarca, and Boccaccio were the trio that first popularized literary Italian. During the Renaissance, writers such as Ludovico Ariosto, Nicolò Machiavelli, and Torquato Tasso blazed new trails with epic poetry, dramas, and political works. Dramatists such as Vittorio Alfieri and Carlo Goldoni and the poet Ugo Foscolo led a literary revival in the eighteenth century.

In the twentieth century, the poet Gabriele D'Annunzio, the dramatist Luigi Pirandello, and writers Alberto Moravia, Cesare Pavese, and Italo Calvino all made their mark in Italian literature. What follows are just a few of the many classics in Italian literature.

- **Canzoniere (Collection of Poems).** Francesco Petrarca, one of the great early Renaissance humanists, wrote love poetry in the "vulgar" tongue. His *Canzoniere* had enormous influence on the poets of the fifteenth and sixteenth centuries. Head over heels in love with Laura, Petrarca wrote 365 poems, one passionate poem a day, dedicated to his true love.
- **La divina commedia (The Divine Comedy).** The epic poem by Dante, begun in exile in 1306, allegorically describes the poet's (and, by implication, mankind's) journey through life to salvation. The *Commedia* is the central and culminating literary work of Medieval Europe. It is systematically structured in *terza rima*, with three *cantiche* (*Inferno*, *Purgatorio*, and *Paradiso*).
- **Il decamerone (The Decameron).** Written by the Italian humanist writer Giovanni Boccaccio almost 650 years ago, *Il decamerone* contains a hundred tales supposedly told in ten days by a party of ten young people who had fled from the Black Death in Florence. Regarded as his masterpiece and a model for Italian classical prose, its influence on Renaissance literature was enormous.
- **Orlando Furioso.** A romance epic by the Italian poet Ludovico Ariosto. Orlando goes mad because his lady, Angelica, marries a Moorish youth, but he is cured in time to defeat Agramante, king of Africa, who has been besieging Paris. Ariosto invents fantastic episodes and complicated romantic intrigues and adventures.

- *I promessi sposi (The Betrothed).* In Alessandro Manzoni's powerfully characterized historical reconstruction of plague-ravaged seventeenth-century Lombardy, the simple attempts of two poor silk weavers to marry are used to explore the corrupt and oppressive rule of the Spaniards and, by implication, of the later Austrians. The novel also forged the literary Italian, which, after the unification of Italy, became standard Italian.

✅ Fact

Italic script was a style of handwriting adopted in fifteenth-century Italy by papal scribes and later (c. 1500) adapted for printing. Italic cursive letters eliminate unnecessary lifts of the pen, permitting rapid legible handwriting.

- *Il fu Mattia Pascal (The Late Mattia Pascal).* Luigi Pirandello's remarkable work focuses on Pascal, a landowner fallen on hard times who gets a chance to create a new life.
- *Non si paga, non si paga (Can't Pay? Won't Pay!).* Nobel Prize–winning playwright Dario Fo tells the story of a Milan housewife Antonia, who steals a large number of groceries from her local supermarket during a mass protest against rising prices. There follows an increasingly frantic series of confusions, police searches, and misunderstandings that spiral into high farce.
- *I rusteghi (The Tyrants).* Carlo Goldoni, a dramatist who wrote 250 plays, based this three-act comedy on the society of his native Venice.

Newspapers and Magazines

Italian publications can be found on the newsstands of many large cities, at airports, and online. *Panorama* and *L'Espresso* are weekly newsmagazines similar to *Time* or *Newsweek*. Both include news, science, politics, medicine, sports, lifestyle, and personalities. Some familiar magazines are also published in Italy, such as *Le Scienze*, which is the Italian version of *Scientific American*.

In Italy, you are what you read, and newspapers are a sign of how important politics are to Italians. Many people swear allegiance to certain publications, depending on their party affiliations.

 Fact

Guglielmo Marconi, an Italian physicist, invented the radio in 1895. He achieved the first successful wireless trans-Atlantic transmission from Wellfleet, Massachusetts, on Cape Cod.

The most popular national daily papers are *Il Corriere della Sera*, a conservative publication from Milan, and *La Repubblica*, a liberal paper from Rome. Other popular papers include *La Stampa* (conservative, published in Torino and owned by Fiat) and *Il Messaggero* (liberal, published in Rome). *Il Sole 24 Ore* is the *Wall Street Journal* of Italian newspapers, while the pink-colored *La Gazzetta dello Sport* is a favorite among *i tifosi* (fans, enthusiasts) to keep track of their favorite soccer team.

The Internet

You can use the web to improve your Italian skills. Whether it's browsing a news site, requesting travel information, or even taking an interactive Italian lesson on a website designed specifically for

English speakers, there are many ways to use the web to advance your language abilities.

TABLE 18-1 VOCABULARY: THE INTERNET

address	l'indirizzo
browser	il navigatore
to click	cliccare
computer	il computer
control panel	il pannello di controllo
dialogue box	la finestra di dialogo
to download	scaricare
e-mail box	la casella di posta elettronica
folder	la cartella
icon	l'icona
Internet	la rete
keyboard	la tastiera
online	in linea
page	la pagina
password	la parola d'accesso
printer	la stampante
to reboot	rifare il booting
search engine	il motore di ricerca
site	il sito

Here are a few online Italian dictionaries that you might find helpful as you browse Italian websites:

www.yourdictionary.com
www.lai.com/lai/glossaries.html
www.garzantilinguistica.it
www.virgilio.it/servizi/dizionario/

Il rock and roll

You might know the Beatles, the Rolling Stones, Britney Spears, and Michael Jackson. But how about Claudio Baglioni, Laura Pausini, Vasco Rossi, Eros Ramazzotti, and Jovanotti? Or Claudio Villa, Mina, Domenico Modugno, Gianni Morandi, and Adriano Celentano? Modern Italian pop stars have been filling the airwaves for decades with their version of rock, soul, funk, and dance music.

INDEX